THE ARDEN SHAKESPEARE

GENERAL EDITOR: RICHARD PROUDFOOT

THE MERRY WIVES OF WINDSOR

THE ARDEN SHAKESPEARE

All's Well That Ends Well: edited by G. K. Hunter
Antony and Cleopatra: edited by M. R. Ridley
As You Like It: edited by Agnes Latham
The Comedy of Errors: edited by R. A. Foakes
Coriolanus: edited by Philip Brockbank
Cymbeline: edited by J. M. Nosworthy
Hamlet: edited by Harold Jenkins
Julius Caesar: edited by T. S. Dorsch
King Henry IV, Parts 1 & 2: edited by A. R. Humphreys
King Henry V: edited by John H. Walter
King Henry VI, Parts 1, 2 & 3: edited by A. S. Cairncross
King Henry VIII: edited by R. A. Foakes
King John: edited by E. A. J. Honigmann
King Lear: edited by Kenneth Muir
King Richard II: edited by Peter Ure
King Richard III: edited by Antony Hammond
Love's Labour's Lost: edited by Richard David
Macbeth: edited by Kenneth Muir
Measure for Measure: edited by J. W. Lever
The Merchant of Venice: edited by John Russell Brown
The Merry Wives of Windsor: edited by H. J. Oliver
A Midsummer Night's Dream: edited by Harold F. Brooks
Much Ado About Nothing: edited by A. R. Humphreys
Othello: edited by M. R. Ridley
Pericles: edited by F. D. Hoeniger
The Poems: edited by F. T. Prince
Romeo and Juliet: edited by Brian Gibbons
The Taming of the Shrew: edited by Brian Gibbons
The Tempest: edited by Frank Kermode
Timon of Athens: edited by H. J. Oliver
Titus Andronicus: edited by J. C. Maxwell
Troilus and Cressida: edited by Kenneth Palmer
Twelfth Night: edited by J. M. Lothian and T. W. Craik
The Two Gentlemen of Verona: edited by Clifford Leech
The Winter's Tale: edited by J. H. P. Pafford

THE ARDEN EDITION OF THE WORKS OF WILLIAM SHAKESPEARE

THE MERRY WIVES OF WINDSOR

Edited by
H. J. OLIVER

METHUEN
LONDON and NEW YORK

The general editors of the Arden Shakespeare have been W. J. Craig (1899–1906), R. H. Case (1909–44), Una Ellis-Fermor (1946–58), Harold F. Brooks (1952–82), Harold Jenkins (1958–82) and Brian Morris (1975–82)

Present general editor: Richard Proudfoot

This edition of *The Merry Wives of Windsor*, by H. J. Oliver,
first published in 1971 by
Methuen & Co. Ltd
11 New Fetter Lane, London EC4P 4EE

First published as a University Paperback in 1973
Reprinted twice
Reprinted 1984

Published in the USA by
Methuen & Co.
in association with Methuen, Inc.
733 Third Avenue, New York, NY 10017

ISBN (hardbound) 0 416 47690 2
ISBN (paperback) 0 416 17780 8

Printed and bound in Great Britain by
Richard Clay (The Chaucer Press) Ltd
Bungay, Suffolk

CONTENTS

INTRODUCTION

The question with which study of *The Merry Wives of Windsor* often begins, and the one with which it too often ends, is the relation of the play to Shakespeare's *Henry IV* and *Henry V*; criticism, understandably enough, centres on Falstaff, and the issue most likely to be debated is whether the Falstaff of *The Merry Wives* is the authentic Falstaff, as that life-like character is assumed to be in the two parts of *Henry IV*. The question, in so far as it is a real question, may be deferred, but the absurdity of pursuing it too far may be commented on even now. The links between the comedy and the Histories are certainly not made systematically, and it is difficult to say when exactly the action of *The Merry Wives* is supposed to take place. To be sure, when the audience needs to be reminded that Fenton is a romantic and desirable suitor, Master Page can reply to the Host's praise ('he capers, he dances, he has eyes of youth; he writes verses, he speaks holiday, he smells April and May') with an objection that the audience will probably interpret as a compliment—'he kept company with the wild Prince and Poins'; and such a statement, if taken literally, would place the action either in the reign of Henry IV, when Prince Hal was nearly breaking his father's heart by consorting with Falstaff and his Eastcheap companions in sin, or, at the latest, in the reign of Prince Hal himself as Henry V. Yet the Mistress Quickly of *The Merry Wives* does not seem to be the Eastcheap hostess of *Henry IV*, but does seem to be the speaker of lines about a Windsor Castle that has apparently just been identified as the home of 'our radiant Queen' who 'hates sluts and sluttery'. Indeed there is an important sense in which *The Merry Wives* is the one of Shakespeare's plays that most obviously deals with life in Elizabethan England, and it may even be not only the most topical of them but also the one most clearly designed for a specific (and royal) occasion. It would, then, be doubly unfortunate if the casual links with the other Falstaff plays, which would have added to the attraction of the comedy for its original audiences, happy to be reminded of old friends, were allowed to limit or spoil modern appreciation of the play.

I. THE TEXTUAL AND THEATRICAL HISTORY OF THE PLAY

Although, as will be shown, there is every reason to believe that the play was written in the last decade of the sixteenth century, the first mention of it is found in the Stationers' Register on 18 January 1602:

> Io. Busby. Entred for his copie vnder the hand of m^r Seton / A booke called. An excellent & pleasant conceited comedie of S^r Io ffaulstof and the merry wyves of windesor[.] vj^d

followed immediately by the transfer, in a different hand:

> Arthure Iohnson[.] Entred for his Copye by assignement from Iohn Busbye / A booke Called an excellent and pleasant conceyted Comedie of Sir Iohn ffaulstafe and the merye wyves of windsor[.] vj^d [1]

It is not known how Busby acquired his right in the text, but Johnson's claim could hardly have been disputed, since the transfer had been entered in the usual acceptable form; and in the same year he engaged Thomas Creede to print his text and duly published it, as a quarto, with the inviting title-page:

> A / Most pleasaunt and / excellent conceited Co- / medie, of Syr *Iohn Falstaffe*, and the / merrie Wiues of *Windsor*. / Entermixed with sundrie / variable and pleasing humors, of Syr *Hugh* / the Welch Knight, Iustice *Shallow*, and his / wise Cousin M. *Slender*. / With the swaggering vaine of Auncient / *Pistoll*, and Corporall *Nym*. / By *William Shakespeare*. / As it hath bene diuers times Acted by the right Honorable / my Lord Chamberlaines seruants. Both before her / Maiestie, and else-where. / [*ornament*] / LONDON / Printed by T.C. for Arthur Iohnson, and are to be sold at / his shop in Powles Church-yard, at the signe of the / Flower de Leuse and the Crowne. / 1602.

An attempt will be made later to show that this Quarto is a most corrupt version of the play not as it was presented before the Queen's Majesty but as it was no doubt divers times acted elsewhere. Nevertheless another printer, William Jaggard, reprinted this text with a few unimportant alterations in 1619 ('Q2'), ostensibly for Johnson but probably for Thomas Pavier, who published a series of genuine and spurious 'Shakespeare' texts in that year. Pavier's venture seems to have led to protests from the King's Men—on whose behalf the Lord Chamberlain wrote to the Stationers' Company forbidding further printing of King's Men plays without consent—and so, indirectly, it led to the publication by William Jaggard, his son Isaac, and others, in 1623, of the first

1. Register C, fo. 78, cited by W. W. Greg, *The Merry Wives of Windsor 1602*, Shakespeare Quarto Facsimiles, No. 3 (Oxford, 1957), p. i.

full collection of Shakespeare's plays, now known as the First Folio.[1] The Quarto text of *The Merry Wives* was not reproduced again until George Steevens in 1766 included a reprint of Q2 in Volume I of his *Twenty of the Plays of Shakespeare, Being the whole Number printed in Quarto During his Life-time, or before the Restoration*; and although every editor of the play must refer to it, the Quarto has not often been republished in the nineteenth and twentieth centuries except in standard series of facsimiles (such as those of Griggs, in 1881, corrected in 1888, and W. W. Greg, in 1939 and 1957) or because of its 'curiosity value' as an inferior or supposedly earlier form of the fuller Folio text (e.g. by Halliwell in 1842 and by Greg in 1910).

The version of the play published in the First Folio of 1623 is almost twice the length of the Quarto text (which is the shortest of all the Shakespearian 'Bad' Quartos) and is in nearly every way markedly superior. Only odd lines or phrases in the Quarto have no counterpart in the Folio, whereas the Folio has at least five scenes that are not represented in the Quarto at all, the most important being the completely detachable 'Latin lesson' (Act IV, Scene i). Not surprisingly, therefore, it was the Folio and not the Quarto version that was republished as a further Quarto ('Q3') in 1630, although the new publisher Meighen did not take the step until Johnson on 29 January of that year had assigned to him his 'estate' in the work. (It would seem that once an Elizabethan stationer, by an entry on the Register, had established his right to one text of a play, however corrupt, his fellows were normally content to allow his right to other versions of that play, however different.) The claim on the title-page that the text had been 'newly corrected' was no doubt intended to mean that this was the first publication of the play *in quarto* to contain the 'corrected', Folio, version and not that the Folio had been further corrected. The First Folio text was reprinted with only the most minor of variations in the later Folios; and the editorial history of the play thereafter is related mainly to the use that each editor has been prepared to make of the Quarto when he found the Folio 'wrong' or, occasionally, inadequate.

The theatrical history of *The Merry Wives* in Shakespeare's own day is harder to trace. There is no reason to doubt either the statement on the title-page of the 1602 Quarto that the play had been acted 'divers times', both for the Queen 'and elsewhere', or its implication that not only Falstaff but also Evans, Shallow, Slender,

1. See, e.g., E. K. Chambers, *William Shakespeare* (Oxford, 1930), I. 133–41; W. W. Greg, *The Editorial Problem in Shakespeare* (Second edition, Oxford, 1951), pp. 131–4.

Pistol, and Nym were popular characters with audiences. As will be seen later, there is also reason to think that the play may have been written for a special occasion as early as 1597. The first record of an actual performance, however, is in the Revels Accounts for 1604 (which seem now to have successfully survived allegations of forgery). Here it is recorded that the King's Men performed on 'Hallamas Day being the first of Nouembar A play in the Banketinge house att Whithall called The Moor of Venis' and 'The Sunday ffollowinge A Play of the Merry Wiues of Winsor'.[1]

There seems to be no substance in H. C. Hart's theory that a reference to the 'true heirs of Master Justice Shallow' in Dekker's *Satiromastix* (1601) means that the Children of Pauls, who are mentioned on the title-page of the 1602 edition of that comedy as having played it 'priuately', had also acted *The Merry Wives of Windsor*. The passage in question occurs in a speech by Horace (a caricature of Ben Jonson) when Horace is boasting to Crispinus that he has 'a set of' letters written to be sent to flatter 'any fresh suited gallant' who comes on the scene, the letters being intended to give impressive evidence of Horace's fluency and genius: 'We must haue false fiers to amaze these spangle babies, these true heires of Master Iustice Shallow'. Hart tries to link Horace's ready-made letters with Falstaff's in *The Merry Wives*, of which Mistress Page says 'I warrant he hath a thousand of these letters, writ with blank spaces for different names ...' (II. i. 71–2); but even if Dekker were thinking of Falstaff, the reference to the true heirs of Shallow seems to mean no more than 'fools like Shallow': Shallow is not connected in any way with Falstaff's letters in *The Merry Wives* and indeed (as Collier had already pointed out) Dekker may be thinking of the Shallow of *2 Henry IV*.[2]

It is just possible that the record of payment to the King's Men on 20 May 1613 for, among 'fowerteene severall playes', one called 'Sir John ffalstaffe' refers to *The Merry Wives*, since the very next entry includes another called 'the Hotspur';[3] but the next certain record is more than thirty years after the first: on 12 March 1638/9, the King's Men, through Lowin, Taylor, and Swanston, were paid for a performance at Court on 15 November 1638.[4]

1. E. K. Chambers, *The Elizabethan Stage* (Oxford, 1923), IV. 171 and 136–40.

2. H. C. Hart ed., *The Merry Wives of Windsor* (the original Arden edition, London, 1904, revised 1932), pp. 66–7; J. P. Collier, *The Works of William Shakespeare* (London, 1844), I. 175. The *Satiromastix* reference is to II. ii. 27–35 in the edition of Dekker by F. T. Bowers (Cambridge, 1953), I. 336.

3. Chambers, *Elizabethan Stage*, IV. 180. The point is made by William Bracy, *The Merry Wives of Windsor* (Columbia, Missouri, 1952), p. 10.

4. G. E. Bentley, *The Jacobean and Caroline Stage* (Oxford, 1941–68), I. 99; W. W. Greg ed., Malone Society *Collections*, II. 3 (Oxford, 1931), pp. 388–9.

After the Restoration in 1660, *The Merry Wives* was one of the first plays to be acted. It was among those allotted to Thomas Killigrew; and Pepys saw a performance in the Vere Street Theatre on 5 December 1660—and was not impressed. He thought 'the humours of the country gentleman [presumably Slender] and the French doctor very well done' but disapproved of Cartwright's Falstaff and 'the rest'. Performances on 25 September in the following year and on 15 August 1667 were no more to his taste. Downes also records a special performance 'at Court at St. *Jame's*', on 23 April 1704 or 1705, with what must have been one of the best casts ever seen in the play: Betterton was Falstaff; Dogget, Evans; Mrs Barry, Mistress Page; and Anne Bracegirdle, Mistress Ford. It may have been the acting rather than the play itself that disappointed Pepys, for Dennis recorded in 1702 that 'all those men of extraordinary parts, who were the Ornaments of that Court; as the late Duke of *Buckingham*, my Lord *Normandy*, my Lord *Dorset*, my late Lord *Rochester*, Sir *Charles Sidley*, Dr *Frazer*, Mr *Savil*, Mr *Buckley*, were in Love with the Beauties of this Comedy', and Downes recalled in 1708 that it was one of the 'Old Plays' which, being old, 'were Acted but now and then; yet being well Perform'd, were very Satisfactory to the Town'. Yet it is not difficult to believe that the Restoration audience would have thought unsophisticated a play in which country virtue triumphed so easily over courtly gallantry. (Indeed Dennis added that 'this Comedy had never upon Revivals had any great success, and that particularly when it was Revived in King *Charles* the Seconds time, the only character that pleased to a height was *Slender* acted by *Wintershal*'.)[1]

An attempt to 'improve' the play for early eighteenth-century audiences—inevitable in spite of its reasonable conformity to the unities of time, place, and action—was made by Dennis. *The Comical Gallant: Or The Amours of Sir John Falstaffe* was presented at Drury Lane in 1702, but not very successfully (Dennis blamed the actor who played Falstaff). As might have been expected, the plot was theoretically tightened up (Dennis complained that 'there are no less than three Actions in it that are independent one of another, which divide and distract the minds of an Audience'): Fenton becomes the principal character and is Mistress Ford's nephew; a second Host, the Host of the Bull Inn, is Mistress Ford's brother; Falstaff is persuaded by Fenton that Mistress Ford and Mistress Page are in love with him; instead of Falstaff's being thrashed as the supposed Witch of Brentford, Ford suffers the punishment at

1. John Downes, *Roscius Anglicanus*, ed. Montague Summers (London, [1928]), pp. 47, 9; John Dennis, Epistle Dedicatory to *The Comical Gallant* (London, 1702), A2, A2v.

the hands of Mistress Page—who is disguised as Captain Dingboy, the supposed lover of Mistress Ford; and, in the interests of symmetry, it is again Ford who is pinched and burnt and beaten by the 'fairies', when he, as well as Falstaff, is disguised as Herne the Hunter. Slender and Caius are tricked by the disguises into being 'married' to one another by the Host of the Garter disguised as a parson; and Fenton, too noble to marry Anne without her parents' consent, gains that consent because of the correctness of his sentiments. After all, as Dennis generously said, 'in so short a time as' Shakespeare was allowed to write his play, 'nothing could be done that is perfect'; but since Shakespeare 'performed more than any-one else could have done in so short a time', all that the reviser had to do was to 'Correct the foresaid Errours' (the plot, and the 'places' where the style was 'stiff and forced and affected').

In the 1720's Shakespeare's play, not Dennis's, became exceptionally popular, and it was produced by most of the famous companies and actor-managers of the eighteenth and nineteenth centuries, though often in an abridged form; Quin, for example, excelled as Falstaff, though Kemble (at first) and Kean preferred to play Ford. Kean's Mistress Ford was, of course, Ellen Tree; and Ellen Terry and Mrs Kendal later played the wives, with Beerbohm Tree as Falstaff. The play was also performed in America as early as 1770, in Philadelphia, and as early as 1773 in New York, and it was never quite lost to the United States theatre thereafter, although George Pope Morris informed the nation in *The New-York Mirror* of 13 November 1824 that 'there is no play in the English language of so exceptionable a character as this indelicate production of Shakespeare'.[1]

There have been many successful revivals in the twentieth century, not only in England and America but also, for example, in Europe (the play has been translated into most European languages); there is even record of a production in Japan. Experimental productions have included Oscar Asche's surprisingly unpopular 1911 'wintry' version, and his calamitous 1929 modern-dress variation (Anne 'rode pillion on Fenton's motor-bicycle'); Komisarjevsky's in 1935 with a Viennese background; a Yale Shakespeare Festival 1953 performance 'in the language of Shakespeare's day' (the actors being coached by Helge Kökeritz); a comic-ballet; and a 1957 production in Russia when 'in order to maintain the spirit of revelry and gaiety throughout the entire

1. Harrison T. Meserole, 'Shakespeare in New York, 1823–24: The *Mirror*, Morals, and The *Merry Wives of Windsor*', in G. R. Smith ed., *Essays on Shakespeare* (University Park, 1965), pp. 228–38. Augustin Daly's late nineteenth-century productions of the play were always carefully expurgated.

performance, a kind of merry fair was organized during the intervals, in which both the actors and the audience took part. This innovation was a great success, but the producer's rather free attitude to the text of the comedy has provoked some disagreement.'[1] Suffice it to add that although some theatre-goers naturally prefer Shakespeare in a more serious mood, such a production of *The Merry Wives* as that by Glen Byam Shaw in the 1955 season at Stratford-upon-Avon showed that even a sophisticated audience can be delighted when the play is presented as the light-hearted comedy it really is. *The Merry Wives* also has the distinction of having been used for the librettos of at least nine operas, including those by Reynolds (1824), Balfe (1838), Nicolai (1849), Vaughan Williams (*Sir John in Love*, 1929), and, above all, Verdi (*Falstaff*, 1893).[2]

2. THE RELATIONSHIP OF QUARTO AND FOLIO

It was inevitable that the Quarto of 1602, which, in approximate figures, has only 1,600 lines, as against the Folio's 2,700, and is in all judgements inferior to it, should once have been taken to be an earlier version of the play or even a first draft.[3] This was commonly thought to be the status of several Shakespeare texts, such as the First Quartos of *Hamlet* and *Romeo and Juliet*, and even *The Taming of a Shrew*; and although Collier, Grant White, P. A. Daniel, and others had reservations and alternative theories, most critics did not abandon the 'first sketch' explanation altogether until A. W. Pollard made his famous distinction between 'good' and 'bad' Quartos and pointed the way to the full demonstration that many published plays once thought to be sources or first versions were in fact later, debased, 'reported' or 'pirated' forms of the authentic Shakespeare texts. As early as 1910, however, W. W. Greg argued

1. Y. Shvedov, in 'International Notes', *Shakespeare Survey 12* (Cambridge, 1959), p. 118. Fuller details of various twentieth-century productions are given in other volumes of *Shakespeare Survey* and *Shakespeare Quarterly* and in J. C. Trewin, *Shakespeare on the English Stage, 1900–1964: A Survey of Productions* (London, 1964). For the earlier stage history, see e.g. E. L. Avery, *The London Stage 1660–1800* (Carbondale, Ill., 1960–); C. B. Hogan, *Shakespeare in the Theatre. 1701–1800* (Oxford, 1952, 1957); G. C. D. Odell, *Shakespeare from Betterton to Irving* (New York, 1920); W. Winter, *Shakespeare on the Stage* (Third series, London, 1916), pp. 383–430; O. J. Campbell and E. G. Quinn ed., *The Reader's Encyclopedia of Shakespeare* (New York, 1966), pp. 536–8; and Harold Child, 'The Stage-History of *The Merry Wives of Windsor*', in Quiller-Couch and J. Dover Wilson ed., *The Merry Wives of Windsor* (Cambridge, 1921, 1954), pp. 135–8.

2. See, e.g., Winston Dean, 'Shakespeare and Opera', in Phyllis Hartnoll ed., *Shakespeare in Music* (London, 1964).

3. This was the opinion of, e.g., Pope (who knew the 1619 Quarto), Theobald (who also knew of the earlier one), Johnson, Capell, and even Malone.

convincingly that the Quarto of *The Merry Wives* was just such a corrupt 'report'.[1] There have, it is true, been dissentients—notably William Bracy, but his '*The Merry Wives of Windsor.*' *The History and Transmission of Shakespeare's Text* (1952), while entering a few caveats, failed to destroy the theory of memorial reconstruction. The facts must be set out in some detail.

P. A. Daniel first pointed out[2] that the Quarto version of the part of the action covered in Folio's Act IV Scene V hardly makes sense and could best be explained as a failure to reproduce correctly a larger version of the scene such as Folio's.[3] In the Quarto, Slender's servant Simple, in quest of 'the wise woman of Brainford', has the following conversation with Falstaff:

> *Sim.* Marry sir my maister *Slender* sent me to her,
> To know whether one *Nim* that hath his chaine,
> Cousoned him of it, or no.
> *Fal.* I talked with the woman about it.
> *Sim.* And I pray sir what ses she?
> *Fal.* Marry she ses the very same man that
> Beguiled maister *Slender* of his chaine,
> Cousoned him of it.
> *Sim.* May I be bolde to tell my maister so sir?
> *Fal.* I tike, who more bolde.
> *Sim.* I thanke you sir, I shall make my maister a glad
> man at these tydings, God be with you sir

(and although no exit is marked, Simple apparently leaves). In Daniel's words, 'Simple, therefore, is made to say that he will make his master a glad man with the news that he has been cozened of his chain'—and, even allowing that Simple is stupid enough for most things, that is rather surprising. The Folio text presents no problems here. When Simple receives Falstaff's answer that 'the very same man that beguil'd Master *Slender* of his Chaine, cozon'd him of it', he is not satisfied but replies 'I would I could haue spoken with the Woman her selfe, I had other things to haue

1. A. W. Pollard, *Shakespeare Folios and Quartos* (London, 1909) and *Shakespeare's Fight with the Pirates* (Cambridge, 1920); Peter Alexander, *Shakespeare's 'Henry VI' and 'Richard III'* (Cambridge, 1929); *Shakespeare's 'Merry Wives of Windsor' 1602*, ed. W. W. Greg (Oxford, 1910). Also valuable, though out of date in some respects, is Alfred Hart, *Stolne and Surreptitious Copies* (Melbourne, 1942). See, too, Leo Kirschbaum, 'An Hypothesis concerning the Origin of the Bad Quartos', *PMLA*, LX (1945), 697–715, and for proof that the Quarto of *Henry V* is a reported text, G. I. Duthie, in *Papers Mainly Shakespearian*, coll. G. I. Duthie (Edinburgh, 1964), pp. 104–30.

2. Preface to William Griggs's facsimile of the First Quarto (London, 1881, revised edition 1888), p. x.

3. The Quarto has no act and scene divisions; the references given are always those of the Folio, with the line-numbering of the present edition.

spoken with her too, from him', and we soon learn what they are, namely, 'they were nothing but about Mistris *Anne Page*, to know if it were my Masters fortune to haue her, or no':

Fal. 'Tis, 'tis his fortune.
Sim. What Sir?
Fal. To haue her, or no: goe; say the woman told me so.
Sim. May I be bold to say so Sir?
Fal. I Sir: like who more bold.
Sim. I thanke your worship: I shall make my Master glad with these tydings.

Obviously this makes better sense; and it is hard to believe either that somebody composed the Quarto version first or that somebody deliberately shortening the Folio version would have omitted the question about Anne Page and retained the one about the chain. It will also be noticed that Simple's 'May I be bold to say so Sir' has been retained in the Quarto version, albeit as a comment on the first, not the second question—as if somebody's memory jumped a few lines—and that the Quarto's 'I tike, who more bolde' could most easily be explained as some kind of corruption of Folio's 'I Sir: like who more bold' (meaning 'be as bold as you please' or 'as bold as the boldest')—possibly a simple misprint ('t' for 'l' in 'like'), perhaps an attempt to 'improve', conceivably even a confusion of the line being recalled with such another as 'Base Tyke, cal'st thou mee Hoste' from *Henry V* (II. i. 31).

There is another tell-tale omission, in the Quarto scene corresponding to Folio's I. iv.[1] When Caius finds Simple hiding in the 'Counting-house' (itself an odd substitution for the Folio 'Closset'), Simple denies being a thief, with the words

O Lord sir no: I am no theefe,
I am a Seruingman:
My name is *Iohn Simple*, I brought a Letter sir
From my M. *Slender*, about misteris *Anne Page*
Sir: Indeed that is my comming

whereupon Caius writes out a challenge not to Slender but to Sir Hugh Evans. Now it is true that the *audience* has already seen Evans send Simple to Quickly with the letter, on Slender's behalf, but there has been nothing whatever to cause Caius to associate Evans with the matter (and Bracy's insistence on 'the skill with which the essential plot is advanced' throughout the Quarto is seen to be quite wrong). Again the Folio makes all clear: the Quarto has omitted Mistress Quickly's volunteering to Caius of the information 'I beseech you be not so flegmaticke: heare the truth of it. He

1. According to Harness's edition of 1825, it was first noticed by James Boaden.

came of an errand to mee, from Parson *Hugh*' and has reproduced only the general sense of Simple's 'Tale' of why he came: 'To desire this honest Gentlewoman (your Maid) to speake a good word to Mistris *Anne Page*, for my Master in the way of Marriage'. No dramatist could have *composed* the Quarto scene as it stands, to tell the story; and no sane reviser of the play trying to save space or time would have left out the only statement that makes sense of the action.

One further instance of Quarto lines that are meaningless in themselves, and can be understood only if the Folio text is taken into account, occurs in II. iii. Caius waits for Evans to appear and fight the duel for which he sent the challenge in I. iv; and Shallow, Page, the Host, and Slender come instead. (At least, the Quarto stage direction says that all four of them come, but Slender does not speak, and Caius asks 'Vat be all you, Van to tree com for, a?'; in the Folio, Slender does speak, and Caius, consistently, asks 'Vat be all you one, two, tree, fowre, come for?') To the Host's question whether Evans has already been killed, Caius replies (in both texts) that Evans has not dared to show his face. In the Quarto, Shallow thereupon comments: 'He hath showne himselfe the wiser man M. Doctor: / Sir *Hugh* is a Parson, and you a Phisition'. Why should a parson not meet a physician, one wonders? The Folio alone gives the answer: in that text, Shallow's reply to Caius is 'He is the wiser man (M. Doctor) he is a curer of soules, and you a curer of bodies: if you should fight, you goe against the haire of your professions', and it is a few lines later in the scene that he says: 'M. Doctor *Caius*, I am come to fetch you home: I am sworn of the peace: you haue show'd your selfe a wise Physician, and Sir *Hugh* hath showne himselfe a wise and patient Churchman'. Whoever was responsible for the Quarto remembered, apparently, that something was said about the professions of Caius and Evans but forgot what was said; and because he forgot exactly what was said, he set down a phrase that misses the whole point of Shallow's first comment.

The only theory that will explain all the corruptions already listed is that somebody (singular or plural) was trying to reconstruct either the Folio text or one similar to it. Although the Quarto text was published first, it cannot possibly represent either an early draft of a text like the Folio's or *only* a version of it shortened for performance. There is no feature of the Quarto that is inconsistent with the theory that it is a 'reported' text; and there are many features that cannot be otherwise explained.

The Quarto stage directions, for example, sometimes bring on characters who have nothing to say and no part in the action: presumably their presence on stage was remembered (and, of course, a reviser preparing a deliberately abridged version of the play would have removed them from the stage directions too). One instance has already been noted—Slender's presence in the Quarto stage direction in II. iii, although his Folio line ''Giue you good-morrow, sir' has been dropped (but Caius does refer to him—in a speech where lines, perhaps by a compositor's error, have been run into those that should be spoken by the Host—'M. *Page* and M. *Shallow*, / And eke cauellira *Slender*, go you all ouer the fields to Frogmore?'). Then in the next scene, corresponding to III. i of the Folio, the Quarto has a stage direction '*Enter Page, shallow, and Slender*' but Slender neither speaks nor is spoken to, whereas in the Folio version he wanders round sighing 'O sweet *Anne Page*'. Even more significant, in the opening scene the Quarto has the stage direction: '*Enter Syr* Iohn Falstaffe, Pistoll, Bardolfe, *and* Nim', but Bardolph does not speak, and Slender does not include him in his accusations of those who robbed him. Where the Folio has 'I haue matter in my head against you [Falstaff], and against your cony-catching Rascalls, *Bardolf*, *Nym*, and *Pistoll*', the Quarto has 'I haue matter in my head against you and your cogging companions, *Pistoll* and *Nym*' and the Folio's later charge that 'he in the red face had it' is missing, as are Bardolph's replies (and Evans's comment on the first of them). Again it is the stage direction that gives the game away.[1]

There are also, as Alfred Hart noted,[2] many of the superfluous and 'descriptive' stage directions that either repeat or replace dialogue and are rarely if ever found in good texts. They include, in the order in which they occur in the Quarto (the Folio act and scene references for comparison being given in parentheses):

(i) *Quic.* . . . For Gods sake step into the Counting-house . . .
He steps into the Counting-house.
. . . Are you come home sir alreadie?
And she opens the doore. (I. iv)

(ii) *Doc.* . . . *Iohn Rugby* giue a ma pen
An Inck: tarche vn pettit tarche a little.
The Doctor writes. (I. iv)

(iii) *Enter Mistresse* Page, *reading of a Letter*
(cf. Folio, II. i: *Mist Page.* What, haue scap'd Loue-letters in the holly-day-time of my beauty, and am I now a subiect for them? let me see? . . .)

1. Curiously, in III. i, although Bardolph is not on the stage, according to either the Folio or the Quarto stage directions, the Quarto has the Host say '*Bardolfe* laie their swords to pawne' where the Folio has only 'Come, lay their swords to pawne'. Presumably any name was good enough for the reporter here.

2. *op. cit.*, pp. 429–31.

(iv) *Ford.* A word with you sir.

Ford and the Host talkes.

(Folio, II. i: *Ford.* Good mine Host o'th' Garter: a word with you. / *Host.* What saist thou, my Bully-Rooke?)

(v) *Mis. For.* O Lord step aside good sir *Iohn.*

Falstaffe stands behind the aras.

(cf. Folio, III. iii: *Fal.* She shall not see me, I will ensconce mee behinde the Arras. / *M. Ford.* Pray you do so, she's a very tatling woman.)

(vi) *Sir Iohn goes into the basket, they put cloathes ouer him, the two men carries it away: Foord meetes it, and all the rest, Page, Doctor, Priest, Slender, Shallow*

(all based on the Folio dialogue, III. iii).

(vii) *Enter mistresse Page.*

[*Mis. For.*] Gods body here is misteris *Page,*
Step behind the arras good sir *Iohn.*

He steps behind the arras.

(cf. Folio, IV. ii, 'Step into th' chamber, Sir *Iohn*'. The Quarto confuses, and weakly repeats, the similar but different action in III. iii.)

(viii) *Enter M. Ford, Page, Priest, Shallow, the two men carries the basket, and Ford meets it.*

(cf. the Folio dialogue, IV. ii, as in this edition; but cf. also vi, above.)

(ix) *Enter Falstaffe disguised like an old woman, and misteris Page with him, Ford beates him, and hee runnes away.* (IV. ii)

(x) The stage directions recorded in the collations to this edition at V. v. 30, 37, and 103.

The Quarto also often confuses and conflates incidents or speeches that are similar but distinct in the Folio—and often gets into the earlier of the two episodes words that belong properly in the later (a phenomenon, incidentally, that practically rules out any theory that the Quarto text is an inaccurate shorthand report of the Folio). For example, in II. i in the Folio, when the proposed 'duel' between Evans and Caius is being discussed, Page says to Shallow, 'I haue heard the French-man [Caius] hath good skill in his Rapier' and Shallow in his reply speaks of the modern technique of fencing ('your Passes, Stoccado's, and I know not what') contrasted with the practice of his own youth: ''tis the heart (Master *Page*) 'tis heere, 'tis heere: I haue seene the time, with my long-sword, I would haue made you fowre tall fellowes skippe like Rattes'. In II. iii, after Shallow has told Caius that Evans 'is the wiser man' for not appearing, Page, to make conversation, comments, 'Master *Shallow*; you haue your selfe beene a great fighter, though now a man of peace' and Shallow, flattered, agrees: 'if I see a sword out, my finger itches to make one . . . we are the sons of women (M. *Page*.)' The Quarto, which has nothing similar in II. iii, gets Page's comment into II. i and conflates the two thus:

> *Pa.* Maister *Shallow* you your selfe
> Haue bene a great fighter,
> Tho now a man of peace:
> *Shal:* M. *Page* I haue seene the day that yong
> Tall fellowes with their stroke & their passado,
> I haue made them trudge Maister *Page*,
> A tis the hart, the hart doth all: I
> Haue seene the day, with my two hand sword
> I would a made you foure tall Fencers
> Scipped like Rattes.

(The weak repetitions of 'tall' and 'I haue seene the day' should be noticed too.)

Again, in Folio III. iv, Slender's unforgettable 'wooing' of Anne Page (which the Quarto manages to botch so badly that it is hardly funny at all) ends with Anne's desperate question 'I meane (M. *Slender*) what wold you with me?' and Slender's equally desperate reply 'Truely, for mine owne part, I would little or nothing with you: your father and my vncle hath made motions: if it be my lucke, so; if not, happy man bee his dole, they can tell you how things go, better then I can: you may aske your father, heere he comes'. The Quarto confuses this with the other time when Anne and Slender are left alone on the stage, in I. i, and 'reproduces' it there thus:

> *Anne.* Now forsooth why do you stay me?
> What would you with me?
> *Slen.* Nay for my owne part, I would litle or nothing with you. I loue you well, and my vncle can tell you how my liuing stands. And if you can loue me why so. If not, why then happie man be his dole.

(Even worse, if worse can be imagined, is the reply that the Quarto gives to Anne—a reply that proves that whoever was responsible for the Quarto had not the least understanding of her character:

> *An.* You say well M. *Slender*.
> But first you must giue me leaue to
> Be acquainted with your humor,
> And afterward to loue you if I can.

Anne love Slender, indeed!)

In Folio IV. ii, after Falstaff, at his second assignation with Mistress Ford, has had to step hurriedly 'into th' chamber' when

Mistress Page appears, Mistress Ford whispers to her fellow-conspirator 'Speake louder' (that Falstaff may not fail to be terrified by what she is saying). The Quarto contrives to get Mistress Ford's 'Speake louder' into the scene of the first assignation with Falstaff when—on the Quarto's own showing—Mistress Page is in no danger of not being heard, since Falstaff is only behind the arras. Equally absurd is the transference of Ford–Brook's flattery of Falstaff in II. ii, 'Sir, I heare you are a Scholler . . .' to Page in III. i: when Page should be saying to Evans, 'We are come to you, to doe a good office, Mr. Parson' and frightening him by telling him how angry his opponent Caius is, he is made to say, astoundingly, not only, 'Well Sir *Hugh*, we are come to craue / Your helpe and furtherance in a matter' but also 'Now Sir *Hugh*, you are a scholler well red, and verie perswasiue, we would intreate you to see if you could intreat him to patience'.

Not to labour the point, there are at least four other instances of Quarto's confusing situations thus. It gets the part of Ford's soliloquy involving devils' names, at the end of II. ii, into his other soliloquy at the end of III. v. It transfers from III. iii both Evans's acceptance of Page's invitation to breakfast, 'If there is one, I shall make two in the Companie' and Caius' unfortunate addition, 'If there be one, or two, I shall make-a-the turd' and puts them both in III. ii, as answers to *Ford's* invitation to *dinner*. It omits from Falstaff's speech in IV. v about being cozened the lines 'if it should come to the eare of the Court, how I haue beene transformed . . . they would melt mee out of my fat drop by drop, and liquor Fishermens-boots with me: I warrant they would whip me with their fine wits, till I were as crest-falne as a dride-peare' (ll. 89–95), and puts a version of them into his reflections in V. v on his being deceived by the supposed fairies 'Well, and the fine wits of the Court heare this, / Thayle so whip me with their keene Iests, / That thayle melt me out like tallow, / Drop by drop out of my grease'. Again, in II. ii, in Falstaff's blustering description of Ford to 'Brooke', for the Folio's 'They say the iealous wittolly-knaue hath masses of money', the Quarto substitutes 'For they / Say the cuckally knaue hath legions of angels', confusing it with Falstaff's earlier account of the Fords to Pistol and company in I. iii, 'Now, the report goes, she has all the rule of her husbands Purse: he hath a legend of Angels' (which the Quarto renders in the right place as 'She hath legians of angels'). It is even likely that the Quarto has Falstaff say to Shallow in I. i 'youle complaine of me to the Councell, I heare?' where the Folio has 'Now, Master *Shallow*, you'll complaine of me to the King?' not because the Folio text was altered after the Quarto was derived from it or because the Quarto was trying to remove any inconsistency between a King's reign and the Queen's, but simply because the Council had been mentioned earlier in the scene and was mentioned again a few lines later. With the possible exception of this last example, none of the transferences is of the kind that can be attributed to a compositor carrying words in his mind from what he has just set up or from reading his copy ahead.

In reported texts it is common to find also the mistaken introduction of, or confusion with, similar lines in other plays—perhaps plays in which the reporter had acted. Such conflation is found in the Quarto of *The Merry Wives* but fewer conclusions than usual can be drawn from it. For example, the line 'What is the reason that you vse me thus?' (spoken by Mistress Ford to her husband, in place of lines to the same general effect but quite different in wording in Folio IV. ii), occurs in *Hamlet* (V. i. 312). It is not an exceptional line, however; conceivably the reporter (half-remembering Mistress Ford's 'You vse me well, M. *Ford*? Do you?', from III. iii[1]) could have invented it, or it could be a standard phrase used frequently in conversation. Some of the other 'inter-play borrowings' listed by Alfred Hart and H. R. Hoppe[2] are unconvincing for much the same reason ('caught you a the hip', for example, 'Haue you importuned her by any means', 'Ifaith I know not what to say', 'led in a fooles paradice', and 'tis not vnknown to you'). It is also far from certain that Mistress Page's 'Why what a bladder of iniquitie is this?' (II. i) is a recollection of Falstaff's 'a plague of sighing and griefe, it blowes a man vp like a Bladder' (*1 Henry IV*, II. iv. 366) as conjectured by E. K. Chambers.[3] More convincing is the hypothesis that Pistol's 'When *Pistoll* lies do this' in the same scene is a transference from *2 Henry IV*, V. iii, of the identical words, spoken by the same character.

More important are lines in Nym's speeches that suggest that the reporter knew *Henry V* and was confused about Nym's speeches in the two plays (and perhaps that the actor who had played Nym in both plays was one of the 'reporters' of the Quarto *Merry Wives*). Editors have spoilt some of the evidence here by introducing lines from the Quarto unnecessarily into their texts (see particularly II. i. 133 and note). In the Folio, Nym constantly uses and misuses

1. In III. iii, what should be Mistress Ford's line is given quite nonsensically to Evans in the form 'You serue me well, do you not?'

2. Hart, *Stolne and Surreptitious Copies*, pp. 393–4; Hoppe, 'Borrowings from *Romeo and Juliet* in the 'Bad' Quarto of *The Merry Wives of Windsor*', *Review of English Studies*, XX (1944), 156–8.

3. *William Shakespeare*, I. 429.

the word 'humour', but he does not once say 'that's the humour of it'. This idiom is his 'signature tune' in *Henry V*, where he uses it at least five times (II. i. 63, 74, 101, and 121; and II. iii. 63). In the Quarto *Merry Wives*, in the form 'there's the humor of it', the phrase is introduced into four of Nym's nine speeches—and of the other five, two are 'Let vs about it then' and 'By *Welkin* and her Fairies' and neither into these nor into the other three could the full phrase easily be fitted even by a reporter. The four speeches in the Quarto in which Nym does say 'There's the humor of it' all have Folio counterparts: the Quarto has simply added the phrase to two of the four, and in the others has substituted it for 'is not the humor conceited?' (I. iii. 21–2) and, perhaps most significant of all, for 'that is the very note of it' (I. i. 152).[1]

The borrowing from *Henry V* seems certain (and incidentally proves that the Quarto *Merry Wives* cannot have been put together until after *Henry V* had been played). With this clue, it then becomes interesting to note other verbal links with *Henry V*, which in themselves could not prove the dependence of one play on the other but perhaps provide a kind of corroborative evidence. Where, for example, in the Folio *Merry Wives*, Pistol says 'word of deniall in thy *labras* here' (I. i. 147), the Quarto has 'I do retort the lie / Euen in thy gorge'—and '*Couple a gorge*, that is the word. I defie thee againe' is found, spoken by Pistol, in *Henry V* (II. i. 75–6 in the 'Globe' division but Act I in the Folio's). In *The Merry Wives* II. ii. 264, where the Folio has 'ther's my haruest-home', the Quarto reads 'there's my randeuowes'—and 'rendezvous' is used twice in *Henry V* (once by Nym, II. i. 18—'that is the rendeuous of it', once by Pistol, V. i. 88—'and there my rendeuous is quite cut off'). Less significant, perhaps, but interesting, is Quarto's 'egregious' in Falstaff's 'I suffered three egregious deaths', where the Folio has 'I suffered the pangs of three seuerall deaths' (III. v. 98–9): 'egregious' occurs twice in *Henry V*, at II. i. 49 and IV. iv. 11—both times spoken by Pistol. One expects Shakespearian characters to have each an idiom of his own, and it is natural that some phrases will tend to be common to plays written about the same time (and there are verbal links of this kind between the Folio *Merry Wives* and *Henry IV* and *Henry V*); but the noted substitution in the Quarto, for different phrases in the Folio, of words spoken in *Henry V*—particularly when so many of them concern Nym and Pistol—seems explicable only as memorial contamination.

1. William Green (*Shakespeare's 'Merry Wives of Windsor'*, Princeton, 1962, pp. 90–4) points out that the 'Bad', 1600, Quarto of *Henry V* similarly substitutes 'there's the humor of it' for comparable phrases of the good, Folio, text. But it does *not* follow that the *Merry Wives* reporter must have known the *Henry V* Quarto.

That so much of the Quarto is printed as if it were verse, when it must be prose, may be the compositor's fault, but there are instances where the Quarto verse corresponds to the Folio verse—and the difference between them is instructive. For example, for the Folio's

> Albeit I will confesse, thy Fathers wealth
> Was the first motiue that I woo'd thee (*Anne*:)
> Yet wooing thee, I found thee of more valew
> Then stampes in Gold, or summes in sealed bagges:
> And 'tis the very riches of thy selfe,
> That now I ayme at (III. iv. 13–18)

the best that the Quarto can do is:

> Thy father thinks I loue thee for his wealth,
> Tho I must needs confesse at first that drew me,
> But since thy vertues wiped that trash away,
> I loue thee *Nan*, and so deare is it set,
> That whilst I liue, I nere shall thee forget.

The tortured syntax and word-order of the Quarto are more easily explained as the price paid in a desperate attempt to recall ideas that were half-remembered (and remembered to be in verse) than as a probable part of a 'first shot' at the speech.

The examples of Quarto's retaining the sense of the Folio, but not the words; of its spoiling the very point of what it is trying to say; and of its omitting the only words and phrases that can make sense of what it retains, are far too numerous to list. The following, however, are typical:

(1) F. I. i. 112. *Eu. Pauca verba*; (Sir *Iohn*) good worts.
Q. *Sir. Hu.* Good vrdes sir *Iohn*, good vrdes.

(2) F. I. i. 40–59, and 187–238. Evans proposes the match between Slender and Anne Page ('there is also another deuice in my praine. . . There is *Anne Page*, which is daughter to Master *Thomas Page*, which is pretty virginity'), and mentions her 'goot gifts'; and Shallow and Evans try to prompt Slender and to 'description the matter' to him, but he is not 'capacity of it'.

Q. *Shal.* . . . M. *Page* . . . For you
Syr, I loue you, and for my cousen
He comes to looke vpon your daughter.
Pa. And heres my hand, and if my daughter
Like him so well as I, wee'l quickly haue it a match

—and this before Slender's idiocy has been demonstrated. (Quarto's words probably represent a confusion with III. ii. 52–6.)

(3) F. I. i. 270–5. *Sl.* I haue seene *Sackerson* loose, twenty times, and haue taken him by the Chaine; but (I warrant you) the women haue so cride and shrekt at it, that it past: But women indeede, cannot abide 'em, they are very ill-fauour'd rough things.

Q. *Slen.* . . . Ile run yon to a Beare, and take her by the mussell,
You neuer saw the like.
But indeed I cannot blame you,
For they are maruellous rough things.

(4) F. I. ii. 2–5. *Eu.* . . . one Mistris *Quickly*; which is in the manner of his Nurse; or his dry-Nurse; or his Cooke; or his Laundry; his Washer, and his Ringer.

Q. *Sir Hu.* . . . one mistris *Quickly*, his woman, or his try nurse.

(5) F. I. iv. 88–99. *Qui.* [to Simple, of Caius] . . . ye French Doctor my Master, (I may call him my Master, looke you, for I keepe his house; and I wash, ring, brew, bake, scowre, dresse meat and drinke, make the beds, and doe all my selfe:)

Simp. 'Tis a great charge to come vnder one bodies hand.

Qui. Are you a-uis'd o' that? you shall finde it a great charge: and to be vp early, and down late: but notwithstanding, (to tell you in your eare, I wold haue no words of it) my Master himselfe is in loue with Mistris *Anne Page*.

Q. *Quic.* . . . my M. hath a great affectioned mind to mistresse *Anne* himselfe. And if he should know that I should as they say, giue my verdit for any one but himselfe, I should heare of it throughly: For I tell you friend, he puts all his priuities in me.

Sim. I by my faith you are a good staie to him.

Quic. Am I? I and you knew all yowd say so:
Washing, brewing, baking, all goes through my hands,
Or else it would be but a woe house.

Sim. I beshrow me, one woman to do all this,
Is very painfull.

Quic. Are you auised of that? I, I warrant you,
Take all, and paie all, all goe through my hands.

(Here it will be noticed that although, exceptionally, the Quarto is not shorter, it is still thinner; the subtler indecencies of the Folio have been reduced to one obvious malapropism; Simple's two comments between them do not provide as good a 'lead' as 'one bodies hand'; and Quickly's twice-used 'all goes through my hands' misses the joke.)

(6) F. II. i. 4–19. Falstaff's letter to Mistress Ford (substantially as in this text).

Q. *Mis. Pa.* Mistresse *Page* I loue you. Aske me no reason,
Because theyr impossible to alledge. Your faire,
And I am fat. You loue sack, so do I:
As I am sure I haue no mind but to loue,
So I know you haue no hart but to grant[.]
A souldier doth not vse many words, where a knowes
A letter may serue for a sentence. I loue you,
And so I leaue you.
Yours Syr Iohn Falstaffe.

(and the Quarto manages only a twenty-line summary of the ensuing discussion of the letter by Mistress Page and Mistress Ford—about seventy lines in the Folio).

(7) F. II. ii. 52–76. Quickly's long-winded attempt to give Falstaff the message from Mistress Ford is followed by Falstaff's plea 'But what saies shee to mee? be briefe my good shee-*Mercurie*'.

Q reduces Quickly's lines to five; and in those five she does give Falstaff some information (that Mistress Ford has received his letter); yet Quarto retains 'Nay prethy be briefe my good she *Mercury*'.

(8) F. II. ii. 259. *Fal.* [to 'Broome', of Ford] Hang him (poore Cuckoldly knaue) I know him not. . .

267–8. *Fal.* Hang him, mechanicall-salt-butter rogue; I wil stare him out of his wits.

Q. *Fal.* Hang him poore cuckally knaue, I know him not. . .
Fal. Hang him cuckally knaue, Ile stare him
Out of his wits.

(9) F. III. ii. The Folio begins with the cross-chat of Ford, Mistress Page, and Robin (not in the Quarto at all), then has a soliloquy by Ford (eighteen lines—reduced to five feeble lines in the Quarto); then has Slender and Shallow decline an invitation to dinner at Ford's home, giving as their excuse their earlier invitation to dine with Anne.

Q. (apparently remembering that Anne was not present but was relevant somehow)
For. Welcome good M. *Page*,
I would your daughter were here.
Pa. I thank you sir, she is very well at home.

(10) F. IV. ii. 113–16. *Page.* Why, this passes M. *Ford*: you are not to goe loose any longer, you must be pinnion'd.
Euans. Why this is Lunaticks: this is madde, as a mad dogge.
Shall. Indeed *M. Ford*, thi[s] is not well indeed.

Q. *Pa.* Fie M. *Ford* you are not to go abroad if you be in these fits.

Sir Hu. By so kad vdge me, tis verie necessarie
He were put in pethlem.

The 'reporting' process that seems to be illustrated by this analysis of the relation of the Quarto to the Folio text may have taken place in different ways and for at least two possible purposes (the preparation of a text specifically for sale to a publisher or the attempt to reconstruct one for acting). The theory that the play was taken down, inadequately, in shorthand would not account for the misplacings or for the kinds of misunderstanding and substitution noted above, whereas a theory of 'memorial reconstruction' does cover them all; and that the reporters were members of a company that had acted the play is made probable by the variation in the quality of the reporting from scene to scene and from character to character.

Of the important parts, those of Page, Ford, Mistress Ford, Mistress Page, Mistress Quickly, and Fenton, in particular, are badly reported; speeches by these characters are nearly always inaccurate and are sometimes cut almost to nothing. (Three of these roles, significantly, may have been played by boys—who are less likely to play the same part over a period of years, if only because the boy's voice 'breaks' in time.) By contrast the lines spoken by the Host are reproduced with remarkable accuracy. A theory that the reporter was the actor who played the Host was modified by its original proponent, Sir Walter Greg, to the form 'Perhaps it would be safer to assume an independent reporter relying generally on mine Host's assistance';[1] in fact, however, the reasons given for withdrawing the original theory are questionable. Greg admitted that the horse-stealing scenes were not evidence either way, for they may also have been known on the stage in a form different from that in which they appear in the Folio; and if 'there are errors in his speeches that perhaps suggest mishearing rather than the blunders of a compositor (IV. v. 85, "I am cozened Hugh and coy Bardolf" for "hue and cry"!)',[2] that need mean no more than that the Host was himself dictating to an amanuensis (and in fact 'coy' may be a printing error for 'cry' or even a misreading of it by the compositor). Greg's other concession that 'the superiority of the scenes in which he appears is not quite uniform (for instance the beginning of II. ii, when he is off, is better than the end of II. i, when he is on)' is even more misleading: the Host's own few words in II. i, as distinct from Shallow's, are repeated with

1. *The Editorial Problem in Shakespeare*, p. 71. 2. *ibid.*

more than reasonable accuracy: 'God blesse you' instead of 'How now', for example, may be an accurate memory of what was in the unexpurgated text—and the omission of 'will you go An-heires?' may signify only that the actor had no more knowledge than have later editors of what the words were supposed to *mean*. More disturbing, perhaps, is another fact, that where the Folio has in the duel scene (III. i. 71–2), '*Host*. Disarme them, and let them question: let them keepe their limbs whole, and hack our English', the Quarto divides the speech thus: '*Host*. Disarme, let them question. / *Shal*. Let them keep their limbs hole, and hack our English'; yet the mistake, if it is one, is not impossible for an actor, or the alteration may have been an attempt by compositor or 'editor' to 'improve', or the Folio may even be in error.

The good reporting of II. ii, of course, is not evidence against the Host as reporter: it is evidence—and only part of overwhelming evidence—that the actor who played Falstaff was *another* of the reporters. Many of his set speeches are reproduced accurately (I. iii and III. v give good examples);[1] and in a scene such as II. ii it is noticeable how much better Falstaff's part is than either Quickly's or Ford's—and that when Falstaff's fails, it is often because the right cue is missing from the other actor's part. (Actors do not always listen carefully to, let alone remember, what is said *to* them on stage.) IV. ii is not as good—but again the main failing is in the words of other characters, and Falstaff himself has relatively little to say anyway.

Allowing, then, for the possibility of assistance from a 'bookholder' or prompter, and for the other possibility (see pp. xxi–xxii above) that the actors who played Pistol and Nym may have had some share in the reporting (since there are conflations of their parts in *The Merry Wives* with their parts in *2 Henry IV* and *Henry V*), the best hypothesis would seem to be that the Quarto text was put together, at some time after *Henry V* had been produced and perhaps not until 1602, by a small group of adult actors, including at least the two who had played (or, conceivably, understudied?) the parts of Falstaff and the Host of the Garter Inn.[2]

The theory that the state of such a text as the Quarto *Merry Wives* can best be explained as memorial reconstruction is not

1. 'A mountaine of money' (for 'mummy') at III. v. 17 is odd, but may be a compositor's misreading.

2. Speculation whether a leading actor such as William Kemp would have stooped to 'reporting' a play, even after he had left a company, is hardly worth while. There is nothing to say that the Chamberlain's Men did not use understudies; and circumstances must have made it necessary sometimes for a minor actor to step into a leading role. Indeed, the actor who normally played the Host may have been the understudy for Falstaff.

weakened at all by a demonstration that the text also contains occasional errors of other kinds, such as foul case, misreading of secretary or italic script, setting out of prose as verse, or even mishearing. What the reporters have reconstructed must still be written down somehow (for example, by one of the actors, or by a separate amanuensis, to whom the speeches are dictated); and what is written down must still be set in type by a compositor. *If*, then, Quarto's '*Hugh*, and coy *Bardolfe*' is a mishearing of 'Hue and cry', that may mean no more than that what the *reporter* said was misheard (and, in addition to the chance of a simple printing error—perhaps foul case—there are the possibilities that the actor learnt some of his part in the first place from dictation, or that the compositor worked for a while from dictation); and the same explanations would cover, if indeed they are mishearings or 'aural' misunderstandings, Quarto's 'gongarian' for 'hungarian' (I. iii. 19); 'by my sword were steele' for 'by my side weare Steele' (I. iii. 72); 'de Hearing be not so dead . . .' for 'de herring is no dead, so . . .' (II. iii. 11); 'is a dead bullies taile' for 'is he dead bully-Stale' (II. iii. 27–8); and 'thou shalt wear her' for 'thou shalt wooe her' (II. iii. 82–3). 'Betmes' for 'buttons' (III. ii. 63) is probably the compositor's misreading rather than the reporter's misremembering; and the constant setting out of prose as verse may be misunderstanding (or attempted inflation) by either compositor or reporters.

A more difficult problem is presented by the omission from the Quarto of passages or whole scenes of the full text. Here there are at least three possibilities: that the reporters simply forgot parts of the original; that they (or their 'editor', if they assigned to one of their number, or to another, the authority to patch up, or put together, the text) deliberately cut the original; or that the version they were trying to recall was itself a cut version of the full text as preserved, for example, in the Folio.

The first explanation covers the omission of many single lines and whole speeches and the general abbreviating where the Quarto dialogue retains the gist of what had been spoken but leaves out much of the detail and most of the colour. It is thus valid for the kinds of inadequacy already noted (pp. xxiii ff.); for the omission of the talk about Page's 'fallow Greyhound' by Slender, Shallow, and Page in I. i and of Quickly's words with and about Rugby before she questions Simple in I. iv; for the truncating of some of Ford–Brook's speeches to Falstaff in II. ii; and possibly for the omission of Mistress Page's discussion with Robin, and discussion of Robin with Ford, at the beginning of III. ii.

One cannot argue that Robin has been deliberately cut from the

Quarto version: his entry and exit in I. iii forbid this. (It is true that he does not speak, but he does not speak here in the Folio either; in both texts he is addressed by Falstaff and given the task of carrying the letters to Mistress Page and Mistress Ford.) Accordingly his omission from II. ii (where his only line in the Folio is to introduce Mistress Quickly—'Sir, here's a woman would speake with you'—and his only other function is to accompany her out) and from III. iii (where in the Folio he announces Falstaff's arrival and later Mistress Page's approach) may both be accidental: in neither scene is he essential to the plot and he certainly has nothing memorable to say. Nevertheless, the possibility that the part had been cut to a minimum before the Quarto was 'reported', in some intermediate version, so that it could be played by—for example—the boy who also played Anne Page, cannot be dismissed (although no company could easily have played *The Merry Wives* if it were short of boys: they are needed as fairies in the final act).

The reduction of Fenton's part in the Quarto raises a similar question. The Quarto omits altogether Fenton's interview with Quickly at the end of I. iv. The first mention of him in the Quarto is thus the Host's question to Page, in III. ii: 'But what say you to yong Maister *Fenton*? . . .' and he first appears, in an abbreviated version of III. iv, with Quickly and Anne. IV. vi is reported well enough, just, to make clear his final plot to marry Anne; and he duly enters with her at the end of the play, but has only two poor lines instead of a formal speech of eleven. Forgetfulness by the reporters may explain this; the alternative explanation is that the reduction has been made to avoid any unnecessary re-telling or fore-telling of what is seen happening on the stage.

This may well be the explanation of the omission from Falstaff's speech in III. v, describing to Ford his sad fate in the buck-basket, of lines 86–98, which recapitulate the stage-action of III. iii—and it will be remembered that Falstaff's part is generally well reported. There can be little doubt that V. i, V. ii, V. iii, and V. iv are omitted because they add nothing to the story. Yet that V. i was not omitted *before* the reporting is proved by the fact that one phrase from it ('this is the third time: I hope good lucke lies in odde numbers') gets into the Quarto version of V. V.

The Latin lesson, IV. i, must have been left out—whether by the reporters or in an intermediate version they were reporting—because it would lose all its fun for an audience that did not know Latin, and most of it for an audience that had not been brought up on William Lilly's Latin grammar text. (The omission of IV. i in turn made necessary the reordering of III. iv and III. v to avoid two consecutive Falstaff scenes.) Presumably Caius' longer French phrases were dropped from I. iv for auditors who could not be assumed to know French; and the jokes in I. i on 'Coram' and '*Cust-alorum*' and on coats of arms with 'Luces' in them would naturally go out for performance before an audience that could not be expected to understand them. Probably, too, such lines as 'What Duke should that be comes so secretly' (IV. iii) and '*Germanes* are honest men' (IV. v) were private or 'in' jokes, not appropriate for all occasions.[1]

Behind the Quarto text, then, there would seem to be a version of *The Merry Wives* that was designed for an audience not aristocratic and not primarily intellectual, whereas the full Folio text has much that would appeal only to the more sophisticated. Here perhaps lies also the explanation of the main differences between the two forms of the final scene (V. v).

In the Quarto, the action may not be convincing but it is relatively straightforward (though rendered hopelessly confusing because of its own confusion over the colours). Falstaff enters and is joined by Mistress Ford and Mistress Page (arriving together); Sir Hugh '*like a Satyre*' and Mistress Quickly '*like the Queene of Fayries*' come on with boys dressed as fairies, and Quickly instructs them to pinch black and blue any mortal they find; Evans gives pointless orders to 'Peane' and 'Pead'; and Falstaff is found, and 'tested' for virtue by tapers put to his fingers' ends. While the fairies '*sing about*' Falstaff, Caius '*steales away a boy in red*' (which is what Fenton had said was Mistress Page's plan); Slender takes another boy '*in greene*' (though Page has previously said that Anne would be in white for Slender, and Fenton had confirmed this); '*And Fenton steales misteris Anne, being in white*'. The entry of Ford, Page, and company immediately disconcerts Falstaff—whose question 'What hunting at this time at night? / Ile lay my life the mad Prince of *Wales* / Is stealing his fathers Deare' does not seem to refer specifically to any action the audience knows of except the appearance of these others. Ford demands the return of £20 borrowed by Falstaff from 'Brooke', but at his wife's request agrees to forgo it. Caius enters complaining that his expected bride turned out to be a boy; Slender likewise has discovered that his wife is a boy, though 'I came to her in red as you bad me'; and Fenton and Anne return, and are forgiven largely because the accomplished fact cannot be undone. But Mistress Page is glad that her husband's plan failed, he is glad that hers miscarried, and Falstaff gets satisfaction from knowing that both their arrows

1. See below, pp. xlvi–xlix.

'glanced'. They are happy to go home to laugh at Slender and Caius. Although this would be far more effective if the reconciliation had not taken place *before* Slender, Caius, Fenton, and Anne returned, the spirit is sustained for the 'happy ending', the interest is entirely in that ending, and there is nothing to connect the scene with any particular occasion or ceremony.

In the Folio, however, not only are the opening speeches fuller and more amusing (Falstaff thinks Mistress Ford is alone and has to be told 'Mistris *Page* is come with me (sweet hart)'), but also there are two specific references to Windsor Castle: one is Pistol's instruction to 'Cricket' to leap to 'Windsor-chimnies' and pinch any lazy maids because 'Our radiant Queene, hates Sluts, and Sluttery', the other is Quickly's long and, in a sense, irrelevant set speech (ll. 56–77) packed with references to the Order of the Garter and apparently directing the elves to prepare the Castle and St George's Chapel for a ceremony connected with that Order. Falstaff is 'discovered' and tested in much the same way as in the Quarto; but he is not let off as easily and is ridiculed and teased by all who are in a position to gloat over him. There is not even the suggestion that he will be let off the repayment of the £20 he had from 'Broome':[1] indeed 'his horses are arrested for it' and 'to repay that money will be a biting affliction'. It is at this point that Page first invites Falstaff 'to be cheerefull', by laughing at Mistress Page who does not know that Slender 'hath married her daughter'. Slender enters and disabuses him: he took a fairy in green, who proved to be a boy. (In IV. vi. 34–7 and V. ii. 5–10, however, it has been made quite clear that Slender should have taken the fairy in *white*.) Mistress Page announces that Caius has taken Anne in white—and Caius enters to complain that the white fairy too was a boy. (And, of course, although Mistress Page originally said in IV. iv. 70–1 that Anne was to be in white—and meant to deceive the others by changing the colour later—the real plan, of IV. vi. 37–41, was for Caius to find Anne in green.) The entry of Fenton and Anne clears up the main mystery and makes it possible for Falstaff for the first time to feel that others cannot afford to laugh at him: 'I am glad, though you haue tane a special stand to strike at me, that your Arrow hath glanc'd'. Mistress Page's 'Good husband, let vs euery one go home, / And laugh this sport ore by a Countrie fire, / Sir *Iohn* and all' saves—so to speak—*everybody's* face.

It would seem, then, that once again the Quarto has all the

1. For discussion of the Brook–Broome problem throughout the play, see below, pp. xxxiv–xxxv and lvi–lviii.

marks of the 'reported' text: the reordering of speeches and events robs them of meaning, and perhaps the Quarto confusion over the colours is a relic of confusion in the original text, helped (in one sense, and made worse in another) by the remembrance that the third colour in the denouement was red.[1] But it is far from certain that what the Quarto is reporting here is the Folio text. The complete omission of the Windsor Castle and Garter speeches (though the action is still left in 'Windsor forrest') may indicate this time that those speeches were not in the text being reported: that, in short, there was an alternative ending to the play for use—probably on the public stage—when, perhaps, the special occasion for which the original text was prepared was simply not relevant.

The general superiority of the Folio does not mean that the Quarto is invariably inferior. No matter how corrupt a reported text may be, there is always the chance that a reporter will have remembered correctly what the scribe who copied the good text, or the compositor who set it up in print, accidentally omitted, misread, or otherwise got wrong; and if the better text had been revised or in any way altered *after* the production or productions that the reporter knew, then the more corrupt text may in some respects be nearer to the original than is the generally superior one. Both these possibilities seem to have been realized with *The Merry Wives*.

The clearest example of the first is towards the end of III. i, where the Host is (he thinks) scoring over Caius and Evans and reconciling them to each other. In the words of the Folio,

> Shall I loose my Doctor? No, hee giues me the Potions and the Motions. Shall I loose my Parson? my Priest? my Sir *Hugh*? No, he giues me the Prouerbes, and the No-verbes. Giue me thy hand (Celestiall) so: Boyes of Art, I haue deceiu'd you both.

1. Interestingly, the Quarto report of IV. iv is particularly poor in *all* respects. In dressing Anne in white when Fenton elopes with her, the Quarto may be influenced by the idea that this is the appropriate colour for a bride; but since there are three specific statements in the Folio that *Slender* must expect her in white (IV. iv. 70–4, IV. vi. 34–7, V. ii. 5–10), and since the boy whom Caius takes must be in green, Anne probably wears a third colour for Fenton—which will be red, if the Quarto reporter, confused as he was, remembered correctly the colours involved. The suggestion, made, for example, by Schücking (*M.L.R.*, XIX, 1924, 338–40), that Fenton distinguished Anne by the 'Ribonds-pendant, flaring 'bout her head'—words that the Quarto puts in the speech in which Fenton describes (to the Host) how he will recognize her—does not explain the Quarto's other confusions about the colours, and does not begin to explain how the words appear in the Folio in Fenton's description of how *Caius* will recognize Anne.

The Quarto, though not right, comes to the rescue here:

> Shall I lose my doctor? No, he giues me the motiōs
> And the potions. Shall I lose my parson, my sir *Hu*?
> No, he giues me the prouerbes, and the nouerbes:
> Giue me thy hand terestiall,
> So giue me thy hand celestiall:
> So boyes of art I haue deceiued you both.

The reporter, although he has apparently forgotten two words ('my Priest'), has remembered the crucial words 'Give me thy hand terrestrial, so' (though either he or the compositor erred over 'terrestrial'), which the Folio omitted, presumably because the compositor's (or scribe's) eye skipped to the parallel word 'celestial'.[1]

Many editors have thought that there are other examples, but these are open to another explanation. For instance, where the Folio has Falstaff say (IV. v. 97–8) 'well, if my winde were but long enough; I would repent', the Quarto has 'and my winde / Were but long inough to say my prayers, / Ide repent', and there is no doubt that the additional words make the joke obvious—but perhaps so obvious that a reporter is more likely to have put them into Falstaff's mouth than is Shakespeare. Similarly, there is no good reason for believing that the Quarto's opening to II. ii

> *Fal.* Ile not lend thee a peny.
> *Pis.* I will retort the sum in equipage.
> *Fal.* Not a pennie

is other than a weaker version of the Folio's

> *Fal.* I will not lend thee a penny.
> *Pist.* Why then the world's mine Oyster, which I, with sword will open.
> *Fal.* Not a penny.

So far from preserving a line dropped from the Folio, the Quarto reporter may be only substituting one semi-proverbial phrase for another.[2] Again, in I. i, Slender's specific charge against Pistol and Nym in the Quarto that 'They carried mee to the Tauerne and made mee drunke, and afterward picked my pocket' has been retained by most editors as a lead to Falstaff's later question in the Folio (and in the Quarto), '*Pistoll*, did you picke M. *Slenders* purse?' Is it not probable, however, that Falstaff's question, since nobody

1. For an illustration of the similar dropping of a necessary line from a good text (*2 Henry VI*) and its preservation in a reported text (*The Contention*) see Alfred Hart's *Stolne and Surreptitious Copies*, pp. 301–2.

2. See note on II. ii. 2–3.

in the Folio text has mentioned the charge, shows a prior knowledge of the crime—because he has been involved in it? (As Pistol afterwards says to him on a similar matter, 'Didst not thou share? hadst thou not fifteene pence?') The Quarto, confusing Falstaff's later question with Slender's accusation, misses the subtlety completely. Finally, if the Quarto's version of Nym's briefing of Page in II. i:

> *Nym.* . . . Farwell, I loue not the humor of bread and cheese:
> And theres the humor of it. *Exit Nym.*
> *Pa.* The humor of it, quoth you:
> Heres a fellow frites humor out of his wits.

is compared with the Folio's far fuller one, ending

> *Nim.* . . . adieu, I loue not the humour of bread and cheese: adieu.
> *Page.* The humour of it (quoth 'a?) heere's a fellow frights English out of his wits

it may be concluded, not that the Quarto preserves a phrase ('And theres the humor of it') wrongly dropped from the Folio, but that the Quarto is monotonously repeating one phrase (possibly imported from *Henry V*)—and that in the Folio Page catches up Nym's single word 'humour', not a whole phrase.[1]

There are two, or perhaps three, examples in the play of Quarto's preserving the original text where the Folio preserves a revised and possibly un-Shakespearian reading. One of these concerns the pseudonym that Ford adopts when in disguise he bribes Falstaff, as he thinks, to demonstrate Mistress Ford's unfaithfulness. In the Folio the pseudonym is, always, 'Broome'; in the Quarto it is 'Brooke'. 'Brooke' or 'Brook' is obviously a more natural second name for a Ford than is 'Broome'; and indeed there are lines in the Folio that make sense only on the supposition that 'Broome' must be replaced by 'Brook'. The best instance is Falstaff's comment (II. ii. 145–6) when he is told that the visitor has sent him 'a mornings draught of Sacke': 'such *Broomes* are welcome to mee, that ore'flowes such liquor'. The Quarto reads 'Such *Brookes* are alwaies welcome to me', which is far better sense, but, most significantly, omits the following words, 'that ore'flowes such liquor', which are necessary to give point to the jest—an almost

1. See above, p. xxi; and see note on II. i. 133. It may be added that in the lines corresponding to I. iii. 90 and 91, the Quarto has Nym and Pistol say that they will report Falstaff's ambitions to Page and Ford, as they later do, whereas the Folio has it the wrong way round. The Quarto may be either rationalizing here or recalling a performance in which the confusion had been 'tidied up'. See, however, the note on I. iii. 90, 95.

certain proof that the Quarto did not invent the name 'Brooke' but was once again recalling a joke without being able to recall the exact words that made it a joke. Other Folio phrases that perhaps lose their point with the substitution of 'Broome' for 'Brooke' are (III. v. 126–8): 'you shall haue her (Master *Broome*) Master *Broome*, you shall cuckold *Ford*' and the final couplet of the play 'To Master *Broome*, you yet shall hold your word, / For he, to night, shall lye with Mistris *Ford*'. The only logical explanation seems to be that Shakespeare wrote 'Brook(e)' and that 'Brooke' was spoken on the stage, since the Quarto remembers it, and that at some *later* time 'Broome' was substituted for it.[1]

The second way in which the Folio text seems to have been altered for the worse after the original performances concerns the oaths and other asseverations. In II. ii. 49–50, for instance, the Folio has Quickly say 'heauen-blesse them, and make them his Seruants', while the Quarto has 'Now God blesse them, and make them his seruants'. In II. iii. 18 in the Folio, Shallow's greeting is ''Saue you Mr. Doctor *Caius*'; in the Quarto the line (given to Page) is 'God saue you M. Doctor *Cayus*'. For Evans's ''Plesse my soule: how full of Chollors I am, and trempling of minde' (III. i. 11–12), the Quarto has 'Ieshu ples mee, how my hart trobes, and trobes'; and for the Folio's ''Mercie on mee, I haue a great dispositions to cry', the Quarto reads 'Now so kad vdge me, my hart / Swelles more and more. Mee thinkes I can cry / Verie well'. The last two examples are perhaps good enough reason for suspecting that the Quarto cannot be trusted to have the oaths exact, since it has only a vague paraphrase of the words that the oaths introduce (and a study of other bad texts such as the First Quarto of *Romeo and Juliet* confirms that reporters improvise asseverations more readily than most other phrasing). Nevertheless the Folio text has obviously been censored. The expurgation of dramatic texts became more common, though not invariable, after the *Acte to Restraine Abuses of Players* (3 Jac. I, c.21–27 May 1606), which provided a penalty of £10 for 'jestingly or prophanely' speaking or using 'the holy Name of God or of Christ Jesus, or of the Holy Ghoste or of the Trinitie' in any 'Stageplayes, Interludes, Maygames, Shewes' or pageants; and there was some 'censorship' of printed plays also, at least after Sir Henry Herbert took office as (virtually) Master of the Revels, in 1623—what Greg calls 'a purely literary tradition of expurgation'. It seems that plays were sometimes expurgated by scribes or 'editors' as a precaution before being presented for licensing; and it is generally said that the expurgating of the plays in the Folio of

1. See below, pp. lvi–lviii.

1623 is more severe in those that were printed, or prepared for printing, after Herbert's succession—i.e. in the Histories and Tragedies.[1] Here, however, in *The Merry Wives*, is a comedy that has been expurgated—which may be some kind of reason for thinking that the offending phrases were removed for stage purposes, after 1606 but before the transcript or other copy was prepared for the printing of the Folio.

The New Cambridge editors have argued (p. 125) that the Quarto's references to '*Horne* the hunter' also preserve an original name that has been corrupted in the Folio to 'Herne'. It is not certain that there was a legend of a former keeper in Windsor Forest who haunted an oak in the neighbourhood (although *after* Shakespeare's day there was an oak that apparently became famous as Herne's or Falstaff's oak, until it was cut down towards the end of the eighteenth century); but whether there was such a tradition or not, it seems far more likely that the Quarto, always ready to make more obvious or otherwise vulgarize, would have substituted 'Horne' for 'Herne' and then invented the line saying that Falstaff was to be persuaded to come 'Disguised like *Horne*, with huge horns on his head', than that Folio would have replaced 'Horne' by 'Herne', for no good reason at all. (Various claims to have discovered the name 'Herne' or 'Horne' 'in the old Windsor Registers of Shakespeare's period' or on a list of yeomen guilty of poaching in Henry VIII's reign seem, like W. S. Gilbert's flowers that bloom in the spring, to have nothing to do with the case.[2]) What is curious is that Mistress Ford's and Mistress Page's explanations to their husbands (IV. iv) of their third and final plan to disgrace Falstaff do not, in the Folio, specify that Falstaff is to be disguised like Herne with horns on his head; many editors, not content with Mistress Page's later 'We'll . . . dis-horne the spirit', therefore incorporate the Quarto line, even if they change 'Horne' to 'Herne' in the process.[3]

One other slight difference between the Quarto and the Folio should be mentioned. In I. iv in the good text, Mistress Quickly hides Simple in the 'Closset' where Caius keeps his green box and his other 'simples'; and it is in the 'Closset' that Caius discovers the hidden visitor. The Quarto refers consistently not to a closet but to a 'Counting-house' (three times in the dialogue and once in a stage direction). Many commentators have found it difficult to believe that a counting-house and a closet were so similar that the

1. See, e.g., Chambers, *Elizabethan Stage*, IV. 338–9; Greg, *The Shakespeare First Folio* (Oxford, 1955), pp. 149–52 and 169–72.

2. H. C. Hart, *The Merry Wives of Windsor*, pp. li–lii.

3. See note on IV. iv. 28–45.

reporter of the Quarto could himself have substituted one for the other and they have suspected that the Quarto is, so to speak, a London version of the play. It has thus also been thought significant that the Quarto replaces some of the references to Windsor Castle in the final scene with the lines 'Where is *Pead*? go you & see where Brokers sleep, / And Foxe-eyed Seriants with their mase, / Goe laie the Proctors in the street, / And pinch the lowsie Seriants face'. Yet it replaces others with lines about 'these shady groues', and 'Peane' is told to go 'to the countrie houses'; John Munro has shown that 'counting houses' were known in country homes (the house-keeping accounts were kept there); and, as he says, 'Brokers, Serjeants, and Proctors were not peculiar to London'.[1] The Quarto's variations again look like poor improvisation rather than logical substitution. It is just possible, however, that the version of the play used on the public stage presented Caius as the kind of dealer in herbs and other medicines with which a typical London audience would have been familiar. Another theory, that the Quarto—for some reason—is closer to a supposed source play about London citizens, is contradicted by all the evidence showing that the Folio text was in fact the earlier.[2]

3. THE PRINTING OF THE QUARTO AND THE FOLIO

The printer of the 1602 Quarto of *The Merry Wives*, T[homas] C[reede], printed two other bad Quartos, *The First Part of the Contention betwixt the Two Famous Houses of Yorke and Lancaster* (1594)—for T. Millington—and *The Cronicle History of Henry the fift* (1600)—for Millington and Busby (and Busby, it will be remembered, assigned *The Merry Wives* to Arthur Johnson, just before the publication of the Quarto in 1602). It might be unwise to infer that either Busby or Creede habitually dealt in pirated texts: apparently publishers and printers did not always inquire into the good faith of those who sold dramatic texts or wanted them printed—although failure to inquire, even in the days before copyright, may itself suggest an incriminating lack of concern.

The printing of the Quarto is careless and also rather odd. There is some reason for thinking that at least two compositors were involved: one preferred the spellings 'Ford' and 'here' and was addicted to the colon as a mark of punctuation (there are some twenty-one colons on E2, for example—counting both dialogue and speech-prefixes); the other normally spelt 'Foord' and 'heere' and

1. 'Some Matters Shakespearian', *Times Literary Supplement*, 13 September 1947.

2. See not only pp. xiii–xxvi above but also pp. lx–lxi.

could set a whole page with but a single colon (E3, for instance). The second seems to have been more willing than the first to set prose as prose—but throughout the Quarto the intention was presumably to set everything possible as verse, largely, perhaps, to spread it all out more, over as great a number of pages as possible, though there are many abbreviations and turned-over lines. (E2^{v}, which is nearly all prose, is quite exceptional.) Probably the existence of the two compositors, working simultaneously but from two different cases of type, is connected also with the curious use of the italic capital '*I*' for the roman on many pages. The italic '*I*' is first found on B3^{v}, but not in the first seven lines, in which there are four roman capital 'I's; Quickly's speech in line 8 begins '*I*s he quoth you' and the italic capital is used in the remainder of that page and throughout B4 (but not at all in B4^{v}—where suddenly there is prose, in the speech by Mistress Page following the reading of Falstaff's letter, although the rest of the page, after Mistress Ford's entrance, is set as 'verse'). This looks like two compositors setting at this stage by formes—with the compositor who set the inner forme running out of the roman capital 'I', and resorting to the italic, before the end of his stint.[1] No such clear-cut pattern emerges in the remainder of the play, although the two compositors may have continued to divide the work, unsystematically, throughout: perhaps once the type was distributed after the printing of the 'B' gathering, and after the setting of some of 'C', the roman and italic capital 'I's were mixed up, in one case: there are pages in which none of the italic capitals occur—namely C1, C1^{v}, and C2, and then C3, C4^{v}, D1, D1^{v}, F1, F1^{v}, G2^{v}, G3, and G3^{v}; at least one which has them only at the top of the page (C4); others which have them only after a certain point (C2^{v}, C3^{v}, D4); and many which have a mixture (D2, D4^{v}, etc.).

Unfortunately there is nothing in the facts or hypotheses concerning the printing of the Quarto to help determine the nature of the copy from which it was set. No one character's speeches, for example, are more consistently in prose than another's, and none has a characteristic spelling. The only useful guess might be that most of the copy was in prose; that the persistent setting out as verse was a matter of 'editorial' or 'compositorial' policy and, occasionally, of *ad hoc* decisions based on the spacing of the page; and that since Fenton, on his few appearances, *always* speaks verse, albeit sometimes very poor verse, the reporter (who was certainly not the actor who played Fenton) may have remembered that the

1. It may be significant of a general scarcity of type that on these same two pages—B3^{v} and B4—the compositor resorts to roman 'VV' for 'W'.

part, exceptionally, was mostly blank verse in the original text.

There are five surviving copies of the Quarto—in the British Museum; the Bodleian Library; the Wren Library of Trinity College, Cambridge; the Folger; and the Huntington.[1] They have all been collated, and no variants have been found, other than a 'variant' apparently caused by the dislodging of a piece of type.

The Folio, although a longer and better text than the Quarto, is certainly not perfect. As has already been shown (pp. xxxii ff.), in at least one speech the Folio dropped, by accident, a line that must have been in the play as written and that, by good luck, is preserved in the Quarto; the text has been expurgated, at some indefinable time between the composition of the play and the publication of the Folio (but probably after 1606); and at the beginning of I. iii either the scribe or the compositor has perpetrated an obvious and understandable error with the stage direction '*Enter Falstaffe, Host, Bardolfe, Nym, Pistoll, Page*': Page does not appear in this scene at all and could not conceivably do so, for he is discussed in his absence, but 'the Page', Robin, is needed and must be meant.

The stage directions in the Folio are all of the kind just cited: that is to say, at the beginning of every scene (and the Folio has a full, systematic, division into acts and scenes) there is a list of all the characters who appear at any time during the scene—i.e. a so-called 'massed entry'; but no other entries or exits are marked during a scene, no matter how many characters may come and go. There is only one exception: '*Enter Fairies*' at v. v. 37—an entry which is still cryptic, for it covers the disguised Evans, Pistol, and Quickly as well as the children.

The massed entries, made 'under the influence of the neo-classical drama of the Continent',[2] are part of the evidence for the generally accepted theory that the 'copy' given to the printer for the Folio *Merry Wives* was a transcript made by the professional scribe, Ralph Crane. Crane—whose transcripts of Middleton's *Game at Chess* and *The Witch* and Fletcher's *Demetrius and Enanthe*, and other works, have survived and been carefully studied for evidence of his scribal habits—is thought to have been employed, as a matter of policy, to transcribe for the printer what were to be the first four plays in the Folio, namely *The Tempest*, *The Two*

1. The original *Short-Title Catalogue*, compiled by A. W. Pollard and G. R. Redgrave in 1926, mistakenly lists four other copies, which are in fact of the 1619 Quarto.

2. Greg, *Editorial Problem*, p. 137. Greg convincingly refutes the earlier theory that massed entries were an indication of a text made up from players' parts and a 'plot' (a summary of exits and entrances, action and properties).

Gentlemen of Verona, *The Merry Wives of Windsor*, and *Measure for Measure*. *The Two Gentlemen of Verona* also has the massed entries (though *The Tempest* and *Measure for Measure* have not). Other characteristics of Crane found in *The Merry Wives* are his addiction to parentheses—'that same knaue (*Ford* hir husband) hath the finest mad diuell of iealousie in him (Master *Broome*) . . .'; his extravagant use of colons; his fondness for hyphens—'an old-fat-woman', 'rag'd-hornes', 'ranting-Host', 'mary-her'; a strange use of the apostrophe—'go't's' (='Got's'), 'do's' (='does'), 'if he ha's'; and some favoured spellings ('troa' for 'trow' may be one: compare 'doa' for 'doe' in both *The Witch* and *Demetrius and Enanthe*).[1] Perhaps too the occasional setting-up as 'verse' of what can only be prose—as in Mistress Page's comments on Falstaff's letter in II. i[2]—occurs because the compositor follows Crane, who, although he does not necessarily begin every line with a capital, has a most confusing trick sometimes of setting out in separate lines like verse what must have been prose in his copy. On the other hand, Crane elsewhere has careful stage directions marking exits and entrances during scenes (notably in *The Witch*). It must be added that *any* inference about what was in the printer's 'copy' for an Elizabethan play is in a sense guesswork, since Elizabethan compositors felt free to space and punctuate as seemed to them fitting at the moment.

That true verse does occur at times in the Folio text of *The Merry Wives* need not mean that there was anything odd about the copy. If, as will be argued later (p. lxxvi), the verse is used appropriately for some of the more romantic or serious parts, there is no necessity for a theory that the verse sections represent copy by a different playwright or copy from an earlier stage of composition (although it is certainly not impossible that *The Merry Wives* involves revision of an earlier play). Nor can much be inferred from the presence in v. v of the only stage direction within a scene. The entry of so many characters at once is itself exceptional in the action of the play; and in other respects Act v Scene v seems to be no different from the rest: it has the massed entry at the beginning of the scene, and other 'Crane' mannerisms. It is true that Evans's Welsh accent is not indicated in the speeches he utters while in

1. On Crane, see, e.g., F. P. Wilson, 'Ralph Crane, Scrivener to the King's Players', *The Library*, 4th Ser. VII (1927), 194–215; W. W. Greg, 'Some Notes on Crane's Manuscript of *The Witch*', *The Library*, XXII (1942), 208–22; Middleton's *A Game at Chesse*, ed. R. C. Bald (Cambridge, 1929); the Malone Society editions of *Demetrius and Enanthe* (1951) and *The Witch* (1950); and T. H. Howard-Hill, 'Ralph Crane's Parentheses', *Notes and Queries*, N.S. XII (1965), 334–40.

2. Even the Quarto, exceptionally, reports this, albeit very badly, as prose—a probable indication that it was prose in the original.

disguise as a fairy or satyr or whatever it is; but since Falstaff does notice some accent ('Heauens defend me from that Welsh Fairy'), the explanation may be that the actor playing Evans is being encouraged to give the impression that he 'tries' to alter his accent while speaking his prepared or given lines, and fails.

The printing of the Folio text has been fully analysed by Charlton Hinman in *The Printing and Proof-Reading of the First Folio of Shakespeare* (Oxford, 1963). That *The Merry Wives* was printed immediately after *The Two Gentlemen* is proved by, for example, the error in using the running title '*The Merry Wives of Windsor*' for the last two pages of the preceding play (D1 and D1^{v}); but there may have been interruptions because of the need to work concurrently on, and sometimes give priority to, another book (Wilson's *Christian Dictionary*). Probably for this reason, several compositors (three or even four) seem to have set parts of the text, and Hinman has more than the usual difficulty in identifying them from spelling habits or from typographical evidence. In such conditions, printing errors are to be expected, but there is nothing to suggest any special care in reading proofs. Only five trivial variants in different copies of the Folio have been found: on D2 the final letter was dropped in the catchword and wrongly replaced (so that some copies have, correctly, '*Shal.*' but others have the point before the 'l' and the 'l' upside down); on E2 uncorrected copies have a wrong character (for which 'y^{e}' had to be substituted) and a blotch (probably an inked quad) that had to be removed; and the uncorrected E5^{v} has 'id' for 'in', and another inked quad. There was obviously some 'casting-off' of copy (i.e. calculating in advance how much copy was required to fill a particular page and forme); and on D2^{v}, for example, the compositor can be seen resorting to abbreviations, as he approaches the foot of the second column, so that he can fit all the necessary words and speeches in.

There is an oddity, at the head of the first column of E1, that makes one wonder whether for the minute the compositor had his eye on the Quarto. The relevant lines, as set out in the Folio, are:

> *Cai.* I, dat is very good, excellant.
> *Host.* Peace, I say: heare mine Host of the Garter,
> Am I politicke? Am I subtle? Am I a Machiuell?
> Shall I loose my Doctor? No, hee giues me the Potions
> and the Motions. Shall I loose my Parson? my Priest?
> my Sir *Hugh*? No, . . .

The setting-up of the Host's first two lines as verse is odd (there is room to spare for 'Am' at the end of the first line, and for 'Shall' at the end of the second); and the Quarto is thus:

[D3] *Doc.* This is verie braue, excellent.
Host. Peace I say, heare mine host of the garter,
[D3v] Am I wise? am I pollitícke? am I Matchauil?
Shall I lose my doctor? No, he giues me the motiõs
And the potions. Shall I lose my parson, my sir *Hu*?
No, . . .

It will be apparent, however, that the differences far outweigh the resemblances (indeed it is later in this speech that the Folio omits the words that the Quarto has in the form 'Giue me thy hand terestiall, / So'); and the probable explanation of the passing similarity is that the Host's lines were set out thus (as in the Folio) in Shakespeare's original script, and in the actor's part transcribed from it, and that the actor who played the Host (and was almost certainly one of the reporters of the Quarto, and a good one) has remembered and reproduced, as actors sometimes do, the *look* of his lines as they were written out for him. The same explanation covers a vague typographical similarity in the Folio (D5) and the Quarto (C2v) of a speech by Falstaff (II. ii. 4–12), noted by the New Cambridge editors.[1] There is, then, no good reason for thinking that the Folio was at any time set up from the Quarto.

4. THIS EDITION

In accordance with the practice of the Arden series, the text of this edition is in modern spelling, with modern punctuation. All possible weight has been given to the seventeenth-century punctuation, but any attempt to retain in a modernized text a system so different from our own leads to hopeless inconsistency and invites misunderstanding of Shakespeare's meaning.

Necessarily, in view of what has been said in the preceding sections of this Introduction, this edition is based on the Folio. Readings from the Quarto are adopted very rarely and only when one can be reasonably certain that the Quarto preserves a reading that is right where the Folio, exceptionally, omits it by accident (e.g. III. i. 97) or gets it wrong through misreading or misprinting (as, probably, in I. iii. 14) or, possibly, through rationalization (as in the speech prefix of II. i. 203). The Quarto has also been followed for Ford's pseudonym 'Brooke' as against the Folio's 'Broome', the justification being that the dialogue shows that Shakespeare must have written 'Brook(e)' and that even if he had to put up with 'Broome' for particular performances, he cannot have preferred it.[2] The oaths present a problem. Undoubtedly the Folio text has

1. pp. 95–6. 2. See above, pp. xxxiv–xxxv, and below, pp. lvi–lviii.

been expurgated and yet only by following it can one achieve any consistency at all; the Quarto may sometimes have the oath that Shakespeare wrote down, but all one's experience with reported texts suggests that the reporter had at best an even-money chance of being right on such a question. For once, then, Bertrand Russell's famous dictum may be reversed: it may be better to be consistently 'wrong' (with the Folio) than to be occasionally right (with the Quarto) at the certain cost of importing actors' improvisations that neither Shakespeare nor Heminge and Condell would necessarily have approved. Nor is it impossible that Shakespeare himself, however reluctantly, made the alterations for the expurgated text.

Whereas the Folio entries are massed at the head of each scene, the Quarto often gives a stage direction in the correct place; it therefore has authority of a kind here, although no Quarto stage direction has been adopted unless it can also be inferred from the full text. Stage directions which are in neither the Folio nor the Quarto are, in accordance with Arden practice, invariably placed in square brackets. Once or twice it happens that an early editor (say, Rowe) has a stage direction similar to a Quarto stage direction, in a scene so badly reported in the Quarto that there is no precise parallel between the Quarto and the full text; the stage direction is then put in square brackets and the collation reads, exceptionally, 'Rowe (as Q)'. Imaginary settings of the scene are not given in the stage directions but the collations include a sampling of those invented by earlier editors, generally in complete misunderstanding of the principles of the bare Elizabethan stage.

The collations are essentially selective. Every Folio reading of any importance not adopted in this edition is collated, but it has not been thought necessary to record aberrant Folio line-division where it is obviously typographical in origin—i.e. where verse lines have been cramped into prose length to save space or where prose lines have been spaced out as if verse, to spread insufficient text over a page. Wrong fount is not retained in citations of either the Folio or the Quarto. It is impossible in collations to give all the different readings of the Quarto; but none have been omitted that are conceivably right or have any special interest as evidence of the reporting process.

Emendations made in the later Folios and by subsequent editors are listed only where they are accepted in this edition, or are plausible, or have been so widely accepted as to be familiar to many readers of the play, or have had their place in the historical process of emendation, pointing the way to a better emendation made by a later editor. The collations do not record, for instance, all Pope's scene divisions (a few examples are given) or the attempts of editors to 'normalize' Shakespeare's syntax or their attempts to 'regularize' Evans's bad English (e.g. by altering 'good' to 'goot' or 'cheese' to 'seese').

The Folio reading is given in the exact spelling (except for the long 's') if it is not adopted, as in

27. Galen] *Rowe; Galien F*

but is not necessarily given exactly when it is adopted, as in

50. will hack] *F*

where the Folio actually reads 'will hacke', or even

ACT II SCENE I] *F*

where the Folio has '*Actus Secundus. Scœna Prima*'. If, however, the Folio spelling could conceivably be otherwise interpreted or could be relevant to a textual (as distinct from a purely bibliographical) theory, it is shown thus:

152. we] *F* (wee).

5. THE PROBABLE OCCASION OF THE PLAY AND THE THEORIES OF PERSONAL SATIRE

The tradition, now often repeated as if it were fact, that *The Merry Wives of Windsor* was written by Shakespeare to please Queen Elizabeth is first recorded in print in John Dennis's dedication to George Granville of *The Comical Gallant* in 1702. Dennis's adaptation had not succeeded on the stage: some of his ill-wishers, he says, believed the original play 'to be so admirable, that nothing ought to be added to it; the others fancied it to be so despicable, that anyones time would be lost upon it'; and it is in this context that he makes his now famous statement:

> That this Comedy was not despicable, I guess'd for several Reasons: First, I knew very well, that it had pleas'd one of the greatest Queens that ever was in the World, great not only for her Wisdom in the Arts of Government, but for her knowledge of Polite Learning, and her nice taste of the Drama, for such a taste we may be sure she had, by the relish which she had of the Ancients. This Comedy was written at her Command, and by her direction, and she was so eager to see it Acted, that she commanded it to be finished in fourteen days; and was afterwards, as Tradition tells us, very well pleas'd at the Representation. (A2)

(He repeats in his Prologue the assertion about the fourteen days.)

A few years later, in the biography published with his 1709 editions of Shakespeare, Rowe added to the details:

> She was so well pleas'd with that admirable Character of *Falstaff*, in the two Parts of *Henry* the Fourth, that she commanded him to continue it for one Play more, and to shew him in Love. This is said to be the Occasion of his Writing *The Merry Wives of* Windsor. How well she was obey'd, the Play it self is an admirable Proof. (pp. viii–ix)

Then in 1710 Gildon, probably relying only on Dennis and on Rowe (whose edition he and his publisher Curll were supplementing unasked) but also at least drawing attention to the relevance of parts of Act v, wrote:

> The *Fairys* in the fifth Act makes a Handsome Complement to the Queen, in her Palace of *Windsor*, who had oblig'd him to write a Play of Sir *John Falstaff* in Love, and which I am very well assured he perform'd in a Fortnight; a prodigious Thing, when all is so well contriv'd, and carry'd on without the least Confusion.[1]

There is no reason to believe that Dennis, Rowe, or Gildon knew of the 1602 Quarto. They were therefore presumably not indebted to its title-page for their information that the play had been presented before the Queen. (It is nevertheless not impossible that the tradition of the Queen's command had begun, years earlier, from that same title-page.) Pope (who knew only the 1619 Quarto) and Theobald (who rediscovered that of 1602) made the connection, but unfortunately concluded that the play written in a fortnight for the Queen must have been the Quarto version, which they thought of as a 'first imperfect sketch'.[2] They thereby started criticism on a wrong track, along which it ran happily for over a hundred years.

Gildon was more probably correct when he associated the royal command with the lines in Act v of the play (v. v. 56–74)—found only in the *Folio* text—that instruct the fairies to prepare Windsor Castle for, apparently, some special ceremony and allude to the Order of the Garter. It does not follow, however, that the play was performed *at* Windsor; and easily the most persuasive explanation of the occasion and date of the play is that advanced by Leslie Hotson in his *Shakespeare versus Shallow* (London, 1931), although unfortunately it falls short of final proof.[3]

Hotson argues that the play was performed at the Garter Feast celebrated not in Windsor but in the royal Whitehall Palace, in

1. 'Remarks on the Plays of Shakespear', in *The Works of Mr. William Shakespear* [ed. Rowe]. *Volume the Seventh.* (London, 1710), p. 291.

2. Pope, *The Works of Shakspear*, I. 233; Theobald, *The Works of Shakespeare*, I. 223.

3. William Green's *Shakespeare's 'Merry Wives of Windsor'* tries to build on Hotson's argument but adds little to it.

Westminster, on St George's Day, 23 April 1597. (A decree made early in Elizabeth's reign permitted the celebration 'Where the *Soveraign* should then happen to be'.) This feast, which marked the first election of knights to the Order of the Garter for four years, preceded by one month the formal installation of the knights in St George's Chapel at Windsor, an installation which the Queen did not attend. The Fairy Queen's speech in Act v of the Folio is thus explained adequately as a direction to the fairies that they must now start getting Windsor Castle, and in particular the Chapel, ready for the installation, by scouring the 'Chaires of Order', cleaning the coats of arms and other insignia, and 'writing' in flowers the motto of the Order of the Garter, '*Hony Soit Qui Mal-y-Pence*'. Nor should one overlook the simple fact that a play about Windsor would have been appropriate for the purpose.

Hotson further pointed out that there was a very special reason for the involvement of Shakespeare's company, the Chamberlain's Men, in the London celebrations in April 1597, for one of the five knights being honoured by election to the Order was George Carey, Lord Hunsdon, who became patron of the company after the death of his father Henry in July 1596, and who on 17 April 1597 had just become Lord Chamberlain following the death in March of his father's successor, William Brooke Lord Cobham. Hunsdon seems to have been a great favourite with the Queen (Hotson quotes, on p. 116, a few of her letters to him, one including, in modernized form, the sentence 'And in what place soever you be, you shall find us a mother and a wife to minister unto you all the best effects of that tender and kind affection which we may possibly extend to one whom for many respects we hold so near and dear unto us'); he had decided to make a grand occasion of his election and is known to have borrowed extensively to do so; and he would thus presumably have been most eager to have his company, through its greatest playwright, obey any command the Queen may have given.[1]

The theory that *The Merry Wives of Windsor* was written for the Garter Feast in 1597 has the added attraction that it alone makes sense of allusions in the play that were first discussed by Charles Knight in his 1839 'Pictorial Edition' of Shakespeare. These are the allusions supposed to be to Frederick, Duke of Württemberg and formerly Count of Mömpelgard, allusions which were once

1. F. P. Wilson (*Shakespearian and Other Studies*, Oxford, 1969, p. 88n.), arguing that there is 'no record of payment to the Chamberlain's men' on this day, and that the Queen would not have been likely to pay for the performance herself, overlooks the probability that, if Hotson's theory is correct, Hunsdon would have borne the expenses.

thought to gain their point from their supposed connection with the stealing of the Host's horses but which are now seen to be humorous rather because of their relevance to the Garter ceremonies in 1597. As Count Mömpelgard, Frederick had visited England in 1592, had travelled to Maidenhead, Reading, and Windsor, among other places, and had afterwards developed a 'burning desire' to be elected to the Order of the Garter; after his return home and his becoming Duke of Württemberg, he kept pestering Elizabeth about an alleged promise she had made him that he would be elected. (She denied this to his envoy in 1595.)[1] Probably for political reasons, he was finally elected, in 1597, but *in absentia*; Elizabeth, thanks to a clause introduced by Henry VIII, was not obliged to tell him immediately of his success and conveniently forgot to do so (and James I had to pay for the insignia in 1603 after her death). To a court audience in April 1597, then, there would be special fun in the Host's reply to Bardolph's statement in IV. iii (of the Folio text only) that 'the Duke himselfe will be to morrow at Court, and they are going to meet him': 'What Duke should that be comes so secretly? I heare not of him in the Court'. Mömpelgard was coming very 'secretly' indeed; since he had not been invited, he was not coming at all. The same jest is to be found in Caius' 'it is tell-a-me, dat you make grand preparation for a Duke *de Iamanie*: by my trot: der is no Duke that the Court is know, to come' (IV. v. 81–4—also only in the Folio). At a time when relations between England and the German states were deteriorating, the Host's earlier comment 'doe not say they be fled: *Germanes* are honest men' (ll. 66–7, Folio only) may also have been as gleefully received as would have been a statement on the English stage in the 1930's that Germans were modest and retiring.

Whether there was further point in associating Mömpelgard in particular, or Germans in general, with horse-stealing or post-horses is far from clear. It will be remembered that in the earlier part of the comedy (III. i. 106–15 and III. iii. 221–5) Caius and Evans vow vengeance on the Host for the practical joke he has played on them by arranging the 'duel' and then making them look silly when it is not fought. Only a very naïve reader, surely, could fail to link this with the gloating way in which, one after the other, they come in (IV. v. 68–84) to add to the Host's misery by giving him corroborative detail about the theft of his post-horses—

1. See Elias Ashmole, *The Institution, Laws & Ceremonies Of the most noble Order of the Garter* (London, 1672); W. B. Rye ed., *England as seen by Foreigners in the Days of Elizabeth and James the First* (London, 1865), pp. iv-ciii and 3–53; Victor von Klarwill ed., *Queen Elizabeth and Some Foreigners*, trans. T. H. Nash (London, 1928), pp. 347–423; Green, *op. cit.*, pp. 121–50.

a theft of which Bardolph (no doubt bribed for the purpose) has just told him. The relevant lines of Caius' contribution have already been quoted; Evans's lines, in the Folio version (70–7), are 'Haue a care of your entertainments: there is a friend of mine come to Towne, tels mee there is three Cozen-Iermans, that has cozend all the *Hosts* of *Readins*, of *Maidenhead*; of *Cole-brooke*, of horses and money: I tell you for good will (looke you) you are wise, and full of gibes, and vlouting-stocks: and 'tis not conuenient you should be cozoned. Fare you well.' The puns on cousins-germane, Germans who could be addressed as 'cousin' (a frequent polite term of aristocratic address), Germans who 'cozen' or cheat, and those who 'cozen' by pretending to be Germans may all be disentangled fairly easily, but that Shakespeare is associating the particular German, Mömpelgard, with any incident involving post-horses is improbable. The corresponding Quarto passage, 'Now my Host, I would desire you looke you now, / To haue a care of your entertainments, / For there is three sorts of cosen garmombles, / Is cosen all the Host of Maidenhead & Readings . . .', has been thought to provide evidence for such a connection, 'garmombles' being taken to be a word invented as a quibble on Mömpelgard's name (and one theory is that the Quarto here retains an original jest removed in a post-1602 revision and not preserved in the Folio). On the other hand, 'garmombles' may be only another bad attempt by the Quarto to recall the general sense of what was spoken on the stage (and perhaps the actors themselves became confused between the jokes on Mömpelgard—which would quickly lose their point—and the others, really distinct, about German horse-thieves). The word 'garmomble' probably did exist—see note on IV. v. 72—and even W. B. Rye (p. xcviii) was prepared to grant that 'if the word be archaic, and a meaning found for it, we are willing to yield the point', i.e. willing to concede that 'garmombles' did not necessarily refer to 'Mömpelgard'.

J. E. V. Crofts[1] has shown that there is no reason for associating Mömpelgard with misappropriation of post-horses; indeed the Duke was given an official warrant enabling him to use them without charge. Crofts's alternative theories, however—that Shakespeare transferred from Frenchmen to Germans a scandal involving de Chastes, the visiting Governor of Dieppe, in 1596 and in revising alluded rather to another, involving only Englishmen, in November 1597—have little to recommend them.[2] There is

1. *Shakespeare and the Post Horses* (Bristol, 1937).

2. Crofts's attempts at textual analysis of the Quarto and the Folio, and Green's further explanation (pp. 169ff.) of how 'the fertile brain of the playwright toyed with the incident' (of de Chastes), have even less.

really no need to suppose that the stealing (or unofficial borrowing) of horses had any topical reference at all; the 'source' for the incident may have been, as the text itself suggests, Marlowe's *Doctor Faustus*, undoubtedly a play about Germans, and whether this sub-plot was ever any clearer in a version of which even the Folio is not a true representation is highly problematical.

The connection of Lord Hunsdon and Count Mömpelgard with the Garter Feast of April 1597 was, paradoxically, less important in the mind of Leslie Hotson, who first showed the connection, than another supposed reference that he thought pointed to the same date—a reference that has not seemed nearly so certain to later writers on the subject. Hotson discovered that in 1596 one William Wayte took out a writ of surety against William Shakespeare, Francis Langley (the owner of the Swan theatre), and two women, and that a writ of attachment was duly issued, returnable on 29 November. He also discovered that, a little earlier, Langley had taken out a writ of surety against Wayte and Wayte's step-father William Gardiner, a Surrey justice of the peace. Finding that Wayte was elsewhere described as 'a certain loose person of no reckoning or value, being wholly under the rule and commandment of the said Gardiner'; building up a not fully convincing case against Gardiner as a rogue;[1] and arguing, also not very convincingly, that Gardiner was one of the chief opponents and prosecutors of the theatre,[2] Hotson went on to suggest that Gardiner and Wayte were satirized in *The Merry Wives* as Shallow and Slender, particularly in the first scene.

It is true that if one could be sure that, exceptionally, Shakespeare was here making fun of living people—and relying on his audience's knowing the facts in so much detail that all the jokes could be appreciated (which is rather harder to believe[3])—this first scene would be more amusing, and what seem to be loose ends in the play, having no connection at all with the later actions of Shallow and Falstaff, would at least be explicable. It is true, for example, that Gardiner, like Shallow (ll. 1–4 and 32), was given to threats of legal action (as were many other Elizabethans!); that

1. J. E. Hannigan, 'Shakespeare vs. Shallow', *Shakespeare Association Bulletin* VII (1932), 174–82, enters some important caveats and shows how, e.g., Hotson takes conventional legal phraseology too literally.

2. Hotson's evidence on this question perhaps proves no more than that as a justice of the peace Gardiner naturally received instructions to put into effect decisions made by his superiors.

3. Cf. Peter Alexander's comment that to see satire here 'is to attribute to Shakespeare a sad deficiency of gall, and to the audience an appreciation of Shakespeare's allusions rivalling that of later investigators' (*Shakespeare*, London, 1964, p. 41).

he was a member of the quorum but could hardly hope to be custos rotulorum, and that William Wayte would probably not have known the difference (ll. 5–8); that he had luces in his coat of arms, and only by quartering, since his first wife was the widow Frances Wayte, née Luce or Lucy; that he had married Wayte off to an heiress, possibly to swindle him of her money; and that he had a deer park, perhaps acquired by shady methods. April 1597 would also be exactly the right time for a caricature of Gardiner, after the writs of November 1596 and well before Gardiner's death on 26 November 1597. It is also true, however, that there are no signs of any satire on Gardiner in the portrait of Shallow in *2 Henry IV*; that Shallow is supposed to be over eighty; that he comes from Gloucestershire; that the setting of the play is Windsor; and that the audience for which the play was first written was probably an aristocratic one. Perhaps Shakespeare was allowing himself a side-glance or two at a pompous opponent; it is difficult to be certain.

If Shakespeare is here indulging, even for a passing moment, in personal satire, Gardiner may be a better candidate for the distinction than is the traditional one, Sir Thomas Lucy. The Lucy story is familiar to most students of Shakespeare in the version of Rowe:

> He [Shakespeare] had, by a Misfortune common enough to young Fellows, fallen into ill Company; and amongst them, some that made a frequent practice of Deer-stealing, engag'd him with them more than once in robbing a Park that belong'd to Sir *Thomas Lucy* of *Cherlecot*, near *Stratford*. For this he was prosecuted by that Gentleman, as he thought, somewhat too severely; and in order to revenge that ill Usage, he made a Ballad upon him. And . . . it is said to have been so very bitter, that it redoubled the Prosecution against him to that degree, that he was oblig'd to leave his Business and Family in *Warwickshire*, for some time, and shelter himself in *London*. (p. v)

Rowe later adds:

> Amongst other Extravagances, in *The Merry Wives of* Windsor, he has made him [Falstaff] a Dear-stealer, that he might at the same time remember his *Warwickshire* Prosecutor, under the Name of Justice *Shallow*; he has given him very near the same Coat of Arms which *Dugdale*, in his Antiquities of that County, describes for a Family there, and makes the *Welsh* Parson descant very pleasantly upon 'em. (p. xviii)

(Rowe is referring here to a coat repeated in four quarterings, so that the three luces of the Lucy coat of arms become twelve, as in the play.)

Rowe can hardly have known that the same tradition had already been recorded in some manuscript notes by Richard Davies, who died in 1708. Davies had written that Shakespeare was

> much given to all unluckinesse in stealing venison & Rabbits particularly from Sr Lucy who had him oft whipt & sometimes Imprisoned & at last made Him fly his Native Country to his great Advancem^{t} but His reveng was so great that he is his Justice Clodpate and calls him a great man & y^{t} in allusion to his name bore three lowses rampant for his Arms.[1]

Obviously Davies knew of, but did not fully understand, the allegation that Mr Justice Shallow was a caricature of Lucy; yet his mention of rabbits, as well as 'venison', and of whipping, and his inability to give Lucy's christian name, suggest that his source of information may not have been exactly the same as Rowe's.

Malone, finding no evidence that Lucy had a deer-park, rejected the story outright and has been followed by others who maintain that the play does not support the tradition and that in fact the tradition arose from the play. Perhaps there was confusion in somebody's mind because Lucy's grandson, the third Sir Thomas Lucy, did bring a charge in Star Chamber in 1610 against 'a gentleman who had stolen deer from his park at Sutton'; and it is true that it was not until 1618 that this Sir Thomas was licensed to impale his park at Charlecote.[2] Yet even as cautious a scholar as Chambers hesitates to reject the deer-stealing tradition. The first Sir Thomas Lucy, he points out, did at least have a free-warren, in which he may have been entitled to run roe-deer, if not fallow deer;[3] and indeed there may have been advantages in not licensing one's park until one had to.

The best reasons for not accepting the opinion that Shakespeare caricatured, or cast side glances at, Lucy in the person of Shallow in *The Merry Wives* are, again, that there are no traces of such allusions in the Shallow of *2 Henry IV*; that Lucy was not the kind of man one could safely satirize in a play written for performance at Court (and there would have been no special reason for thinking of him in 1597); and that not even the Court audience could have been expected to see the point (if indeed there is one: 'satire' is almost a misnomer for cryptic references of the kind suspected in the opening scene). It may perhaps be confessed, nevertheless, that if ever there were a place in Shakespeare's art for laughing comment on individuals (comment that most readers would feel to be

1. The MS is reproduced by Chambers, *William Shakespeare*, II. 257.
2. Recorded in Mark Eccles, *Shakespeare in Warwickshire* (Madison, 1961), p. 75.
3. *William Shakespeare*, I. 18–20.

foreign to his ways of thought), then, provided that he could have relied on his audience to identify the persons concerned, that place would have been in such a topical play as *The Merry Wives* seems to have been.

6. THE RELATIONSHIP OF THE PLAY TO SHAKESPEARE'S HISTORIES; AND THE 'BROOKE'–'BROOME' PROBLEM

Inevitably, since many of the characters of *The Merry Wives* appear also in the better-known First and Second Parts of *Henry IV* or in *Henry V*, there has been considerable discussion of the connection of the comedy with the 'Histories'. The discussion has taken two main forms: an attempt to determine when the action of *The Merry Wives* is supposed to have occurred, in relation to the events dramatized in *Henry IV* and *Henry V*; and an attempt to establish the exact order of composition of the four plays.

The first question is answerable only if it is assumed, in an old-fashioned way, that Shakespeare thought of the characters as real people whose biographies could, as it were, be written from the plays—and may not be answerable even then. That *The Merry Wives* presupposes an audience familiar with *1 Henry IV* is made certain by Page's comment on Fenton that 'he kept company with the wild Prince and Poins' (III. ii. 66–7)—which if taken seriously would date the action in the reign of Henry IV or V; yet elsewhere, as has been shown, the action seems rather to be in Elizabethan England, and not only does Fenton not know Falstaff (perhaps not as inconsistent a fact as Wheatley supposed) but also Falstaff does not know Mistress Quickly. Moreover while Quickly has both the same name as the character in *Henry IV* and *Henry V* and the same manner of digressive speech larded with malapropisms, she is in many other ways a different person. The most that can be said is that Falstaff's 'If it should come to the ear of the court how I have been transformed, and how my transformation hath been washed and cudgelled, they would melt me out of my fat drop by drop, and liquor fishermen's boots with me; I warrant they would whip me with their fine wits till I were as crest-fallen as a dried pear' clearly presupposes a time when he is on jesting terms with Prince Hal, a time *before* his disgrace at the end of *2 Henry IV*.

Whether the words may have been more easily *written* before the end of *2 Henry IV* is another question; but some evidence does suggest that *The Merry Wives* may have been composed at the same time as the second part of the trilogy, and none of the available facts contradicts such an hypothesis.

The First Part of *Henry IV* is now normally dated in the winter of

1596–7. The play, which must be later than *Richard II*, was entered on the Stationers' Register on 25 February 1597/8 (and published in 1598); and Meres, in his *Palladis Tamia* (S.R. 7 September 1598) mentions it, though he lists it as proving Shakespeare's ability in tragedy (he has no separate category of 'history').[1] It is known that Falstaff in Part I was originally called 'Oldcastle' ('my old lad of the Castle' survives in the dialogue as a form of address to him); and in the epilogue to the Second Part, there occurs the famous promise and retraction: 'If you be not too much cloyed with fat meat, our humble author will continue the story, with Sir John in it, and make you merry with fair Katharine of France: where, for any thing I know, Falstaff shall die of a sweat, unless already a' be killed with your hard opinions; for Oldcastle died a martyr, and this is not the man.'[2] (In fact Falstaff does not appear in *Henry V*—except for the announcement of his death—although it has been conjectured that he was originally in the play and was taken out on second thoughts.[3]) The generally accepted theory is that the name 'Oldcastle' was changed because of protests from the influential Cobham family, who objected to the denigration of a distinguished ancestor (and of course *if* the protest came from William Brooke, Lord Cobham, when as Lord Chamberlain he was in a strong position to see that his objection was not overruled, it must have been before his death in March 1597; but there is nothing to prove that his son, Sir Henry, was not the one to speak up: it was he who was satirically called 'S^r^ Io. Falstaff' in a private letter by Essex in February 1598).[4]

1. For discussion of the dating of *1 Henry IV*, and further evidence suggesting the 1596–7 date, see *King Henry IV Part I*, the (New) Arden edition, ed. A. R. Humphreys (London, 1960), pp. xii–xiv. It has been conjectured that because Meres lists the play as tragedy, he must have been thinking of 'the dark tone of Part II'. May he not rather have been thinking of the death of Hotspur? Incidentally, Meres does not mention *The Merry Wives*, but it has long been clear that his list is made up more from a desire for neat parallels than from any desire for completeness; and if *The Merry Wives* had been originally produced at Court and not quickly transferred to the public stage, he may not have seen it or known of it by, say, early 1598.

2. There may or may not have been an earlier version of the epilogue without these lines. Even if there were one, it does not follow that the name 'Oldcastle' was not altered until the later version; an apology is never *too* late.

3. See *King Henry V*, the (New) Arden edition, ed. J. H. Walter (London, 1954), pp. xli–xliii.

4. Humphreys, *op. cit.*, p. xii. The hypothesis, advanced by H. N. Paul, Humphreys, and others, that Shakespeare chose 'Falstaff' as the substitute name because in *1 Henry VI* he had (wrongly) associated the historical Sir John Falstaff (1378–1459) with conduct unworthy of a knight of the Garter is incapable of proof. Incidentally 'Falstaff' was just as unfair, if one thought of the man of the same name in history, as was 'Oldcastle'.

The alteration of 'Oldcastle' to 'Falstaff' must have been made before the entry of *1 Henry IV* on the Stationers' Register on 25 February 1597/8, for the entry mentions 'the conceipted mirthe of Sir Iohn Falstoff'; and there is really nothing to suggest that the character in *The Merry Wives* or *2 Henry IV* was ever called anything but 'Falstaff', although the name 'Oldcastle' may well have remained, as it were, in Shakespeare's subconscious after it was officially abandoned. It would be natural for him to *think* of the character as 'Oldcastle'; and this is sufficient explanation of the occurrence of the speech prefix '*Old.*' at I. ii. 137 in the Quarto of Part II and is also sufficient explanation, if explanation is needed, of the pun, if any, in *Merry Wives*, IV. v. 5, 'There's his chamber, his house, his castle' (but would anybody ever have seen a pun on 'Oldcastle' here, or in the Quarto version of the lines, if not going out of the way to look for it?).

Queen Elizabeth could have seen *1 Henry IV* at Court on 26 or 27 December 1596, 1 or 6 January, or 6 or 8 February 1597: on all those dates the Lord Chamberlain's Men played before her.[1] She could then have expressed a wish to see Falstaff in love, and a performance of *The Merry Wives* would have followed most opportunely in April.[2] The unlucky 'Oldcastle' name had probably already been changed (why would the Brookes wait until the offence had been repeated before protesting?); and by this time Shakespeare may well have been working on *2 Henry IV* (a second part having been in his mind from the beginning or—as Harold Jenkins has argued[3]—having become necessary as he found he had too much material while writing Part I). There is no good reason for putting the completed *2 Henry IV* before late 1598 (and some slight reasons—e.g. a possible use of Gerard's *Herball*—for not putting it earlier); and it is difficult to agree that '*The Merry Wives* . . . assumes that the spectators already know Justice Shallow, and they could do so only through *2 Henry IV*. Similarly, Pistol is elaborately introduced into *2 Henry IV* whereas in *The Merry Wives* Slender mentions him, with Nym and Bardolph, as a matter of course'.[4] The introduction of Shallow in *The Merry Wives* is even more 'elaborate' than that of Pistol in *2 Henry IV*, which could be interpreted as the fanfare to introduce an old friend; and no earlier knowledge of Pistol, Nym, and Bardolph is neces-

1. Chambers, *Elizabethan Stage*, IV. 165.
2. To this extent, I agree with a suggestion made by H. N. Paul in a letter to the editor of the New Variorum edition of *1 Henry IV* (Philadelphia and London, 1936), p. 355; I cannot accept other parts of his theory.
3. *The Structural Problem in Shakespeare's 'Henry the Fourth'* (London, 1956).
4. Humphreys, *op. cit.*, p. xiii.

sary for an understanding or appreciation of their roles in the comedy.

The theory that *2 Henry IV* and *The Merry Wives* were being written at the same time—the composition of the former having been interrupted for the hasty writing of the latter—has two minor advantages. It 'explains' the occurrence in the two plays of words and phrases not found elsewhere in Shakespeare ('by cock and pie'; 'pippin'; 'tester'; 'red-lattice'; 'cavalier(o)'; 'Ephesian'; 'said I well?', plus perhaps the Jove–bull joke and the pun on 'cheater' and 'escheator'[1]); and it perhaps solves the problem of Falstaff's curious out-of-the-way journey to Gloucestershire on his way north from London that has so puzzled editors of *2 Henry IV*. A. R. Humphreys has written: 'The conscientious insertion of locations by editors has concealed the fact . . . that Shakespeare makes no mention of Gloucestershire as Justice Shallow's habitat until *2 Henry IV*, IV. iii. 80, 126–7. Shallow is "a poor esquire of this county" in III. ii, but no county is named [though Lincolnshire is implied]. . . When . . . [Falstaff] is due to return, it transpires that his second visit to Shallow is to take place in Gloucestershire, and thereafter the place-names relate to that county. . . Why [Shakespeare] apparently shifted the location thus can hardly be ascertained'.[2] The answer may be that, having meanwhile made Shallow a justice of the peace in Gloucestershire (which is not so far from Windsor) in *The Merry Wives*, Shakespeare decided that he might as well live with it.[3] For the little it is worth, one other observation may be made: any request from the Queen for Falstaff to be shown 'in love' may have been more easily made if she had not yet seen the Doll Tearsheet scenes of *2 Henry IV*.

It would seem, then, that the weight of probability, including not only Hotson's interpretation of topical allusions most relevant on a particular occasion but also the relationship of *The Merry Wives* to the Henry IV plays, favours as the date of the comedy not 1599 or 1600 or even 1602, as once thought, but 1597, after the production of the first part of *Henry IV* and probably before the

1. *Wiv.*, I. i. 279 (Page); I. ii. 12 (Evans); I. iii. 83 (Pistol); II. ii. 25 (Falstaff); II. i. 186 etc. (Host); IV. v. 16 (Host); I. iii. 11 (Host); V. v. 3 (Falstaff); I. iii. 66 (Falstaff); *2H4*, V. i. 1 (Shallow); V. iii. 2 (Shallow); III. ii. 297 (Falstaff); II. ii. 86 (a page); V. iii. 62 (Shallow); II. ii. 164 (a page); III. ii. 227 (Shallow); II. iii. 192 (Hal); II. iv. 111 (Quickly).

2. *The Second Part of King Henry IV*, the (New) Arden edition (London, 1965), pp. 235–6.

3. Although he does not say so, H. N. Paul perhaps had this in mind when he suggested, with unnecessary precision, that Shakespeare interrupted *2 Henry IV* at IV. iii. See above p. liv, n. 2. Humphreys also mentions the possibility (*2 Henry IV*, p. xvii, n. 3).

completion of the second. *Henry V* certainly followed *2 Henry IV* and thus almost certainly, for the reasons already given, *The Merry Wives*.[1] It is not possible to say whether the final omission of Falstaff from the action of *Henry V* had anything to do with his having been used for another full play, *The Merry Wives*, that was not part of the historical sequence as originally contemplated. On the whole it is unlikely, particularly if *2 Henry IV* was not completed until after *The Merry Wives*; and the Falstaff comedy of the latter is too far removed from the Histories to make acceptable the otherwise tempting theory that Falstaff scenes first planned or written for *Henry V* were hurriedly transferred from it and adapted for the play that had to be written in 'a fortnight'. Yet another conjecture, that the omission was forced on Shakespeare when Kemp left the acting company, carries weight only if one believes firmly both that Kemp played Falstaff and that nobody else could have done so.

To add to the confusion, there is the problem of Ford's pseudonyms, 'Brooke' in the Quarto, 'Broome' in the Folio. It has been shown (p. xxxiv) that Shakespeare must originally have written 'Brook(e)'; and in the days when the Quarto was thought of as a first sketch of the play, it was natural to argue that 'Brooke' was used in the first performances and altered to 'Broome' for later performances—in particular at Court—because of protests, or feared protests, from the Cobham family who, having objected to the name of their ancestor 'Oldcastle' in *1 Henry IV*, were similarly put out by the occurrence of their family name in *The Merry Wives* (although exactly why its use should have offended them, or been thought likely to do so, has never been made clear). Now that the 1602 Quarto is seen to be a later, debased version of the play, and the 1623 Folio probably very close to the text of a first Court performance, the problem is more difficult. The Quarto could hardly read 'Brooke' unless that was the name spoken on the public stage;[2] and so one must infer *either* that 'Brooke' was altered to 'Broome' for the original Court performance and altered back to

1. There may also be something in the argument that Nym is taken for granted when first seen in *Henry V* (II. i), as if he were already known from *The Merry Wives* (he does not appear in *2 Henry IV*). The contrary reasoning, that he would not have been called 'Corporal' in *The Merry Wives* if he had not earlier been seen on the battlefield in *Henry V*, is not conclusive, for he is associated with Bardolph, who is seen serving under 'Captain' Falstaff in *1 Henry IV*. The title-page of the Quarto, which has been dragged into the discussion, is irrelevant. All that it proves is that *by 1602*, Pistol, Nym and the others were well known, from performances on the stage of any of the plays—not excluding *The Merry Wives*.

2. Green's theory (p. 119) that the Host-reporter restored in the Quarto the name that he had first learnt but had later had to abandon *during rehearsal* is surely desperate.

'Brooke' for the public theatre—and that the Folio was printed from the still unchanged Court text—*or* that 'Brooke' was spoken on all stages until at least the time of the compilation of the Quarto but was subsequently altered in the text that finally became, directly or indirectly, 'copy' for the Folio (if only in the sense that a transcript was made from it, by Crane or somebody else, for the printer). The second explanation seems the better. If 'Brooke' once gave offence, it could hardly have been put back, before 1602, while Sir Henry was still able to take offence (certainly 'Oldcastle' was never restored and in 1600, when *2 Henry IV* was printed, in a good text, the apology for it stood); and if 'Brooke' ever had been restored on the stage, it is also difficult to believe that it would not have been put back in the acting company's texts of the play. It is not as if the manuscript behind the Folio had been left unchanged in all other respects since, shall we say, April 1597; for one thing, as has been shown, it had been expurgated. Even accepting, then, that the Folio text is a 'Court' text, and that the Quarto is based on a 'public' one, an hypothesis of alteration to the former *after* the latter had been published is the more acceptable. Two such explanations have been proposed. One, proffered by Crofts, that 'Broome' was substituted during the printing of the Folio, to placate the York Herald, Ralph Brooke, who had fallen out with the publisher Jaggard over the printing of his book in 1619, has been convincingly rejected by Green, for the very good reason, among others, that Jaggard was more concerned to score off Brooke than to placate him.[1] The other, first proffered by Alfred Hart,[2] that the substitution was made in 1604, at least has nothing against it. *The Merry Wives* was performed before James I on 4 November 1604; in December 1603 George Brooke (brother of Henry, Lord Cobham) had been executed for his part in the Bye Plot, and Sir Henry Brooke had been arrested and sentenced to death for his in the Main Plot, to depose James and put Arabella Stuart on the throne, and in February 1604 Sir Henry, although reprieved from death and imprisoned instead, had been expelled from the Order of the Garter. Hart's reasoning that 'Brooke' would be removed in November 1604 from the text of a play presented before the King, lest the name 'revive unpleasant memories', is certainly not answered by Green's demonstration that the King had shown some clemency to Brooke; and Hart's theory does

1. *Shakespeare and the Post Horses*, p. 103; Green, p. 109.

2. *Stolne and Surreptitious Copies*, pp. 89–90. David M. White was apparently developing the same idea at the same time in an unpublished thesis, and later published a note on it, 'An Explanation of the *Brook–Broome* Question in Shakespeare's *Merry Wives*', *Philological Quarterly*, XXV (1946), 280–3.

explain both why the Quarto reads 'Brooke' and why the Folio, if based on a manuscript that had been used for the 1604 revival of the full original Court play, should have the inferior reading.

7. LITERARY SOURCES OR ANALOGUES

The search for the work or works on which Shakespeare may be presumed to have based *The Merry Wives* has been so unsuccessful, in one sense, that Kenneth Muir, in a standard book on Shakespeare's sources, notes the suggestions made by others and is content to add 'In the present state of our knowledge it is useless to pursue the matter further.'[1] In another sense, no further investigation is necessary, inasmuch as for nearly every incident and situation in the plot of the play an analogue or a vaguely possible source has been found in earlier European fiction and farce or in English stories and translations.[2]

The Falstaff–Ford–Brook story belongs to a group of tales in which a lover unwittingly tells a husband of the progress of an affair with the latter's wife. The closest analogue is probably the second 'novella' of the second day of Ser Giovanni Fiorentino's *Il Pecorone* (a collection that also seems to have given Shakespeare the idea for the 'pound of flesh' in *The Merchant of Venice*).[3] A young man Buccivolo, a student in Bologna, consults a professor about the science of love, follows the advice, and reports his progress, until the assignation is made with the lady who is, of course, the professor's wife. The husband suspects the truth and follows the lover, who has to be concealed under a heap of damp washing ('un monte di panni di bucato, i quali non erano ancora rasciutti'); but after the search for him is unproductive, the gallant is successful with the wife and duly tells the professor so. Interrupting the second assignation, the husband stabs the pile of washed clothes—as Ford searches the buck basket—and is similarly considered mad (and treated accordingly). The lover, however, now identifying the professor as the husband, visits the house a third time, to console him, and then leaves the city to return to his native Rome. No English translation of this story is known to have been available to Shakespeare, but it is at least closer to *The Merry Wives* than is the

1. *Shakespeare's Sources. I. Comedies and Tragedies* (London, 1957), p. 260.

2. Most of these are discussed, and some are given, in Geoffrey Bullough, *Narrative and Dramatic Sources of Shakespeare*, Vol. 2 (London, 1958), pp. 3–58. Earlier studies not listed elsewhere in these notes include K. M. Lea, *Italian Popular Comedy* (Oxford, 1934), II. 431–3.

3. The relevance for *The Merry Wives* was first pointed out by Carlo Segré in 1911. See S. G. Thomas, 'Source of *The Merry Wives of Windsor*', *Times Literary Supplement*, 11 October 1947, p. 528.

'source' favoured by H. C. Hart and others, 'The Tale of the two Lovers of Pisa' in *Tarltons Newes out of Purgatorie* (1590), another version of the lover's confiding in the husband, but with the difference that the lover is unsuccessful (until after the husband's death). That this husband, like Caius, is an elderly foolish doctor, who is chosen by the wife's parent (her father, in fact), hardly strengthens the case for 'borrowing'.

Not fully convincing either is the claim that the tale 'Of Two Brethren and their Wives' in Barnaby Riche's *Riche his Farewell to the Militarie Profession* (1581) is a direct source.[1] Here a wife plays off against each other three unwanted (but previously acceptable) lovers; and one, a lawyer, is nearly suffocated when he is persuaded to allow himself to be wrapped in a bag or knapsack, and is beaten, while the second lover is a doctor, who is employed to carry the bag from the house, believing it to contain the wife, and is startled to find that 'she' has a beard. The third lover, a soldier, is used to disconcert and beat the other two, but is later sent to foreign wars—and the lady and the husband live happily ever after. The differences between this and *The Merry Wives* far outweigh any resemblances, although a few verbal 'parallels' have been suspected; and in any case Riche is known to have based others of his stories on Italian originals, which may have come independently to Shakespeare's notice.

The evidence may be summarized by saying that Shakespeare did not need to *invent* a husband who receives 'progress reports' on the attempted seduction of his wife; a lover who is the victim of a clever wife's schemes, involving near-suffocation in her washing; a jealous husband who, having learnt how he has been tricked once, assumes that he is being tricked a second time in the same way; women who tell each other of the approaches made to them by the one man; or a lover who escapes by pretending to be a woman. All these, however, may have leapt to his mind when required, from reading done over a period of years; a source, in the stricter sense, was unnecessary.

Similarly, it seems superfluous to propose as the source of the Anne Page story a play by Plautus, *Casina* (of which there was no available English translation):[2] again the differences far outweigh

1. Dorothy Hart Bruce, '*The Merry Wives* and *Two Brethren*', *Studies in Philology*, 39 (1942), 265–78. Of course this tale is generally accepted as a source for part of the Malvolio story in *Twelfth Night*.

2. R. S. Forsythe, 'A Plautine Source of *The Merry Wives of Windsor*', *Modern Philology*, 18 (1920), 401–21. Bullough, *op. cit.*, p. 9, understates the difficulties, but still has to admit that 'The *Casina* could not be followed closely because Falstaff, unlike Lysidamus, was not meant to lust after Anne Page'.

the resemblances, and there must have been many such plots where the suitor favoured by the young lady wins the day against suitors favoured by her parents. It remains barely possible that Shakespeare, had he been able to examine his subconscious, might have been prepared to admit that schoolboy memories of Plautus gave him the 'idea' for the disguises and confusion of Slender and Caius and their 'wives' in the final scene.

Not content with 'sources' for parts of the plot, some commentators have argued that the whole play is only a rewriting of an undiscovered, non-extant, original. The favourite candidate, proposed by F. G. Fleay and adopted by the New Cambridge editors, is *The Jealous Comedy*, a lost play that Shakespeare's company had acted in 1593;[1] and the 'evidence' includes the loose ends, such as the deer-stealing allegations of the first scene; Ford's telling Falstaff (II. ii. 174) 'Sir, I hear you are a scholar' (apparently flattery never extends to improbabilities); and speeches that are said to be uncharacteristic of the 'real' Falstaff (i.e. Falstaff as some readers think him to be in *1 Henry IV*), such as (v. v. 127–9) 'See now how wit may be made a Jack-a-Lent, when 'tis upon ill employment!' (apparently Falstaff is considered incapable of a wry and rueful glance at his own folly—in spite of 'No more of that, Hal, an thou lovest me!' after the Gadshill exposure in *1 Henry IV*, III. iv. 312–13). The Quarto also is dragged in, the references to sergeants and proctors in Act v being taken as relics of a 'London' original;[2] and even the preponderance of prose, with only sparing and uneven use of verse, is said to indicate a source in verse that Shakespeare had not time or energy to rewrite fully in blank verse—as if his predecessors, such as Greene, had not pointed the way to the use of prose for comedy in certain tones, including the farcical, and as if Shakespeare was never to write *As You Like It*[3] or Dekker *The Shoemaker's Holiday* and *The Honest Whore*.

J. M. Nosworthy would go further and would identify the source of *The Merry Wives* as *The Two Merry Women of Abingdon*, an unfinished play that Henslowe in 1599 commissioned from Henry Porter, presumably because of the rather inexplicable success of his *Two Angry Women of Abingdon*.[4] Obviously, since the proposed

1. F. G. Fleay, *A Chronicle History of the Life and Work of William Shakespeare* (London, 1886), pp. 210–13.

2. See above, pp. xxxvi–xxxvii.

3. See below, p. lxxvi. At the time of the earlier volumes in the New Cambridge series, of course, the editors did argue—consistent in this—that *As You Like It* was a revision of a verse play. The theory was later withdrawn. Fleay (*op. cit.*, p. 211) maintained that the predominance of prose in *The Merry Wives* was proof of haste, as in *Much Ado* (and forgot *As You Like It* altogether).

4. *Shakespeare's Occasional Plays* (London, 1965), pp. 86–127.

source does not survive, the 'evidence' must consist mainly of alleged parallels in incident, setting, and phrasing between *The Merry Wives* and the surviving Porter play; and, again, the argument depends partly on the Quarto, which is said to be in some respects, and particularly in the last scene, closer to the lost source. Beyond recording the opinion that another plot as thin as that of *The Two Angry Women of Abingdon* would have given Shakespeare next to nothing to work on, there is little that one can say in reply to so tenuous an argument; presumably it is no use protesting that Porter's deliberate and often humourless style is at the opposite extreme from the gaiety of *The Merry Wives*, for the answer will be that vivacity was precisely what Shakespeare may have added to his hypothetical original.

Nothing is more likely, if the story of the royal command to write a play in a short time is correct, than that the dramatist should have made use of any materials that were at hand; but until stronger evidence is produced, the theory that he rewrote an earlier play falls far short of proof. If the 1597 date for *The Merry Wives* is right, Nosworthy's nomination of the supposed lost source is automatically wrong; and perhaps the signs of inadequate 'revision' that others have found in Shakespeare's play also indicate no more than hasty composition.

Literary sources may have played minor parts in the writing of some sections of Shakespeare's comedy. For example, Tyrwhitt thought that the merry Host of the Garter was indebted to the immortal Harry Bailly, Chaucer's host of the Tabard Inn in Southwark and 'governour' of his Canterbury pilgrims.[1] No doubt Harry Bailly's jovial and exclamatory manner of speech and his general character, intolerant of fuss and hypocrisy, are like Shakespeare's Host; but we may have to allow for a tradition of merry Hosts before *The Merry Wives*, as there was certainly such a tradition after it, including the Host in *The Merry Devil of Edmonton*,[2] and extending at least to Farquhar's Boniface in *The Beaux' Stratagem* (1707).

The fairy scene in Lyly's *Endimion* may or may not have contributed something to the punishment of Falstaff by the 'fairies' in the last act of *The Merry Wives* (see note on v. v. 103). Perhaps, too,

1. Malone was sceptical of the verbal echo ('said I well?') that Tyrwhitt thought he had found, but granted the possible general indebtedness. (The point is made by Sailendra Kumar Sen, '"The noblest Roman of them all": Malone and Shakespearian Scholarship', *Shakespeare Commemoration Volume*, Presidency College, Calcutta, 1966, pp. 67–8.)

2. Noted by Chambers, *Elizabethan Stage*, iv. 30. The date is probably between 1599 and 1604.

there was some lost account of a 'wise woman' of Brentford that suggested Falstaff's method of escape when he is trapped for the second time in Ford's house. Again, however, the Quarto may be responsible for a red herring. In the Folio, Mistress Ford begins the relevant section with the line 'My Maids Aunt the fat woman of *Brainford*, has a gowne aboue'; we are told that Ford, who 'cannot abide' her, 'sweares she's a witch' (IV. ii. 67–8, 77–8); and Ford addresses 'her' in appropriate language, and outlines her methods of witchcraft (158–65). Simple and Slender also know of the repute of 'the Wise-woman of *Brainford*' (IV. v. 24–5), but the only name that she is ever given is when Mistress Page addresses her as 'mother *Prat*' (IV. ii. 168)—and the name may have suggested itself to Shakespeare for the sake of Ford's reply.[1] It is the Quarto that has Mistress Page twice identify the old woman as 'my maids Aunt *Gillian* of *Brainford*' (though the second time it is 'my maidens Ant')—and so it may have been the reporter and not Shakespeare who made the connection between the 'character' in the play and the perhaps proverbial Gillian of Brentford whose comic 'Testament' had been written by Robert Copland, in 1560 or thereabouts, and who is referred to thrice by Nashe (though he once calls her 'Joane'), and once by Harington (both probably recalling Copland) and was apparently to have been a character in a play 'called fryer fox & gyllen of branforde' written by—or possibly only commissioned by Henslowe from—Samuel Rowley and Thomas Dowton in February 1598/9.[2] (It must be pointed out, however, that Copland's Gillyen is in no sense a witch—she is a 'mery widow' and is notable only for the curse-like series of legacies she dictated to her Curate.) Alternatively, the Quarto reporter may merely have made explicit what Shakespeare assumed could safely be left to the audience—the identification of the old woman named in the play with a notorious practiser of fortune-telling 'and such dawbry as this is', of whose doings they had read or heard in ballad and story.

For the Latin lesson (IV. i), Shakespeare could have found a model—had he needed one—not in earlier English drama but in the French. M. L. Radoff has shown that 'by the beginning of the sixteenth century this comic device had become very popular in the [French] farces' and has argued that since John Heywood drew on

1. See note on IV. ii. 170.

2. Robert Copland, *Gyl of braintfords Testament. Newly Compiled* (n.d.); Thomas Nashe, *The Works*, ed. R. B. McKerrow, supp. F. P. Wilson (Oxford, 1958), III. 235, 314; IV. 421; V. 195; [Sir John Harington] *Vlysses vpon Aiax* (London, 1596), B4; *Henslowe's Diary*, ed. R. A. Foakes and R. T. Rickert (Cambridge, 1961), p. 104.

these French plays, Shakespeare could have known them too.[1] At least it can be said that the parallels are closer than one normally finds in alleged sources: they include not only the schoolboy, his master, his mother, and a female who asks unfortunate questions but also some of the indecencies.

In one other way *The Merry Wives* may have been indebted to earlier literature, and particularly drama, for comic material. During the last quarter of the sixteenth century, writers began to see the literary possibilities arising from the theory of 'humours'—the four fluids that existed in different proportions in the composition of different men and thus determined a man's character or disposition. The word 'humour' achieved a 'vogue' comparable with the popularity of 'complex' in the psychology or pseudo-psychology of, say, the second quarter of the twentieth century; fools boasted of their 'humours', and took comfort from them, as their successors did from their 'inferiority complexes' and even 'Oedipus complexes'.

'Humour' appears frequently in the work of writers such as Thomas Nashe (in e.g. *Christ's Tears over Jerusalem*, in 1593); and Nashe may have coined 'humorously' (in the same work) and, in the corresponding sense, the noun 'humourist'.[2] In drama, Lyly, for one, had found the word convenient for naming phases of character; and Shakespeare himself had adopted it in some of his early comedies, including *Love's Labour's Lost* (III. i. 23–4) and, notably, *The Taming of the Shrew*, where it is used often, and at least three times of Kate's shrewishness or of Petruchio's imitation of it: Peter says 'He kills her in her own humour' (IV. i. 183); Petruchio, 'And thus I'll curb her mad and headstrong humour' (IV. i. 212); and Baptista, 'Such an injury would vex a very saint, / Much more a shrew of thy impatient humour' (III. ii. 28–9). Chapman was thus perhaps not so very original when he made great play with the word in *The Blind Beggar of Alexandria*, one of the most popular dramas of 1596, and had Irus use it of his assuming the role of one 'Count Hermes', noted for his 'mad-brain' conduct, mood, or 'humour'. Chapman may have been the first, however, to see the possibilities of fun in the abuse and over-use of the cliché; and presumably (the text is truncated and corrupt) the Spaniard Bragadino is comic partly because of this verbal mannerism: 'you know my intent, my humour is insophisticated and plain'; 'put up thy pistol; 'tis a most dangerous humour in thee'; 'I do not like this

1. 'Influence of the French Farce in *Henry V* and *The Merry Wives*', *Modern Language Notes*, 48 (1933), 427–35.

2. See, e.g., Jürgen Schäfer, '"Humour" in the *O.E.D.*', *Notes and Queries*, N.S. 13 (1966), 290–2; and Bracy, *op. cit.*, pp. 115–17, citing, particularly, C. R. Baskervill, *English Elements in Jonson's Early Comedy* (Austin, Texas, 1911).

humour in thee in pistoling men in this sort; it is a most dangerous and stigmatical humour'.[1] Here, if precedent is needed, is precedent for Nym's murdering of the word in *The Merry Wives*.

Chapman's influence is thought by some to go beyond the mere word and to extend to the dramatic method of basing characterization on 'humours', the method that Jonson was to make his own in *Every Man in his Humour* (1598) and *Every Man Out of his Humour* (1599). In the final Jonsonian formula, the comic characters each had one mannerism or eccentricity; and only when that eccentricity became, or was caused to be, extreme could the possessor be made aware of it or otherwise be brought 'out' of it, and so cured. In earlier versions of the formula, any character with a predominating mannerism, mood, passion, or affectation—or even a character in disguise pretending eccentricity—could be presented for laughter, in what came to be known as a 'humours comedy'; and perhaps the first of these was Chapman's *An Humourous Day's Mirth* (first acted in May 1597) in which Lemot virtually describes the play when he says 'thus will I sit, as it were, and point out all my humourous companions' (ii. 20–1). In this sense, however, it is debatable whether *The Merry Wives of Windsor* should be called a humours comedy at all; and it may be suspected that Nym's abuse of the word, combined with uncertainty in dating the play, has given a false lead. Pistol, with his speech made up of quotation from, and imitations of, earlier popular drama, may possibly be thought of as a 'humours' character, but he has other qualities, such as bluster and an affected sense of honour, that make such simple classification difficult; and although jealousy is a favourite 'humour' with Chapman and Jonson, Shakespeare's drawing of Ford is really too subtle to be reduced to one-dimensional presentation of character.

If *The Merry Wives* is correctly dated April 1597, then the connections between it and Jonson's *Every Man in his Humour* can only be Jonson's emulation of Shakespeare, or friendly rivalry, or (if one must think in terms of opposition) Jonson's attempt, with his portraits of the jealous husband Thorello (Kitely in the 1616 version) and the country fool Stephano (Stephen) to show Shakespeare how such humours ought to have been displayed in Ford and Slender. The further suggestion made by the New Cambridge editors[2] that Shakespeare caricatured Jonson, as Nym, 'prating of

1. *The Comedies of George Chapman*, ed. T. M. Parrott (London, 1914), Scene i, ll. 326–43; Scene ii, ll. 74, 82–3, 114–16.

2. *op. cit.*, pp. xxxi–xxxii. The New Cambridge editors apparently overlooked Sarrazin's 1904 article, 'Nym und Ben Jonson' (*Shakespeare Jahrbuch*, 40, pp. 213–22). Sarrazin argued that Nym may have been taken by Jonson as a caricature but was not necessarily meant as one.

his "humours", reiterating the word until its boredom became comic, under a make-up which ridiculed Jonson in person and even in face' would similarly be ruled out by date, even if it had not already been ruled out by improbability. (Why, one may ask, should Shakespeare have wished at this time to ridicule Jonson? Another tradition says that it was Shakespeare who persuaded his company to act Jonson's play. And how could Shakespeare have afforded to be critical of Jonson for over-frequent use of a word that, as has been shown, he had not failed to exploit himself?)

Similarly, the resemblances between *The Merry Wives* and Chapman's probably contemporaneous *An Humourous Day's Mirth* seem to come to no more than comedy deriving from misuse of the word 'humour', together with another jealous husband, Labervele (but his suspicions of his wife's frailty are in fact justified, if he only knew it, and his manner of speech and his final resolve never to 'be suspicious more' owe so much less to observation than to the 'humours' theory that they clearly had nothing to teach Shakespeare). Chapman's still later *All Fools* (1599?) hardly comes into the story at all: it too has a jealous husband, Cornelio—or, if we believe his final pronouncement, as probably we should not, a husband who merely pretends to be jealous—but while it is conceivable that Chapman took some hints from Shakespeare in showing how the jealous man can 'justify' his jealousy as the alternative to foolishness ('No, let me still be pointed at, and thought / A jealous ass and not a wittolly knave', II. i. 286–7), Chapman had sufficient precedent in his own earlier portraits of the type.

The alleged 'humours' content of *The Merry Wives*, then, is so slight that even if the order of the relevant plays were shown somehow to be quite different, there would be no reason to suspect Shakespeare of indebtedness to either Chapman or Jonson and no reason to alter one's opinion of his originality or of his superiority when he chose to use fashionable literary material.

8. THE PLAY

Whether the tradition of the royal command is true or not, *The Merry Wives of Windsor*, in the Folio text, may be seen as a superb medley of all that would be likely to amuse an aristocratic audience towards the close of the sixteenth century. First and foremost there was a revival, in whatever sense, of Falstaff, the finest comic character the English stage had yet known or was perhaps ever to know; and with him from the merry gang of *1 Henry IV* came not only his red-nosed crony Bardolph but also, albeit in a different role, Mistress Quickly, whose unlucky uses of the English tongue, both decent ('I am nothing to thank God on, I would thou shouldst know it') and indecent, must have made her immediately popular with audiences, though her part was small. For good measure there was a first taste (or—if the dating be disputed—further taste) of loud-mouthed Pistol, Falstaff's colleague in a memorable scene (II. iv) in *2 Henry IV*, and of Mr Justice Shallow, and also of Corporal Nym, who was to ring further changes on his favourite word and add to his qualifications as a humorist in *Henry V*. Then to assist Quickly, Pistol, and Nym in what we must nowadays refer to as 'the cold-blooded murder of the English tongue', there were introduced a jovial Host, a Welsh parson-schoolmaster, and a French doctor—all conceivably variations on types of character already popular on the stage.

For the educated audience that could be flattered by the assumption that it was educated, there were included for good measure the Latin scene (showing Quickly at her best, or worst) and occasional wit of a literary kind, such as Parson Evans's confusion of a Marlowe lyric with a psalm, and the essentially unromantic Falstaff's incongruous accosting of Mistress Ford with a line from Sir Philip Sidney's sonnet sequence *Astrophel and Stella*.

Perhaps Shakespeare added the spice of personal satire, with passing suggestions of living people, in Shallow and even Slender; certainly he put in the all-but-compulsory dash of romance, with the story of 'sweet Anne Page' and her wooer Fenton, who, by carrying her off in spite of the rivalry of less worthy suitors favoured by otherwise likeable parents, shows once again that though the course of true love never did run smooth, love will prevail. Yet *The Merry Wives* is not primarily satiric comedy, nor is it—whatever John Dennis might think about the desirability of making Fenton the central character—either comedy of intrigue or romantic comedy as Shakespeare had already developed that genre in *The Two Gentlemen of Verona* or *A Midsummer Night's Dream* and was to develop it further in *As You Like It* and *Twelfth Night*. *The Merry Wives* is in essence citizen comedy, of the kind also made famous by Dekker in *The Shoemaker's Holiday*, by Chapman, Jonson, and Marston in their fine collaborative work *Eastward Ho* (and by Webster and Dekker in the rival comedies *Westward Ho* and *Northward Ho*) and later by Middleton, and by Massinger in, for example, *The City Madam*. Instead of being set in London, however, it has the added charm of being a portrait of life in an English country town; the characters cross fields and climb over stiles, match their greyhounds or go a-birding, and can always go home to laugh the sport o'er by a country fire, even at the close of a 'raw rheumatic day'.

Gravely to discuss the theme of a play put together in this way is to risk breaking the butterfly upon the wheel. In so far as *The Merry Wives* may be said to have one theme, however, it is the old one of the natural superiority of plain 'honesty' or virtue to the sophisticated or sophistical arts of the gallant or courtier; or if true comedy always involves incongruity, the humour may be said to be based on the incongruity between Falstaff as he sees himself and Falstaff as he is seen by Mistress Page and Mistress Ford, with whom he never stands a chance.

That Falstaff should come off second best in any encounter is, in the eyes of some critics, the height of Shakespeare's offending. Allan Gilbert has answered this in part: it is, he points out, 'the nature of comedy' that 'demands his discomfiture, or a repentance that to his idealizers is still more distasteful. The objection to Falstaff's defeat in the *Merry Wives* is, then, an objection to the very nature of comic drama.'[1] It is also necessary to insist, however, that the Falstaff of *Henry IV* is likewise often discomfited: in spite of 'the incomprehensible lies' that the fat rogue tells when he meets the Prince and others at supper, he loses the battle of wits over the Gadshill robbery and is not allowed to forget it (as when Hal tells him 'I lack some of thy instinct'); even Hal loses patience with him when he has a bottle of sack instead of a pistol in his holster on the battlefield ('What, is it a time to jest and dally now?'); and if the Prince's contemptuous 'Why, thou owest God a death' does not discomfort him, since he is hardly capable of shame, it does lower him for ever in the eyes of any perceptive audience; and though he gets away with his monstrous lie that he killed Hotspur, that is only because Hal is above contradicting it. There is not such a gap as has often been alleged between that Falstaff and the one who can so easily be made to look foolish by the kind of honest woman of whom he has little experience, or between the Falstaff who is frightened of being found by a jealous husband and the one who ran away at Gadshill. Nor is the Falstaff who admits to beating the servants of a justice of the peace, killing his deer, and breaking open his lodge, and at another time (II. ii) to having used influence to keep guilty cronies out of gaol and to sharing the profits of their crimes, a different man from the one who on hearing the news that Hal had become king announces 'Let us take any man's horses; the laws of England are at my commandment. Blessed are they that have been my friends; and woe to my lord chief-justice!'

1. *The Principles and Practice of Criticism* (Detroit, 1959), p. 88.

Shakespeare has also been gravely censured for obeying the Queen's command and showing Falstaff in love.[1] Of course, he did no such thing; the Queen might give what commands she pleased but if she did give this one, Shakespeare sidestepped it, and showed Falstaff pretending to be in love *because* he was hard-up: 'I will be cheaters to them both, and they shall be exchequers to me: they shall be my East and West Indies, and I will trade to them both'. Dr Johnson saw this quite clearly and in a 'general observation' contributed to the 1773 Steevens edition wrote: 'Shakespeare knew what the queen, if the story be true, seems not to have known, that by any real passion of tenderness, the selfish craft, the careless jollity, and the lazy luxury of Falstaff, must have suffered so much abatement, that little of his former cast would have remained. Falstaff could not love, but by ceasing to be Falstaff. He could only counterfeit love, and his professions could be prompted, not by the hope of pleasure, but of money.' The Quarto reporters, incidentally, also had no illusions on this point: having proclaimed that he must 'cheat' and 'cony-catch', Falstaff first mentions the wives with the announcement of his policy: 'I do intend to *make loue* to Foords wife' (my italics).

Falstaff, then, is not 'infatuated' at all but is the victim of another disease, that incurable 'consumption of the purse' that he suffers from again in *2 Henry IV*; and he is prepared to play a different role in the hope of 'earning' money. The audience awaits the result. The fun will be in the ways in which he is victimized, and the laughs will come partly from the conflicts of character and from the farce-like incidents. They come also, however, not from the lies that the fat rogue tells of his adventures (indeed, in *The Merry Wives* he often tells the truth) but from the incomparable idiom in which he tells of them. And if the Falstaff of *The Merry Wives* shares one quality above all others with the Falstaff of *Henry IV*, that quality is, surely, the idiom.

It is heard immediately on his entrance: 'I will answer it straight: I have done all this. That is now answered'; it is clear in his description of Mistress Ford's and Mistress Page's alleged interest in him, with its characteristic trick of seeming to deprecate, or depreciate, himself without really doing so ('sometimes the beam of her view gilded my foot, sometimes my portly belly'—compare, for example, from *2 Henry IV*, 'I do here walk before thee like a sow that hath overwhelmed all her litter but one', and the following

1. M. R. Ridley has complained, for example, that we are 'apparently being solemnly, or at least seriously, invited to suppose' that the old Falstaff 'could . . . be no better than an infatuated gull' (*William Shakespeare: A Commentary*, London, 1936, p. 74).

interview with the Chief Justice); and it is unmistakable when, equally characteristically, he parodies his own style, among others, and, tongue in cheek, writes a letter: 'I love thee. I will not say pity me—'tis not a soldier-like phrase—but I say, love me. By me, / Thine own true knight, / By day or night / . . . *John Falstaff*'. This could not be more like his letter to Hal in *2 Henry IV*, II. ii. 136ff., 'I commend me to thee, I commend thee, and I leave thee. . . Thine, by yea and no, which is as much as to say, as thou usest him, *Jack Falstaff* . . .'.

He is made to speak with exactly the same gift for the unexpected nouns in the most vivid of similes and the repetition of a word to form a startling pun: 'I have *grated* upon my good friends for three reprieves for you and your *coach-fellow* Nym—or else you had looked through the *grate*, like a *geminy* of *baboons*'. In the wry self-communion that is as close as he comes to self-pity, the phrases 'you may know by my size that I have a kind of alacrity in sinking... The water swells a man; and what a thing should I have been when I had been swelled! I should have been a mountain of mummy' are comparable with 'I were better to be eaten to death with a rust than to be scoured to nothing with perpetual motion' (*2 Henry IV*, I. ii. 246–8). Of his subsequent retelling to Ford of his ducking in the Thames (III. v. 75–113), one need say perhaps only that there is no finer comic prose in the whole of English drama. It is ungracious to ask for more, and Hazlitt was surely wrong when he said that Falstaff's 'wit and eloquence have left him'.[1]

One other aspect of Shakespeare's 'revival' of Falstaff in *The Merry Wives* should be noticed—its masterly avoiding of what could have become major problems. For example, Mistress Quickly's second interview with Falstaff (III. v), to invite him to visit Mistress Ford the second time, is kept very short; and the main part of the third, when obviously it would be more difficult for her to evade questions about his earlier discomfiture, takes place off-stage (it is merely introduced in IV. v). Finally, Falstaff's face is saved after the Herne the Hunter farce, when the disclosure is made that those who have played tricks on him have themselves been deceived: Anne has married neither her father's nor her mother's choice, so that her parents, trying to trick each other, have both been tricked, and Caius and Slender have failed to marry their promised brides. Page's invitation to Falstaff to laugh at Mistress Page falls flat, and indeed nobody can afford to laugh at anybody else. Not only has the previously realistic play been turned in Act V into a kind of courtly masque, in which characters

1. *Characters of Shakespeare's Plays* (1818, rep. London, 1890), p. 230.

can step out of their main roles to play other parts, particularly for the purpose of compliment, in true masque style; but also now the masque has, as it were, been allowed to fade out, that the characters of the main play may step forward again and *all* be seen in their true colours. As J. W. Mackail once put it, 'it is a wonderful feat of sleight-of-hand. . . . Managed light-handedly as it is, and taken light-heartedly as it should be, it is as good reading as it is a uniform and certain success on the stage. Mrs. Page's concluding words:

> Let us every one go home
> And laugh this sport o'er by a country fire,
> Sir John and all,

are in effect Shakespeare's own criticism on it—whose else can we require?—and the sufficient answer to the higher critics who have deplored in it the degradation of Falstaff: forgetting that the best of them are but shadows, and the worst no worse if imagination amend them.'[1]

Over a hundred years before Mackail, Oxberry had pointed out that it is in any case an error to concentrate on Falstaff, and the comparison with the Falstaff of the Histories, and to overlook all the other comic characters who helped, in Oxberry's opinion, to make 'this delightful comedy' 'perfect'.[2] Probably the most interesting of these are the wives, in whom Shakespeare showed conclusively, in the words of one of them, that 'wives may be merry, and yet honest too'. They are indeed 'honest' and not only in the sense of 'chaste'; equally appealing is their loyalty to, and understanding of, each other. Even that, however, is not a matter on which they can be solemn: when Ford says to Mistress Page, 'I think, if your husbands were dead, you two would marry', he receives the reply he perhaps deserves: 'Be sure of that—two other husbands'. There is no ambiguity or ambivalence in their attitude to Falstaff's letters; it is summed up in one phrase, 'What doth he think of us?' and their only other thought is 'Let's be revenged on him':

> *Mrs. Ford.* Nay, I will consent to act any villainy against him that may not sully the chariness of our honesty. O that my husband saw this letter; it would give eternal food to his jealousy.

1. *The Approach to Shakespeare* (Oxford, 1930), p. 59. The opposite view is nowhere more strongly stated than by H. B. Charlton, who, in his *Shakespearian Comedy* (London, 1938, rep. 1961), pp. 192–3, said that Shakespeare's treatment of Falstaff here was a 'crime worse than parricide—the slaughter of one's own offspring', adding 'there can be no clearer evidence of his own rejection of Falstaff' or of 'the bitterness of its author's disillusionment'.

2. *The Merry Wives of Windsor*, ed. W. Oxberry (The New English Drama, Vol. 9, London, 1820), p. i.

Mrs. Page. Why, look where he comes; and my good man too. He's as far from jealousy as I am from giving him cause; and that, I hope, is an unmeasurable distance.
Mrs. Ford. You are the happier woman.

The touch of pathos in that last comment should not be missed, but of course Shakespeare will not allow himself to dwell on pathos in such a comedy as this; the sorrow of the woman married to a jealous husband has not been overlooked, but it has been treated with the reserve with which a Mistress Ford would herself treat it.

Above all, the portraits of the wives are significantly unmarred by the fulsomeness that too often accompanies portraits of domestic virtue. Shakespeare has made the point that a woman can be virtuous without taking herself or the world too seriously; and with such a woman a Falstaff is hopelessly out of his element. The phrase that perhaps best describes his predicament is Mistress Ford's 'What tempest I trow threw this whale, with so many tuns of oil in his belly, ashore at Windsor?' A Falstaff is more in his 'natural' environment with an Eastcheap hostess—or with Doll Tearsheet.

Page and Ford are also interestingly drawn. Page is little more than an average decent citizen, above suspecting his wife but not above choosing his daughter's husband; he must therefore be taken down a peg, by discovering that the daughter is quite capable of running off with the man she wants and so escaping the fool to whom her father would rashly have married her. The skill with which the dramatist portrays the jealousy of Ford, however, has not sufficiently been noticed.

When Elizabethan dramatists did not portray jealousy as tragic, they tended to portray it as a 'humour', dominating a man's character and leaving no room for other aspects of temperament. In Ford, jealousy is depicted 'in the round', and the dramatist has shown that a man may be jealous and still not be worthless or beneath contempt. This is achieved by revealing the way in which Ford's mind works. There is, as it were, an intellectual basis for his jealousy, in the sense that he convinces himself, by rationalization, that he would be foolish not to be jealous—that jealousy is, so to speak, a risk worth taking, since the alternative is seen as obstinate unwillingness to acknowledge what could conceivably happen. The line of thought, once Pistol has told him that Falstaff 'affects' his wife—and we know already from the wives that Ford is prone to jealousy—is: 'I do not misdoubt my wife; but I would be loath to turn them together; a man may be too confident; I would have nothing lie on my head; I cannot be thus satisfied' or again 'Though Page be a secure fool, and stands so firmly on his wife's frailty, yet

I cannot put off my opinion so easily: she was in his company at Page's house; and what they made there, I know not. Well, I will look further into't, and I have a disguise to sound Falstaff. If I find her honest, I lose not my labour; if she be otherwise, 'tis labour well bestowed.' It is also perfectly 'in character' that as Brook he should continue to torture himself by hearing of Falstaff's aspirations and progress: a strain of masochism is gently hinted at (and no more than that).

Alfred Harbage has written that 'Master Ford's soliloquy when he thinks he is to be cuckolded does not express the anguish which Shakespeare would give a character actually in such danger'.[1] It may be so, but the anguish seems deep enough, and realistic enough: the difference between Ford's anguish and Othello's may be not so much in the 'tone' (to use Harbage's word) as in the audience's already established attitude to the characters. It knows that Othello's jealousy is groundless but knows also that it is dangerous, whereas in the comedy knowledge both of the stratagem being used by the wives and of the characters of all concerned removes any possibility that Ford will long continue to believe the worst. *While* he suffers, however, his suffering is acute, and certainly dramatically credible.

Of the others, Fenton is little more than the youthful romantic lead, saved from insipidity by the information that he kept company with the wild Prince and Poins and by his dignity and his willingness to do something about the difficulties that beset his wooing. By a dramatic device known from many a play, he also gains by contrast with his rivals for the hand of Anne. Anne is herself both 'sweet' and desirable; her two exchanges with Slender, at the end of I. i and in III. iv, could be played to show a gay sense of humour but in any case reveal firmness and sense ('Good Master Shallow, let him woo for himself'), as do her brief dialogue with Fenton at the beginning of III. iv and her indignant answer to the suggestion that she marry Caius: 'Alas, I had rather be set quick i' th' earth, / And bowl'd to death with turnips!' Perhaps too the imagery of that rejoinder is intended to remind us that we are dealing with a country girl.

Caius is most amusing, with his pugnacity (often expressed through his favourite oath, 'by gar') and his ability to do greater harm to the English language than he ever manages to do to his opponents; there is, however, no reason to question his courage, and his final threat 'by gar, I'll raise all Windsor' need not be seen

1. *As They Liked It* (New York, 1947), p. 135, referring to the soliloquy at the close of II. ii.

as empty. It has exactly the same effect as has Malvolio's 'I'll be revenged on the whole pack of you' at the close of *Twelfth Night:* the joy of the majority is never achieved without the unhappiness of one. In the world of comedy, fools who aspire to the hands of desirable young women must run the risk of being treated as fools and must take whatever is coming to them. Nor in *The Merry Wives* is there an Olivia to say that 'he hath been most notoriously abused' or a Duke to say 'Pursue him, and entreat him to a peace'.

No audience ever sorrowed over Slender, perhaps the finest comic portrait in the play and certainly one of the finest Shakespeare ever painted on a small canvas. It has been well said that the very name is almost too substantial for the character, and F. S. Boas has written that 'In Slender not only do we see intellect flickering with its last feeble glimmer, but the will attenuated almost to vanishing point. Palpitating on the brink of nonentity, he clings for support to the majestic personality of Shallow.'[1] As a dramatic character, however, he is no nonentity, any more than a bore (such as Jane Austen's Miss Bates would have been in real life) need be a bore as a figure in fiction; indeed he is, as Hazlitt put it, 'a very potent piece of imbecility'.[2]

Slender's knowledge is confined to bears and greyhounds; his courage is not even enough to stand up to the bluster of Pistol and Bardolph. He is completely without initiative ('I had rather than forty shillings I had my book of Songs and Sonnets here'); and although Evans tries patiently to explain to him the 'matter' of the wooing of Anne Page, 'if you be capacity of it', the capacity is quite lacking, and the enthusiasm rises only to 'Why, if it be so, I will marry her upon any reasonable demands . . . that I am freely dissolved, and dissolutely'. Yet he wanders through one scene doing nothing but sigh, quite irrelevantly, 'O sweet Anne Page'—playing the part of the love-sick swain as unsuccessfully as he played the part of the polite guest in I. i. His proposal to Anne, in III. iv, competes with Mr Collins's offer to Elizabeth Bennet in *Pride and Prejudice* for the honour of being the funniest proposal in English literature. It can end only as it does, with an immense sigh of relief at being saved from the necessity for further conversation: 'Your father and my uncle hath made motions. If it be my luck, so; if not, happy man be his dole! They can tell you how things go, better than I can. You may ask your father; here he comes.'

Conceivably the portrait of Slender, incapable of acting without the prodding of his uncle the Justice, would have even more humour if it were seen to be aimed at William Wayte, that 'certain

1. *Shakspere and his Predecessors* (London, 1896), p. 298. 2. *op. cit.*, p. 231.

loose person of no reckoning or value, being wholly under the rule and commandment of the said Gardiner', but it does not need that support. Rather, one other quality of the sketch must be praised: its superb restraint. How many dramatists, having thought up Slender, could have been content to make such sparing use of him and have refused to carry him (or Shallow's crony in *2 Henry IV*, Silence) into a second play?

Sparing use is similarly made of Justice Shallow, although the humour of this part was more varied and thus allowed repetition in a 'sequel'. Leaving aside again the possibility of personal satire, the fun of Shallow comes largely from his vanity—particularly that form of it that depends, as in *2 Henry IV*, on unreliable memories of his prowess when he was young; on his trick of repeating the most trivial of phrases ('And I thank you always with my heart, la, with my heart'; 'Sir, he's a good dog, and a fair dog: can there more be said? He is good and fair'; 'He hath wronged me, indeed he hath; at a word, he hath, believe me. Robert Shallow, Esquire, saith he is wronged'); and on his inability either to avoid platitude or to strike the right tone and give no more than the proportionate emphasis to a remark ('Though we are justices, and doctors, and churchmen, Master Page, we have some salt of our youth in us; we are the sons of women, Master Page').

The Welsh parson Evans is there mostly to 'make fritters of English' and, with his cowardice and generally over-anxious good nature, to serve as a foil to his original foe and later collaborator, Caius. He is also unforgettable in the Latin lesson. Caius' 'dry nurse', Mistress Quickly, is yet another enemy of the English language, and has even less control over her tongue: her thoughts pour out, in no semblance of order (and incidentally give headaches to editors who have to punctuate what she says). Add the jovial bluster of the Host; the less good-natured bluster of Pistol, trying to speak in the manner of the hero, or anti-hero, of Elizabethan drama, or melodrama; the 'humours' of Nym; and the blunders of young William Page—and we have one of the most astonishing galleries of perpetrators of verbal fun that even Shakespeare ever put in a play.

It is not surprising, with so many 'comics'—and particularly if the play was in fact written hurriedly—that the plotting should not be tight.[1] Nothing comes of the charge of killing deer brought by Shallow against Falstaff at the beginning of the play, and no

1. Dryden, however, found the play unique among Shakespeare's comedies for 'the mechanic beauties of the plot', 'the observation of the three Unities' ('The Grounds of Criticism in Tragedy', the preface to *Troilus and Cressida*, 1679); and George Colman and other eighteenth-century critics agreed with him.

more is heard of the rather ridiculous threat to make a Star Chamber matter of it. Unless there was indeed some special relevance in all this for purposes of personal satire, one can do no more than assume that it is one way of bringing Mr Justice Shallow up from Gloucestershire to Windsor—and even that is less likely if this play preceded *2 Henry IV*. It is probably not true, however, that nothing comes of the trick played by the Host on Caius and Evans; one must believe that they take their revenge by paying somebody to impersonate visiting German dignitaries and steal the Host's horses.[1] This part of the play nevertheless remains a sub-plot, not connected in any way with the two main 'intrigue' plots—other than that they are all variations on the tale of the biter bit and that all three involve the deflating of a character who thinks himself safe from deception. The intrigue stories—i.e. the tricks played on Falstaff by the merry wives and the outwitting of Page and his wife, Caius, and Slender, by Fenton and Anne—are most skilfully linked at the end when the revealing of Fenton's success prevents the Pages from gloating further over their exposing of Falstaff. (There is also the less important connection of Quickly's acting as go-between in both plots.)

It may be worth pointing out too that the play has been carefully composed for presentation on the most simple of stages. A disclosure space of some kind is required for the hiding of Simple from Caius in I. iv and to serve as the 'arras' behind which Falstaff stands in III. iii, and as the 'chamber' into which Falstaff steps in IV. ii; but there is no need for the audience to *see* the actors 'ascend' in III. iii or 'run up' in IV. ii, and while Falstaff could speak from a higher level in IV. v when the Host calls to him to let the 'fat woman' 'descend', it is not necessary. There is then no commitment to an 'upper stage', and even the last scene can be produced on a simple platform. The play could thus easily have been transferred from public stage to Court, or vice versa, with a minimum of bother and without the problem of transporting clumsy 'properties'.

Of the 'style' of the comedy, something has already been said in discussing the Falstaff idiom. That most of the play is in prose need not mean that prose was easier for Shakespeare (the state of the text of *Timon of Athens*, if that is indeed an unfinished play, may well suggest that it was not); nor is prose in any sense inferior for the purposes of such broad comedy as this. The effect of colloquialism is easily obtained, and sustained; and Shakespeare has

1. Daniel may still be correct in saying that conjecture whether Pistol and Nym were the men in disguise is 'somewhat idle speculation' (Introduction to the Griggs facsimile, p. xii).

no difficulty in covering the necessary range of mood, even to Ford's jealousy. The prose also has some most subtle rhythms, and not only when Shallow is using his characteristic repetitions, or when Caius is piling up threats, or Evans ticking off facts on his fingers: 'there is three umpires in this matter, as I understand; that is, Master Page (fidelicet Master Page); and there is myself (fidelicet myself): and the three party is (lastly and finally) mine host of the Garter'. Falstaff, too, is fond of a singing parallelism ('she discourses, she carves, she gives the leer of invitation') and even Quickly's meanderings often have their own kind of balance ('His worst fault is that he is given to prayer; he is something peevish that way; but nobody but has his fault; but let that pass'). The mingling of speeches of one or two sentences with the longer passages such as Ford's soliloquies, or his addresses (as Brook) to Falstaff, or Falstaff's accounts of his adventures to Ford–Brook, provides another interesting study in variation of dramatic pace.

The occasional modulating into verse is not as arbitrary as has sometimes been maintained. It is nearly all associated either with Fenton, to distinguish the romantic 'plot', or with the Herne the Hunter masque, as a sign of its lesser reality. So Fenton speaks verse, appropriately, in a serious conversation with Anne in III. iv, and not only Anne but also Page and Mistress Page use it when addressing him; similarly both Fenton and the Host talk in verse in IV. vi when discussing the elopement. Ford speaks verse when announcing his reformation, in IV. iv, and Page replies to him in kind—the farce for the minute is over—and then Mistress Page and company use verse when developing the plan to have Falstaff tricked as Herne the Hunter. In the last scene, Quickly and her allies speak verse while playing their parts in the masque, but prose significantly returns when the characters resume their own persons; and the entry of Fenton with his bride naturally demands verse again. Pistol, of course, often lapses into, or imitates, verse when he is trying to emulate Marlowe or the writers of less reputable heroics; and couplets may be used, as so often in Elizabethan drama, to gain the effect of epigram or Q.E.D. at the close of a scene or a distinctive part of one—as with Mistress Page's

> We'll leave a proof, by that which we will do,
> Wives may be merry, and yet honest too.
> We do not act that often jest and laugh;
> 'Tis old but true: 'Still swine eats all the draff'
> (IV. ii. 95–8).

The only 'problem' even worth comment is Falstaff's use of three blank verse lines followed by a couplet, at I. iii. 76–80—and the point here may be that he is imitating and parodying Pistol, exactly as he speaks a few lines of verse 'in King Cambyses' vein' in *1 Henry IV*, II. iv.

To search for thematic imagery in *The Merry Wives* would be folly: the play has neither the intellectual nor the emotional intensity for that. There are, however, some interesting groups of imagery that influence one's attitude to story and characters, and certainly there are some that help to establish atmosphere.[1]

The main group, not surprisingly, could be described as that arising from the typical domestic life of a family in a country town. 'Choked with a piece of toasted cheese' (and other cheese references), 'one that makes fritters of English', 'half stewed in grease like a Dutch dish', 'have my brains ta'en out and buttered', 'rain potatoes', 'bowl'd to death with turnips', 'as blue as bilberry', 'as crest-fallen as a dried pear', 'laid my brain in the sun and dried it', 'knit a knot in his fortunes with the finger of my substance', 'Welsh flannel', 'a cockscomb of frieze', 'cannot creep into a half-penny purse, nor into a pepper box', 'cooled, glowing hot, . . . like a horse-shoe', 'to the forge with it, then; shape it: I would not have things cool', 'like a barrow of butcher's offal', 'like a glover's paring knife' are representative; and, not to forget the out-of-doors, there are the delightful 'these lisping hawthorn-buds' and 'he smells April and May'. While not strictly an image, perhaps, 'plucked geese, played truant, and whipped top' gains the same effect. Amusingly some of the oaths and terms of abuse have this country flavour too: 'You Banbury cheese', for example, or 'mechanical salt-butter rogue'.

In these middle-class surroundings, the characters, not excluding Falstaff, speak most appropriately in homely proverbs or choose their allusions from the better-known parts of scripture. 'The story of the Prodigal', 'a legion of angels', 'Cain-coloured beard', 'a Herod of Jewry', 'Goliath with a weaver's beam', 'as poor as Job', 'all Eve's daughters', 'the hundred Psalms', and 'as firm as faith' are some of these. Classical allusions are correspondingly rare. Several, but by no means all, of these are used by the more highly educated Falstaff; and many are sexual in connotation, such as Actaeon, Jove and Europa, Jupiter and Leda, 'Cupid's carriers', and 'my good she-Mercury'. (The Host throws in 'bully Hercules', 'bully Hector', and 'Hector of Greece'.) If Pistol's constant attempts to be literary are put on one side, and they are all early in the play, other literary references are relatively few: the most memorable

1. 'Image' will be used in a wide sense in the following discussion, much as Caroline Spurgeon used it in *Shakespeare's Imagery* (Cambridge, 1935), to include 'imaginative picture'.

are the Marlowe song, the quotation from Sidney, the Host's 'Am I a Machiavel?', and 'like . . . three Doctor Faustuses'. As befits a play given so much to intentional and unintentional misuse of language, however, there are several linguistic images, such as 'I can construe the action of her familiar style', the 'voice of her behaviour', 'translated her will—out of honesty into English', and 'keep the terms of my honour precise'. ('Spoke the prologue of our comedy', 'puts into the press', and 'second edition' are not unrelated to these.)

A very prominent group of images belongs to the animal–bird class. 'Like rats', 'polecats', 'unkennel the fox', 'cat-a-mountain looks', 'Jack-dog priest', 'jack-an-ape', 'geminy of baboons', and 'rotten bell-wether' come to mind, not to mention 'with as little remorse as they would have drowned a blind bitch's puppies, fifteen i' the litter', 'come cut and long-tail', 'eyas-musket', and 'know turtles from jays'. The effect of these, however, is not basically to lower the world of the play to the level of the animal kingdom (as the images are alleged to lower that of *King Lear*, or as the 'dog', 'boar', and other animal images used of him influence our judgement of Richard III); they work in exactly the opposite way and make the audience smile at the idiosyncrasy of the speaker who indulges in them, as does 'the world's mine oyster, which I with sword will open'. The occasional medical image tends to have the same effect—for example, the Host's 'bully stale' and 'Mounseur Mock-water' and Falstaff's 'as cold as if I had swallowed snowballs for pills to cool the reins', and the references to Hippocrates, Galen, and Æsculapius.

The legal and financial group is not so easily explicable: that love and marriage are so often seen as arrangements to be made formally is only a partial explanation. 'Lay to pawn', 'fee-simple, with fine and recovery', 'the register' (of follies), 'fee'd every slight occasion', 'exhibit a bill in the parliament', references to (legal) 'suits' and inheriting, and, particularly, 'like a fair house built on another man's ground, so that I have lost my edifice by mistaking the place where I erected it' and 'build upon a . . . promise' may even have an autobiographical rather than a dramatic significance (although 'I will be cheaters to them both, and they shall be exchequers to me' is clear enough). Military images help to reinforce the idea that some see woman's purity as an object to be attacked and defended (e.g. 'lay an amiable siege to the honesty of this Ford's wife', 'the ward of her purity', and 'her defences which now are too too strongly embattled against me').

Some of the most vivid images have to do with ships and places and exploration. A few of these link with the previous group (e.g. 'this voyage toward my wife', 'board', 'above deck', and 'under my hatches') and those used by Falstaff reinforce the notion of his exploring for treasure ('sail like my pinnace to these golden shores', 'they shall be my East and West Indies', and 'she is a region in Guiana', for instance). The Host's, however, are far more exotic, and build up the impression of his ebullience—such as 'my Ethiopian', 'Castalian-king-Urinal', 'Anthropophaginian', and 'Bohemian-Tartar'. Falstaff's 'Pickt-hatch', 'like Bucklersbury in simple time', and 'the Countergate'—together with 'red-lattice phrases'—are distinctly English and from his own background.

Falstaff's bulk is the cause of many images, used by him and of him, mentioning oil, fat, and grease, and these, of course, add considerably to the fun as well as to the physical picture. They include 'till the wicked fire of lust have melted him in his own grease' and 'this whale, with so many tuns of oil in his belly', both from Mistress Ford, and, from Falstaff himself, 'lest the oil that's in me should set hell on fire', 'melt me out of my fat drop by drop, and liquor fishermen's boots with me', and 'stinking clothes that fretted in their own grease'. A similar effect, from the 'domestic' class, is gained by 'gross watery pumpion'.

Last but not least, there are all the images related to the horns of the cuckold, leading to a whole range of references to buck and other horned beasts—Ford fearing that he is being reduced to the level of one, and Falstaff equally erroneously thinking to make him one. These reach a deliberate crescendo in Falstaff's anticipations as, wearing horns, he awaits the arrival of his 'doe' at the beginning of the final scene; and the extravagance of 'send me a cool rut-time, Jove' makes him most laughable when it is necessary that he least be pitied.

The language, in short, is superbly adapted to the purposes of the play, and examination of it too suggests that the producers and actors who have continued to present *The Merry Wives*, and the audiences who have continued to enjoy it, may be making sounder literary judgements than those who write whole books on Shakespeare or his comedies and either neglect the play altogether or mention it only in passing.

ABBREVIATIONS AND REFERENCES

The following abbreviations are used in the collations and explanatory notes:

EDITIONS

Q	*A Most pleasaunt and excellent conceited Comedie, of Syr Iohn Falstaffe, and the merrie Wiues of Windsor. Entermixed with sundrie variable and pleasing humors, of Syr Hugh the Welch Knight, Iustice Shallow, and his wise Cousin M. Slender. With the swaggering vaine of Auncient Pistoll, and Corporall Nym. By William Shakespeare.* London, 1602.
Q2	*A Most Pleasant and Excellent Conceited Comedy, of Sir Iohn Falstaffe, and the Merry Wiues of Windsor. With the Swaggering Vaine of Ancient Pistoll, and Corporall Nym. Written by W. Shakespeare.* London, 1619.
Q3	*The Merry VVives of Windsor. With the humours of Sir Iohn Falstaffe, As also the swaggering vaine of Ancient Pistoll, and Corporall Nym. Written by William Shake-Speare. Newly corrected.* London, 1630.
F	*Mr. William Shakespeares Comedies, Histories, & Tragedies.* London, 1623.
F2	*Mr. William Shakespeares Comedies, Histories, and Tragedies.* London, 1632.
F3	*Mr. William Shakespear's Comedies, Histories, and Tragedies . . . The third Impression.* London, 1664.
F4	*Mr. William Shakespear's Comedies, Histories, and Tragedies . . . The Fourth Edition.* London, 1685.
Rowe	*The Works of Mr. William Shakespear . . . Revis'd and Corrected . . . By N. Rowe, Esq.* (Vol. 1) London, 1709.
Rowe[2]	*The Works of Mr. William Shakespear . . . Revis'd and Corrected . . . By N. Rowe Esq.* (Vol. 1) London, 1709.
Rowe[3]	*The Works of Mr. William Shakespear . . . With his Life, by N. Rowe Esq.* (Vol. 1) London, 1714.
Pope	*The Works of Shakespear . . . Collected and Corrected . . . by Mr. Pope.* (Vol. 1) London, 1723.
Theobald	*The Works of Shakespeare . . . Collated with the Oldest Copies, and Corrected; With Notes . . . By Mr. Theobald.* (Vol. 1) London, 1733.
Theobald[2]	*The Works of Shakespeare . . . Collated . . . and Corrected: With Notes . . . By Mr. Theobald. The Second Edition.* (Vol. 1) London, 1740.
Hanmer	*The Works of Shakespear . . . Carefully Revised and Corrected by the former Editions.* (Vol. 1) Oxford, 1744.

Warburton	*The Works of Shakespear. The Genuine Text . . . settled . . . By Mr. Pope and Mr. Warburton.* (Vol. 1) London, 1747.
Johnson	*The Plays of William Shakespeare . . . To which are added Notes by Sam. Johnson.* (Vol. 2) London, 1765.
Capell	*Mr William Shakespeare his Comedies, Histories, and Tragedies* [edited Edward Capell]. (Vol. 1) London, [1767].
Steevens	*The Plays of William Shakespeare . . . To which are added notes by Samuel Johnson and George Steevens.* (Vol. 1) London, 1773.
Steevens[2]	*The Plays of William Shakspeare . . . The Second Edition, Revised and Augmented.* (Vol. 1) London, 1778.
Reed	*The Plays of William Shakspeare . . . The Third Edition, revised and augmented by the Editor of Dodsley's Collection of Old Plays.* (Vol. 1) London, 1785.
Rann	*The Dramatic Works of Shakespeare . . . with notes by Joseph Rann.* (Vol. 1) Oxford, 1786.
Malone	*The Plays and Poems of William Shakspeare . . . With . . . notes . . . By Edmond Malone.* (Vol. 1 Pt 2) London, 1790.
Steevens[3]	*The Plays of William Shakspeare . . . The Fourth Edition.* (Vol. 3) London, 1793.
Reed[2]	*The Plays of William Shakspeare . . . The Fifth Edition. Revised and augmented By Isaac Reed.* (Vol. 5) London, 1803.
Reed[3]	*The Plays of William Shakspeare . . . Revised and augmented by Isaac Reed . . . The Sixth Edition.* (Vol. 5) London, 1813.
Harness	*The Dramatic Works of William Shakspeare; with notes . . . By the Rev. William Harness.* (Vol. 1) London, 1825.
Singer	*The Dramatic Works of William Shakspeare. With Notes . . . by Samuel Weller Singer.* (Vol. 1) Chiswick, 1826.
Knight	*The Pictorial Edition of the Works of Shakspere. Edited by Charles Knight. Comedies* (Vol. 1) London, [1839].
Collier	*The Works of William Shakespeare . . . with the various readings, notes . . . by J. Payne Collier.* (Vol. 1) London, 1844.
Halliwell	*The Complete Works of Shakspere, Revised . . . by J. O. Halliwell.* London and New York, [1850].
Hudson	*The Works of Shakespeare . . . with Introductions, Notes . . . by the Rev. H. N. Hudson.* (Vol. 1) Boston, 1851.
Collier[2]	*The Plays of Shakespeare: The text regulated by the old copies, and by the recently discovered Folio of 1632, containing early manuscript emendations. Edited by J. Payne Collier.* London, 1853.
Dyce	*The Works of William Shakespeare. The Text revised by the Rev. Alexander Dyce.* (Vol. 1) London, 1857.
Grant White	*The Works of William Shakespeare . . . edited . . . by Richard Grant White.* (Vol. 2) Boston, 1857.
Staunton	*The Plays of Shakespeare. Edited by Howard Staunton.* (Vol. 1) London, 1858.
Camb.	*The Works of William Shakespeare edited by William George Clark . . . and John Glover.* (Vol. 1) Cambridge and London, 1863.
Keightley	*The Plays of William Shakespeare. Carefully edited by Thomas Keightley.* (Vol. 2) London, 1864.

Dyce[2]	*The Works of William Shakespeare . . . Second edition.* (Vol. 1) London, 1866.
Hudson[2]	*The Works of Shakespeare . . . with Introductions, Notes . . . by the Rev. H. N. Hudson . . . Revised edition.* (Vol. 1) Boston, 1871.
Wheatley	*The Merry Wives of Windsor . . . edited . . . by Henry B. Wheatley.* London, 1886.
Craig	*The Complete Works of William Shakespeare. Edited . . . by W. J. Craig.* The Oxford Shakespeare. Oxford, [1892].
Hart	*The Merry Wives of Windsor. Edited by H. C. Hart.* The Arden Shakespeare. London, 1904, rep. 1932.
Chambers	*The Merry Wives of Windsor. Edited by E. K. Chambers.* The Red Letter Shakespeare. London, 1906.
New Camb.	*The Merry Wives of Windsor. Edited . . . by Sir Arthur Quiller-Couch and John Dover Wilson.* The New Shakespeare. Cambridge, 1921, rep. 1954.
Yale	*The Merry Wives of Windsor. Edited by George Van Santvoord.* The Yale Shakespeare. New Haven, 1922.
Ridley	*The Merry Wives of Windsor. Edited by M. R. Ridley.* The New Temple Shakespeare. London, 1935.
Kittredge	*The Complete Works of Shakespeare. Edited by George Lyman Kittredge.* Boston, [1936].
Alexander	*William Shakespeare The Complete Works . . . edited . . . by Peter Alexander.* The Tudor Shakespeare. London, 1951.
Sisson	*William Shakespeare The Complete Works . . . Edited by Charles Jasper Sisson.* London, [1954].
Munro	*The London Shakespeare . . . edited by . . . John Munro.* (Vol. 2) London, 1958.
Bowers	*The Merry Wives of Windsor. Edited by Fredson Bowers.* The Pelican Shakespeare. Baltimore, 1963, rep. 1969.

OTHER WORKS

Abbott	E. A. Abbott. *A Shakespearian Grammar.* Third edition, London 1873.
Ashmole	Elias Ashmole. *The Institution, Laws & Ceremonies Of the most noble Order of the Garter.* London, 1672.
Baldwin	T. W. Baldwin. *William Shakspere's 'Small Latine & Lesse Greeke'.* Urbana, Ill., 1944.
Bullough	Geoffrey Bullough. *Narrative and Dramatic Sources of Shakespeare.* (Vol. 2) London, 1958.
Capell (1783)	[Edward Capell]. *Notes and Various Readings to Shakespeare.* London, [1783].
Cartwright	Robert Cartwright. *New Readings in Shakspere.* London, 1866.
Cotgrave	Randle Cotgrave. *A Dictionarie of the French and English Tongues.* London, 1611.
Daniel	P. A. Daniel. *Notes and Conjectural Emendations Of certain Doubtful Passages in Shakespeare's Plays.* London, 1870.
Douce	Francis Douce. *Illustrations of Shakespeare.* London, 1807.
Dyce (*Remarks*)	Alexander Dyce. *Remarks on Mr. J. P. Collier's and Mr. C. Knight's editions of Shakespeare.* London, 1844.

Eliot — [John Eliot]. *Ortho-Epia Gallica. Eliots Fruits for the French.* London, 1593.

Greg — Sir Walter Greg. Private letter to J. Dover Wilson (*New Camb.*, p. 134).

Grey — Zachary Grey. *Critical, Historical and Explanatory Notes on Shakespeare.* London, 1754.

Heath — [Benjamin Heath]. *A Revisal of Shakespeare's Text.* London, 1765.

Hotson — Leslie Hotson. *Shakespeare versus Shallow.* London, 1931.

Hulme — Hilda M. Hulme. *Explorations in Shakespeare's Language.* London, 1962.

Jackson — Zachariah Jackson. *Shakespeare's Genius Justified.* London, 1819.

Jonson — *Ben Jonson*, ed. C. H. Herford, and Percy and Evelyn Simpson. Oxford, 1925–52.

Kinnear — B. G. Kinnear. *Cruces Shakespearianæ.* London, 1883.

Kökeritz — Helge Kökeritz. *Shakespeare's Pronunciation.* New Haven, 1953.

Lambrechts — Guy Lambrechts. 'Proposed New Readings in Shakespeare', *Bulletin de la Faculté des Lettres de Strasbourg*, LXIII (1965), 946–7.

Lilly — [William Lilly, John Colet, *et al.*]. *A Shorte Introduction of Grammar.* London, 1549, 1557, 1577.

Mason — J. M. Mason. *Comments on the Last Edition of Shakespeare's Plays.* Dublin, 1785.

Muir — Kenneth Muir. *Shakespeare's Sources. I. Comedies and Tragedies.* London, 1957.

Nashe — *The Works of Thomas Nashe*, Edited by Ronald B. McKerrow (1904–10) . . . With supplementary notes . . . by F. P. Wilson. Oxford, 1958.

Noble — Richmond Noble. *Shakespeare's Biblical Knowledge.* London, 1935.

O.E.D. — *The Oxford English Dictionary, being a corrected reissue of 'A New English Dictionary upon Historical Principles'.* Oxford, 1933.

Onions — C. T. Onions. *A Shakespeare Glossary.* Second edition 1919, reprinted with enlarged addenda, Oxford, 1958.

Parsons — Howard Parsons. *Emendations to Three of Shakespeare's Plays.* London, [1953].

Partridge — Eric Partridge. *Shakespeare's Bawdy.* New edition, revised, 1955; rep. London, 1961.

Ray — J. Ray. *A Compleat Collection of English Proverbs . . . To which is added A Collection of English Words Not Generally Used.* Third edition, Augmented, London, 1742.

R.E.S. — *The Review of English Studies.* Oxford.

Schmidt — Alexander Schmidt. *A Shakespeare Lexicon.* Third edition, revised Sarrazin, 1902; rep. Berlin, 1962.

Sisson *N.R.* — C. J. Sisson. *New Readings in Shakespeare.* 1956; rep. London, 1962.

Tilley — M. P. Tilley. *A Dictionary of the Proverbs in England in the Sixteenth and Seventeenth Centuries.* Ann Arbor, Michigan, 1950.

Turberville	[George Turberville]. *The Noble Arte of Venerie or Hunting.* London, [1575].
Walker	W. S. Walker. *A Critical Examination of the Text of Shakespeare.* (Vol. 3) London, 1860.
Walter	*King Henry V.* Edited by J. H. Walter. The Arden Shakespeare. Corrected edition, London, 1960.
Whiter	Walter Whiter. *A Specimen of a Commentary on Shakespeare* (1794). Ed. Alan Over and Mary Bell. London, 1967.
Wright	Joseph Wright. *The English Dialect Dictionary.* London, 1896–1905, rep. Oxford, 1961.

The conjectures of Farmer, Tollet, and Tyrwhitt are those recorded by Steevens in his second and third editions.

Abbreviations used for the titles of Shakespeare's other plays are those of C. T. Onions, *A Shakespeare Glossary*, second edition, Oxford 1919, reprinted 1958, p. x; and act, scene, and line references are to the Globe edition. *The Two Noble Kinsmen* is cited from the edition by Clifford Leech (The Signet Classic Shakespeare, New York, 1966).

THE MERRY WIVES OF WINDSOR

DRAMATIS PERSONÆ

Sir John Falstaff.
Fenton, *a young gentleman.*
Shallow, *a country Justice.*
Abraham Slender, *Shallow's kinsman.*
Frank Ford, } *citizens of Windsor.*
George Page, }
William Page, *a boy, son of Page and Mistress Page.*
Sir Hugh Evans, *a Welsh parson.*
Doctor Caius, *a French physician.*
Host of the Garter Inn.
Bardolph, }
Pistol, } *followers of Falstaff*
Nym, }

DRAMATIS PERSONÆ] *This ed.; not in F, Q.* 4. *Shallow's kinsman*] *This ed.; Cousin to* Shallow *Rowe.* 5–6. *citizens of Windsor*] *Chambers; two Gentlemen, dwelling at* Windsor *Rowe.* 11–13. *followers of Falstaff*] *As Capell; Sharpers attending on* Falstaff *Rowe.*

Dramatis Personæ] First tabulated by Rowe. Lists of names are exceptional in the Folio, and the absence of one for this play is therefore of no significance.

4. Shallow's kinsman] Probably Slender is Shallow's nephew, in view of III. iv. 36–41; but the term 'uncle' by which Slender addresses Shallow may have been used loosely of other relationships, as were 'cousin' and 'nephew' (cf. *Oth.*, I. i. 111–14). The description of Slender on the Quarto's title-page as Shallow's 'wise Cousin' is therefore of no assistance in determining the exact relationship.

6. *GEORGE PAGE*] Page is called 'Thomas' at I. i. 42 but 'George' in three other lines, II. i. 143 and 151 and v. v. 199.

8. *EVANS*] The character can hardly have been based on the Stratford schoolmaster of 1575–9, Thomas Jenkins, as is sometimes said. Jenkins was born in London (Mark Eccles, *Shakespeare in Warwickshire*, Madison, 1961, p. 56).

9. *CAIUS*] Normally pronounced 'Keys' or 'Kays', but IV. vi. 27 and the Q spelling 'Cayus' may indicate a dissyllable. There can be no direct connection with the famous founder of Gonville and Caius College in Cambridge, who was an Englishman; and C. J. Sisson's suggestion that the real-life original may have been Dr Peter Chamberlain (a French gynaecologist practising in London before 1611 and probably by 1596) was made only in passing and was not supported by further evidence (*Essays and Studies*, XIII, 1960, 10–11). Nor is it easy to see how the presence of Caius in the play amounts to 'satire on the fad for foreign doctors'.

11. *BARDOLPH*] Probably to be pronounced 'Bardle' (it is spelt 'Bardol' in the Q of *1H4*, II. iv. 329). In *2H4* (III. ii. 235 and 244) he seems to be addressed as a corporal, a rank

ROBIN, *Falstaff's page.*
PETER SIMPLE, *Slender's servant.*
JOHN RUGBY, *Caius' servant.*
JOHN *and* ROBERT, *Ford's servants.*
MISTRESS FORD (ALICE).
MISTRESS PAGE (MARGARET).
ANNE PAGE, *daughter of Page and Mistress Page.*
MISTRESS QUICKLY, *Caius' servant.*
Three or four children (dressed in the last Act as fairies).

17. *John and Robert, Ford's servants*] *As New Camb.; Servants to* Page, Ford, *&c. Rowe.*
22. *Three or four children . . . fairies*] *This ed.*

he retains in *H5*, III. ii. 3. (Nym calls him 'Lieutenant' in *H5*, II. i. 2 but perhaps ironically.) Presumably only a Falstaff could have promoted such a man to such a rank (higher in Shakespeare's day than in ours).

12. *PISTOL*] Perhaps pronounced as 'pizzle' or in such a way as to make a pun on that word possible. Cf. *2H4*, II. iv. 121–6 and 174 ('Peesell' in Q, '*Peesel*' in F). In *2H4* (e.g. II. iv. 75) and *H5* (e.g. II. i. 3) and on the title-page of Q *Wiv.* Pistol is called 'Ancient' or ensign, a rank for which he, too, hardly seems qualified. Jorgensen has pointed out the joke also on 'ancient pistol'—a very noisy and often ineffective weapon (*Redeeming Shakespeare's Words*, Berkeley and L.A., 1962, pp. 70–4).

13. *NYM*] The name is almost certainly derived from 'to nim' in the sense of 'steal' or 'pilfer', although *O.E.D. v.*[3] gives no instance earlier than 1606. In *H5* Nym and Bardolph are said to be 'sworn brothers in filching' (III. ii. 47–8). *New Cambridge* saw also a reference to 'Nym' as an alleged short form of 'Hieronimo', the hero of Kyd's *Spanish Tragedy*, and so, particularly as Nym misuses the word 'humour', interpreted him as Shakespeare's caricature of Ben Jonson, who was taunted with having played the Kyd role. (A 1597 date for *The Merry Wives* would make this suggestion less plausible still.) As in *H5* Nym's rank is that of corporal.

21. *QUICKLY*] Kökeritz sees a quibble on 'quick-lie' (cf. her colleague in *2H4*, Doll Tearsheet). In *H4* Quickly is hostess of the Boar's Head Inn in Eastcheap. See Introduction, pp. vii, lii.

THE MERRY WIVES OF WINDSOR

ACT I

SCENE I

Enter JUSTICE SHALLOW, SLENDER, *and* SIR HUGH EVANS.

Shal. Sir Hugh, persuade me not: I will make a Star Chamber matter of it. If he were twenty Sir John Falstaffs, he shall not abuse Robert Shallow, Esquire.

Slen. In the county of Gloucester, Justice of Peace and Coram.

ACT I

Scene I

ACT I SCENE I] *F* (*Actus primus, Scena prima*); . . . *The* Scene *before* Page's *House in* Windsor. *Pope*. S.D. *Enter . . . Evans*.] *Rowe; Enter Iustice* Shallow, Slender, *Sir* Hugh Euans, *Master* Page, Falstoffe, Bardolph, Nym, Pistoll, Anne Page, *Mistresse* Ford, *Mistresse* Page, Simple. *F; Enter Iustice* Shallow, *Syr* Hugh, *Maister* Page, *and* Slender. *Q*.

1. *Sir Hugh*] For 'Sir' as a normal form of address to a clergyman (perhaps originally ironical, to one *not* entitled to be called 'dominus' as holding a University degree), cf. 'Sir Oliver Martext' in *AYL.*, III. iii. 43. Q misunderstands when on the title-page it refers to 'Syr *Hugh* the Welch Knight'.

1–2. *Star Chamber matter*] The Court of Star Chamber derived its name from the chamber in the royal palace at Westminster, with stars painted on the ceiling, in which the King's Council sat as a judicial body. It did exercise jurisdiction over such matters as riot (l. 32), particularly when men of title were involved; and justices of the peace were empowered and indeed enjoined to use their authority to repress crimes of this kind. (The Elizabethan Star Chamber does not seem to deserve the reputation the Court later obtained as autocratic, tyrannous, and generally not bound by law.) Shallow is thus not exceeding his authority but is, of course, taking himself very seriously. See also Introduction, p. xlix.

4. *Esquire*] Not, as now, a practically meaningless title, but a title of dignity for those one degree below knighthood. Shallow would legitimately call himself 'Esquire', not by birth but as a justice of the peace.

6. *Coram*] A common corruption of 'quorum', used in its original sense of

Shal. Ay, cousin Slender, and Custalorum.

Slen. Ay, and Ratolorum too; and a gentleman born, Master Parson, who writes himself 'Armigero' in any bill, warrant, quittance, or obligation—'Armigero'.

Shal. Ay, that I do, and have done any time these three hundred years.

Slen. All his successors, gone before him, hath done 't, and all his ancestors, that come after him, may: they may give the dozen white luces in their coat.

Shal. It is an old coat.

Evans. The dozen white louses do become an old coat well; it agrees well, passant; it is a familiar beast to man, and signifies love.

Shal. The luce is the fresh fish; the salt fish is an old coat.

8. Ratolorum] *F; Rotulorum Q3.* 18. louses] *F* (Lowses). 21.] *F* (The Luse is the fresh-fish, the salt-fish, is an old Coate.)*;* The luce is the fresh fish, the salt-fish is not an old coat. *conj. Johnson;* The luce is the fresh fish—the salt fish is an old cod. *New Camb.;* The luce is the fresh fish, the salt fish—is an old coat. *Sisson.*

those special justices of the peace at least two of whom had to be present before a felony could be tried.

7. *Custalorum*] A contraction of 'custos rotulorum' or keeper of the rolls, the office of the principal justice of the peace in each county. If Hotson is correct in seeing satire of William Gardiner in Shallow (see Introduction, p. xlix), the point would seem to be that this is an office of dignity which Gardiner could *not* have attained.

8. *Ratolorum*] Slender, not understanding that 'custalorum' means 'custos rotulorum', tries to bring that office in, and, typically, gets it wrong.

9. *Armigero*] Steevens (1793) may be right in suspecting that Slender mistakes the Latin ablative for the nominative. 'Armiger', once synonymous with 'Esquire', originally meant one of gentle birth who carried a knight's shield for him, but came to mean one entitled to a coat of arms.

10. *quittance*] formal release from a debt or obligation.

obligation] written contract or bond.

16. *give*] In the heraldic sense: use in a coat of arms.

luces] pike (normally, only when fully grown)—but in ll. 18ff. there is a pun on louses or lice. For the possible reference to the coat of arms of William Gardiner, or Sir Thomas Lucy, see Introduction, pp. xlix–lii.

19. *passant*] In heraldry, the word means 'walking, and looking towards the dexter side, with . . . the dexter fore-paw raised' (*O.E.D.* 4). Its use of a fish would therefore be comically inappropriate, but Evans is thinking only of lice 'walking'. There may be also a pun on an old meaning of 'passant': 'exceedingly' or 'surpassingly' (*O.E.D.* 1).

familiar] well known; 'part of the family'; *and* intimate, sociable, perhaps even 'unduly intimate' (*O.E.D.* A 2c). Tilley sees a connection with the proverb 'A louse is a man's companion' (L471). Cf. also 'familiar angel', for guardian angel.

21.] The joke, if any, would seem to depend on Evans's mispronunciation

Slen. I may quarter, coz.
Shal. You may, by marrying.
Evans. It is marring indeed, if he quarter it.
Shal. Not a whit.
Evans. Yes, per-lady: if he has a quarter of your coat, there is but three skirts for yourself, in my simple conjectures; but that is all one. If Sir John Falstaff have committed disparagements unto you, I am of the church and will be glad to do my benevolence, to make atonements and compromises between you.
Shal. The Council shall hear it; it is a riot.
Evans. It is not meet the Council hear a riot: there is no fear of Got in a riot. The Council, look you, shall desire to hear the fear of Got, and not to hear a riot; take your vizaments in that.

22. coz.] *As F; coz? Steevens*[3]. 24. marring] *F1; marrying F2.* 26. per-lady] *F;* py'r-lady *Capell.* 31. compromises] *F* (compremises).

of 'coat' as 'cod' or 'coad': he asserts that luces go well with an old 'coad', and perhaps Shallow, misunderstanding because of the mispronunciation, 'corrects' him by 'explaining' that luces are not louses and that luces (fresh-water fish) and cod (salt-water fish) are quite distinct. It is difficult to see further puns on 'cod' in the other sense, or on 'salt' meaning 'lecherous', as *New Cambridge* suggested, or on 'fresh fish' in the sense of 'novice' or 'beginner' (Hart, comparing *H8,* II. iii. 86); but the line is certainly obscure.

22. *quarter*] add another coat of arms to one's own (e.g. after marriage). Evans misunderstands and takes the word in another sense, 'dividing into quarters'. The difficulty is in the relationship of l. 22 to the preceding line, although any connection is obviously through 'coat'; perhaps Slender imagines that Shallow would like the salt fish too on his coat and suggests a way of getting it there.

coz] A contraction of 'cousin', meaning 'kinsman'. See note on *Dramatis Personæ*, l. 4, and III. iv. 36–41 and notes.

23–4. *marrying . . . marring*] 'Marrying is marring' was proverbial (Tilley M701). Shakespeare echoes it again in *Rom.*, I. ii. 12–13, and in *All's W.*, II. iii. 315.

26. *per-lady*] by our Lady. Here and elsewhere in this edition no attempt is made to 'regularize' or 'improve' F's indication of Evans's Welsh speech (most editors read 'py'r').

27. *skirts*] Evans is thinking of a man's garment, probably a kind of top-coat, divided at the bottom, back and front, so that it has four 'skirts' or tails. Cf. 'skirted page' in I. iii. 80.

31. *atonements*] agreements, reconciliation (at one + ment). Cf. *R3*, I. iii. 36.

compromises] *New Cambridge* pointed out that F's 'compremises' is probably only a variant spelling, not a further indication of Evans's confusion or mispronunciation. It compared *Mer. V.*, I. iii. 79, 'compremyzd' ('compremyz'd' F).

32. *Council*] the King's Council sitting as the Court of Star Chamber (cf. ll. 1–2 and note)—but Evans perhaps takes it to mean a church council or synod, as *New Cambridge* suggested.

36. *vizaments*] Evans's version of

Shal. Ha! O' my life, if I were young again, the sword should end it.

Evans. It is petter that friends is the sword, and end it; and there is also another device in my prain, which peradventure prings goot discretions with it. There is Anne Page, which is daughter to Master Thomas Page, which is pretty virginity.

Slen. Mistress Anne Page? She has brown hair, and speaks small like a woman.

Evans. It is that fery person for all the 'orld, as just as you will desire; and seven hundred pounds of moneys, and gold, and silver, is her grandsire upon his death's-bed (Got deliver to a joyful resurrections!) give, when she is able to overtake seventeen years old. It were a goot motion if we leave our pribbles and prabbles, and desire a marriage between Master Abraham and Mistress Anne Page.

Slen. Did her grandsire leave her seven hundred pound?

Evans. Ay, and her father is make her a petter penny.

Shal. I know the young gentlewoman; she has good gifts.

42. Thomas] *F; George / Theobald.* 45. woman.] *F;* woman? *conj. Lambrechts.* 54. *Slen.*] *F; Shal. Capell.* 56. *Shal.*] *Capell; Slen. F.*

'advisements'. He probably means 'take that into consideration'.

41. *discretions*] Evans prides himself on his discretion and judgement of what is 'discreet' or wise for others: cf. l. 132 and IV. iv. 1.

42. *Thomas*] Elsewhere he is 'George': see note on *Dramatis Personæ*, l. 6. 'Thomas' can hardly be a transcriber's error, as Hart suggested, and need not imply hasty revision, as *New Cambridge* argued: Shakespeare was often careless with names (notably in *Tim.*, but not only there).

45. *small*] i.e. in a voice the opposite of 'deep'; cf. *Tw.N.*, I. iv. 32–4, where the Duke, commenting on the disguised Viola's un-masculine qualities, says 'thy small pipe / Is as the maiden's organ, shrill and sound, / And all is semblative a woman's part' and *MND.*, I. ii. 52.

46. *just*] exact or exactly. Cf., e.g., *AYL.*, III. ii. 281.

51–2. *pribbles and prabbles*] Perhaps Evans's improvement on mere 'brabbles' or quarrels. He repeats the phrase at v. v. 160–1 (but uses 'prabbles' alone at IV. i. 42).

54.] Most editors give this line, as well as l. 56, to Shallow; but while 56 would sound rather odd from Slender, who has already said that he knows Anne, l. 54 is not inappropriate to him, and the misattribution of 56 is more easily explained if the scribe or compositor were carelessly repeating the speech prefix of 54.

55. *a petter penny*] The phrase would seem to have been proverbial, as used after specified amounts to mean 'and much more as well' (Tilley P189).

Evans. Seven hundred pounds, and possibilities, is goot gifts.

Shal. Well, let us see honest Master Page. Is Falstaff there?

Evans. Shall I tell you a lie? I do despise a liar as I do despise one that is false, or as I despise one that is not true. The knight Sir John is there; and I beseech you be ruled by your well-willers. I will peat the door for Master Page. [*Knocks.*] What hoa? Got pless your house here!

Page. [*Within*] Who's there?

[*Enter* PAGE.]

Evans. Here is Got's plessing and your friend, and Justice Shallow, and here young Master Slender, that peradventures shall tell you another tale, if matters grow to your likings.

Page. I am glad to see your worships well. I thank you for my venison, Master Shallow.

Shal. Master Page, I am glad to see you: much good do it your good heart! I wished your venison better; it was ill killed. How doth good Mistress Page? And I thank you always with my heart, la, with my heart.

59, 65. Master] *F* (M[r]). 65. *Knocks*] *Rowe* (*before* 'for', *l. 64*); *not in F.* 67. *Within*] *Dyce; not in F; Above, at the window Collier*[2]. *Enter Page*] *As Rowe* (*after l. 66*); *not in F;* Scene II. *Enter Mr.* Page *Pope* (*Pope's scene divisions not listed hereafter*); *after l. 71 Collier*[2]. 69. here] *F1* (heere); here's *F2.* 72. worships] *F;* Worship's *Rowe.*

64. *well-willers*] those who wish you well. Hart was able to cite several other uses (in Holland's *Plinie*, Greene's *Mamillia*, and Howell's *Arbor of Amitie*) to refute the allegation that the word is another of Evans's errors.

70. *tell you another tale*] A folk-saying or 'proverb' (Tilley T49).

71. *likings*] Again, not Evans's error but a recognized form: cf. *Oth.*, III. i. 51.

72. *worships*] The F plural is justified by ll. 244 and 254, where Anne addresses Slender as 'your worship'.

74–5. *much . . . heart!*] A common polite greeting, used again e.g., in a slightly corrupted form, in *Tim.*, I. ii. 73.

76. *ill killed*] A technical phrase, of a deer killed in such a way as to make the meat less good (e.g. by draining too much blood too soon). Probably Shallow also means that Falstaff had done the killing (and been caught in the act).

77. *la*] Slender is fond of this intensive, which has been thought effeminate. Biron's use of it in *LLL.*, V. ii. 414 (where it is made to rhyme, perhaps badly, with 'flaw'), and Whit's in Jonson's *Bartholomew Fair*, IV. v. 30, do both seem to imply some criti-

Page. Sir, I thank you.
Shal. Sir, I thank you; by yea and no I do.
Page. I am glad to see you, good Master Slender.
Slen. How does your fallow greyhound, sir? I heard say he was outrun on Cotsall.
Page. It could not be judged, sir.
Slen. You'll not confess, you'll not confess.
Shal. That he will not. 'Tis your fault, 'tis your fault; 'tis a good dog.
Page. A cur, sir.
Shal. Sir, he's a good dog, and a fair dog: can there be more said? He is good and fair. Is Sir John Falstaff here?
Page. Sir, he is within; and I would I could do a good office between you.
Evans. It is spoke as a Christians ought to speak.
Shal. He hath wronged me, Master Page.
Page. Sir, he doth in some sort confess it.
Shal. If it be confessed, it is not redressed: is not that so, Master Page? He hath wronged me, indeed he hath; at a word, he hath, believe me. Robert Shallow, Esquire, saith he is wronged.

98. hath; at] *F* (hath, at). hath, believe me.] *As Dyce*[2]*;* hath: beleeue me, *F.*

cism of the speaker; cf. also *Tim.*, III. i. 22.

79. *by yea and no*] Such phrases as this and 'la' and 'much good do it your good heart' are used to emphasize Shallow's effusive desire to be pleasant. Perhaps this one also is comically inappropriate in his mouth; cf. Falstaff's use of it in his letter to Prince Hal in *2H4*, II. ii. 142. Quickly uses a similar phrase in *Wiv.*, I. iv. 88.

81. *fallow*] light brown.

82. *Cotsall*] the Cotswold hills (a local pronunciation). It seems unnecessary to see a reference to some regular Cotswold Games, such as those later established in James I's time.

85. *your fault*] the normal check caused when the dog loses the scent (*O.E.D.* 'fault' *sb.* 8; 'your' as in *Ant.*, II. vii. 46, 'What manner o' thing is your crocodile?'). This explanation, first given by *New Cambridge*, is more satisfactory than taking 'your fault' as 'your own misfortune' and comparing III. iii. 202.

88, 89. *good . . . and . . . fair*] Shallow is apparently again airing his knowledge of coursing terms. *New Cambridge* aptly cites, from Turberville's *Book of Hunting*, ch. 6, 'the tokens whereby a man may knowe a good and fayre Hounde'.

96. *If . . . redressed*] The allusion is to the proverb 'A fault confessed is half redressed' (D. C. Browning, *Everyman's Dictionary of Quotations and Proverbs*, 1951, No. 6453) rather than to 'Confession of a fault pardons it', as Tilley suggests (C590). Ray and Tilley also record 'Confession of a fault is half amends' (C589).

Page. Here comes Sir John.

Enter SIR JOHN FALSTAFF, BARDOLPH, NYM, *and* PISTOL.

Fal. Now, Master Shallow, you'll complain of me to the King?

Shal. Knight, you have beaten my men, killed my deer, and broke open my lodge.

Fal. But not kissed your keeper's daughter?

Shal. Tut, a pin; this shall be answered.

Fal. I will answer it straight: I have done all this. That is now answered.

Shal. The Council shall know this.

Fal. 'Twere better for you if it were known in counsel: you'll be laughed at.

Evans. *Pauca verba*; Sir John, good worts.

Fal. Good worts? Good cabbage! Slender, I broke your head: what matter have you against me?

Slen. Marry, sir, I have matter in my head against you, and against your cony-catching rascals, Bardolph, Nym, and Pistol.

100. S.D.] *As Q; not in F.* 102. King] *F;* Councell *Q.* 109. Council] *F* (Councell). 110. counsel] *F* (councell)*;* counsell *Q;* Council *Rowe.* 116–17. Bardolph, Nym, and Pistol.] *As F; Pistoll* and *Nym.* They carried mee to the Tauerne and made mee drunke, and afterward picked my pocket. *Q.*

102. *King*] Since elsewhere in the play there are attempts to place the action in the reign of Henry IV or Henry V, this certainly need not imply revision of the play after the death of Elizabeth. Cf. I. iv. 5 and note.

103. *my men*] Hart assumes from ll. 113–14 that Slender was one of them, but Shakespeare does not say so; it would be no more rash to infer that 113–14 are to be connected with the stealing of Slender's purse, since—unless words are imported from Q at l. 117—Falstaff shows a perhaps incriminating knowledge of that episode at l. 137.

105.] As earlier editors have suggested, this seems to be a quotation from some lost deer-stealing ballad.

106. *a pin*] a trifle, 'nothing to do with the question'.

110. *in counsel*] in secret, in confidence (*O.E.D. sb.* 5. c). Emendations such as Pope's 'if it were not known in council' are thus unnecessary.

112. Pauca verba] few words. Cf. Holofernes in *LLL.*, IV. ii. 172; Pistol's use of 'pauca' in the same sense in *H5*, II. i. 83; and Nym's 'pauca, pauca' in l. 122.

113. *Good . . . cabbage!*] 'Wort', common as the second element in words like 'colewort', also meant specifically a plant of the cabbage family: hence Falstaff's pun on Evans's mispronunciation of 'words'.

114. *matter*] cause of complaint (but Slender probably misunderstands).

116. *cony-catching*] Literally 'rabbit-catching', metaphorically 'cheating', as in Robert Greene's exposure of underworld techniques in his 'Cony-

Bard. You Banbury cheese!

Slen. Ay, it is no matter.

Pist. How now, Mephostophilus?

Slen. Ay, it is no matter.

Nym. Slice, I say; *pauca, pauca*; slice, that's my humour!

Slen. Where's Simple, my man? Can you tell, cousin?

Evans. Peace, I pray you. Now let us understand: there is three umpires in this matter, as I understand; that is, Master Page (fidelicet Master Page); and there is myself (fidelicet myself); and the three party is (lastly and finally) mine host of the Garter.

Page. We three to hear it and end it between them.

Evans. Fery goot; I will make a prief of it in my note-book, and we will afterwards 'ork upon the cause with as great discreetly as we can.

Fal. Pistol!

Pist. He hears with ears.

127. three] *F;* third *Pope.* 128. Garter] *Q3;* Gater *F.*

catching' pamphlets. Cf. the modern idiom 'to be the bunny'. Falstaff uses the phrase again at I. iii. 31; and cf. *Shr.*, v. i. 102.

117. *Pistol*] Most editors add here the sentence from Q given in the collations. It is not necessary—see ll. 137–66 and the note on l. 103—and may be only the spelling-out of the obvious often found in reported texts. Sisson, *N.R.*, p. 64, on similar grounds argued against inclusion of the Q line (he had originally adopted it in his 1954 text).

118. *Banbury cheese*] The town later more famous for its cakes was renowned then for another reason also: 'as thin as Banbury cheese' was proverbial (Tilley C268). (Tewkesbury provided the corresponding simile for thickness: Falstaff tells Doll in *2H4*, II. iv. 262, that Poins's wit is 'as thick as Tewksbury mustard'.)

120. *Mephostophilus*] Lucifer's fellow-devil, probably best known from Marlowe's *Dr Faustus* (which, although not published until 1604, was already most successful on the stage). As Leslie Hotson has shown, Pistol sees himself as 'a player King' (*Yale Review*, 38, 1948, 51–68); and in this play as in both parts of *H4*, his head is full of phrases, quotations, and misquotations from the popular drama of the day, not all of which have been traced. See also IV. v. 65.

122. *Slice*] Probably Nym is carrying on the 'cheese' metaphor and suggesting that Slender be sliced up.

humour] For the topical interest in the word, and Nym's characteristic abuse of it, see Introduction, p. lxiii. Here it means apparently either 'mood' or 'temperament'.

126, 127. *fidelicet*] Evans's mispronunciation, and misuse, of the Latin *videlicet*, 'namely'.

128. *Garter*] There was apparently a real Garter Inn at Windsor in the sixteenth century.

134.] Pistol may be alluding to the Bible (e.g. Psalms 44:1: 'We have heard with our ears') and so, as Noble points out (p. 181), the joke may be on the Parson, who does not recognize the source.

Evans. The tevil and his tam! What phrase is this, 'He hears with ear'? Why, it is affectations.

Fal. Pistol, did you pick Master Slender's purse?

Slen. Ay, by these gloves, did he, or I would I might never come in mine own great chamber again else, of seven groats in mill-sixpences, and two Edward shovel-boards that cost me two shilling and two-pence apiece of Yead Miller, by these gloves.

Fal. Is this true, Pistol?

Evans. No, it is false, if it is a pick-purse.

Pist. Ha, thou mountain foreigner! Sir John and master mine,
I combat challenge of this latten bilbo.
Word of denial in thy labras here!
Word of denial: froth and scum, thou liest!

Slen. [*Pointing at Nym*] By these gloves, then, 'twas he.

137. Master] *F* (M.). 145–8.] *Verse as Pope; prose F.* 149. S.D.] *As New Camb.; not in F.*

135. *The tevil and his tam!*] Proverbial for 'the devil and worse' (Tilley D225). Cf. IV. v. 101.

139. *great chamber*] Apparently, main living room ('bedchamber' and 'reception room' have also been suggested).

140. *seven groats in mill-sixpences*] Probably the phrase is not meant to make perfect sense: 'groats' were small four-penny coins (Fluellen insults Pistol by offering him one 'to heal' his broken head in *H5*, v. i. 61–7); mill- (or milled-) sixpences were silver sixpences stamped in the 'mill' and in time came to have more than their nominal value.

140–1. *Edward shovel-boards*] shillings minted in the reign of Edward VI and afterwards used for the game of shovel-board—which is presumably why Slender was foolish enough to pay more than twice their face-value for them.

142. *Yead*] A familiar or jocular form of 'Ed' or 'Ned' (Falstaff once calls Poins 'Yedward' in *1H4*, I. ii. 149).

145. *mountain foreigner*] foreigner from the (wild) Welsh mountains.

145–6. Either with 'Sir John and master mine' or with the following words, Pistol apparently breaks into verse, perhaps quoting from plays again. It is almost impossible to decide whether some of his lines are meant as verse or prose.

146. *combat challenge*] A 'poetic' reversal of verb and object: challenge combat, demand the ancient right of trial by combat (Pistol is showing off his knowledge of the technical language of chivalry).

latten bilbo] (person who has only a) brass sword. 'Latten' may not even have been 'brass'; it came to mean tin-plate. Bilbao became known in England as 'Bilboa' and gave its name not only to its own good swords but also to swords generally, as did Toledo.

147. *labras*] Pistol apparently thinks the Latin *labra* ('lips') is a singular and makes the same error as those who speak nowadays of 'stratas'. The confusion may also arise from false analogy with the Spanish *palabras* ('words'), frequent in Elizabethan drama.

Nym. Be avised, sir, and pass good humours: I will say 'marry trap with you', if you run the nuthook's humour on me; that is the very note of it.

Slen. By this hat, then he in the red face had it; for though I cannot remember what I did when you made me drunk, yet I am not altogether an ass.

Fal. What say you, Scarlet and John?

Bard. Why, sir, for my part, I say the gentleman had drunk himself out of his five sentences.

Evans. It is his 'five senses'. Fie, what the ignorance is!

Bard. And being fap, sir, was, as they say, cashiered; and so conclusions passed the careers.

151. 'marry trap with you'] *This ed.;* marry trap with you *F; marry trap* with you *Johnson.* 160. fap] *F;* sap *Parsons.* 160–1. cashiered; and so] *As F;* cashiered. *Nym.* And so *Kittredge.* 161. careers] *F* (Car-eires).

150. *Be avised*] Either 'think carefully' (cf. *O.E.D.* 'advise' *v.* 5 and French *s'aviser*; and *Tw.N.*, IV. ii. 102, Feste to the incarcerated Malvolio, 'Advise you what you say') or 'take my advice', 'be counselled' (*O.E.D.* 'advised' *ppl. a.* 6, citing *1H4*, IV. iii. 5).

pass good humours] Here (and in l. 152) 'humour' becomes almost meaningless, as Shakespeare ridicules the over-use of it: presumably, 'put a good face on it'. Cf. l. 161 and note.

151. *marry trap with you*] Not satisfactorily explained. 'Marry' (a corruption of 'By Mary') is a common asseveration, and often harmless. Johnson, suspecting a once-familiar saying, explained the full phrase as an 'exclamation of insult', 'when a man was caught in his own stratagem'. Alternatively a later proverb listed by Tilley (T469) may be relevant: 'to understand trap', deriving from the slang use of 'trap' for 'fraud' or 'sharp practice', meant 'to know one's own interest'; hence, Nym may be saying 'mind your own business'. If 'trap' were also used as slang for a thief-taker earlier than *O.E.D.* records, the transition to 'nuthook' in l. 151 would be even easier.

151–2. *nuthook's humour*] 'Nuthook', originally a hooked stick for pulling down nuts, became a nickname for a beadle or constable. Thus, 'the game of trying to capture thieves'.

152. *note*] Kökeritz sees a kind of jingling pun on 'nut' and 'note'.

156. *Scarlet and John*] Will Scarlet and Little John (Robin Hood's companions). Bardolph is apparently addressed by both names, the first being suggested by his red nose, of which so much fun is made in *2H4* and *H5*. The allusion may be specifically to the old ballad 'Robin Hood and the Jolly Pinder of Wakefield', one line of which Silence sings in *2H4*, v. iii. 107.

158. *sentences*] Bardolph's blunder for 'senses', as Evans points out—but it has meaning of a sort, since 'sentences' may be paraphrased as 'moral precepts'. (Indeed, Baldwin, I. 708, thinks that Bardolph *means* that.)

160. *fap*] Although *O.E.D.* listed no other instance of the word, meaning 'drunk', before the nineteenth century, Sisson, *N.R.*, p. 64, records that Hilda Hulme has since found it in seventeenth-century West Midlands churchwardens' accounts. Emendation (e.g. Parsons's 'sap', as in 'sap-money',

Slen. Ay, you spake in Latin then too; but 'tis no matter. I'll ne'er be drunk whilst I live again, but in honest, civil, godly company, for this trick: if I be drunk, I'll be drunk with those that have the fear of God, and not with drunken knaves.

Evans. So Got 'udge me, that is a virtuous mind.

Fal. You hear all these matters denied, gentlemen; you hear it.

Enter ANNE PAGE, [*with wine; then*] MISTRESS FORD *and* MISTRESS PAGE.

Page. Nay, daughter, carry the wine in; we'll drink within. [*Exit Anne Page.*]

Slen. O heaven, this is Mistress Anne Page.

Page. How now, Mistress Ford?

Fal. Mistress Ford, by my troth, you are very well met: by your leave, good mistress. *Kisses her.*

Page. Wife, bid these gentlemen welcome. Come, we have a hot venison pasty to dinner; come, gentlemen, I hope we shall drink down all unkindness.

Exeunt all except Slender.

169. S.D.] *As Capell; not in F; Enter Mistresse* Foord, *Mistresse* Page, *and her daughter* Anne *Q; Enter Mistress* Anne Page, *with Wine Rowe.* 171. S.D.] *Theobald; not in F or Q.* 172.] *Rowe adds* '*Enter Mistress* Ford *and Mistress* Page'. 175. S.D.] *Q; not in F.* 178. S.D.] *As New Camb.; not in F; Exit all, but* Slender *and mistresse* Anne. *Q; Ex.* Fal. Page, *&c. Manent* Shallow, Evans *and* Slender. *Rowe.*

money allowed to servants for liquor) is therefore unnecessary.

cashiered] As R. H. Case pointed out in an appendix to Hart's edition, this cannot mean 'robbed' unless Bardolph means 'robbed by others'—or unless Falstaff is guilty of deliberate misunderstanding in l. 168. The normal meaning (*O.E.D.*) was 'dismissed' or 'discarded', as in I. iii. 6. (It is some slight consolation that Bardolph's words make no sense to Slender.)

161. *passed the careers*] got out of hand. It is a technical term from horsemanship (strictly, a short gallop, perhaps with quick turns, at speed), and a good parallel is *H5*, II. i. 131–3, where Nym comments, of the King's alleged responsibility for Falstaff's death, 'The king is a good king; but it must be as it may; he passes some humours and careers', i.e. he sometimes does odd things or lets events run away with him.

172, 173. *Mistress*] 'Mistress' was applied to both married and unmarried women until at least the eighteenth century, as was the written 'Mrs'.

175 and S.D.] That the kiss was no more than a polite salutation is shown by, e.g., *H8*, I. iv. 94–6.

178. *drink . . . unkindness*] In accordance with the maxim 'Drink and be friends' (Tilley F732).

Slen. I had rather than forty shillings I had my book of Songs and Sonnets here.

[*Enter* SIMPLE.]

How now, Simple, where have you been? I must wait on myself, must I? You have not the book of Riddles about you, have you?

Sim. Book of Riddles? Why, did you not lend it to Alice Shortcake upon All-hallowmas last, a fortnight afore Michaelmas?

[*Enter* SHALLOW *and* EVANS.]

Shal. Come, coz; come, coz; we stay for you. A word with you, coz. Marry, this, coz: there is, as 'twere, a tender, a kind of tender, made afar off by Sir Hugh here. Do you understand me?

Slen. Ay, sir, you shall find me reasonable; if it be so, I shall do that that is reason.

Shal. Nay, but understand me.

Slen. So I do, sir.

Evans. Give ear to his motions. Master Slender, I will description the matter to you, if you be capacity of it.

Slen. Nay, I will do as my cousin Shallow says. I pray

180. S.D.] *Rowe; not in F.* 186. Michaelmas] *F; Martlemas Theobald.* S.D.] *As New Camb.; not in F.* 195. motions. Master Slender, I] *F* (motions; (M[r]. *Slender*) I)*;* Motions, Mr. *Slender:* I *Rowe.*

179–80. *book of Songs and Sonnets*] Probably the *Songs and Sonnets* of Henry Howard, Earl of Surrey, and others ('Tottel's *Miscellany*'), published in 1557 and at least eight times in the next thirty years. Slender needs some such volume, or his book of Riddles, either as reading matter because he cannot entertain himself even for a minute or as a source of quotations and small talk.

182–3. *book of Riddles*] Not necessarily any identifiable volume: there may have been two or three such collections available.

185–6. *All-hallowmas . . . Michaelmas*] Simple's knowledge is appropriately as slender as his master's: All-hallowmas (1 November) is not a fortnight before Michaelmas (29 September).

187. *stay*] wait.

189. *afar off*] not directly, only as an intermediary.

195. *motions*] proposals; but for the probable pun, not intended by Evans, cf. III. i. 95.

198. *Nay . . . says*] Perhaps Slender does not understand at all but thinks Evans is trying to make peace between him and Falstaff's retainers (*New Cambridge*).

you pardon me; he's a Justice of Peace in his country, simple though I stand here.

Evans. But that is not the question: the question is concerning your marriage.

Shal. Ay, there's the point, sir.

Evans. Marry, is it; the very point of it—to Mistress Anne Page.

Slen. Why, if it be so, I will marry her upon any reasonable demands.

Evans. But can you affection the 'oman? Let us command to know that of your mouth or of your lips; for divers philosophers hold that the lips is parcel of the mouth. Therefore, precisely, can you carry your good will to the maid?

Shal. Cousin Abraham Slender, can you love her?

Slen. I hope, sir, I will do as it shall become one that would do reason.

Evans. Nay, Got's lords, and His ladies! You must speak possitable, if you can carry her your desires towards her.

Shal. That you must. Will you, upon good dowry, marry her?

Slen. I will do a greater thing than that, upon your request, cousin, in any reason.

Shal. Nay, conceive me, conceive me, sweet coz: what I do is to pleasure you, coz. Can you love the maid?

Slen. I will marry her, sir, at your request; but if there be no great love in the beginning, yet heaven may decrease it upon better acquaintance, when we are married and have more occasion to know one

211. mouth] *F;* mind *Pope.* carry] *F1;* marry *F2.* 219–20.] *Prose as Pope;* That you must: / Will . . . *F.*

200. *simple . . . here*] A common mild asseveration: 'as sure as I stand here'.

216. *Got's . . . ladies*] It is true that F has 'got's' but it does not follow, *pace* Hart, that Jupiter is meant. The Q gives some reason for believing that other oaths in the original text of the play were also not mild. See Introduction, p. xxxv.

217. *possitable*] A blunder for 'positively'.

carry her] Apparently, 'convince her of'. Cf. ll. 211–12; cf. also III. ii. 63 and note.

223. *conceive me*] understand me (*O.E.D.* 'conceive' II. 9).

225–9.] This is Slender's version of the popular saying, 'Marry first and love will come after' (Tilley L534).

another. I hope upon familiarity will grow more content: but if you say 'Marry her', I will marry her; that I am freely dissolved, and dissolutely.

Evans. It is a fery discretion answer; save the fall is in the 'ord 'dissolutely': the 'ort is, according to our meaning, 'resolutely'. His meaning is good.

Shal. Ay, I think my cousin meant well.

Slen. Ay, or else I would I might be hanged, la!

Shal. Here comes fair Mistress Anne.

[*Enter* ANNE PAGE.]

Would I were young for your sake, Mistress Anne!

Anne. The dinner is on the table; my father desires your worships' company.

Shal. I will wait on him, fair Mistress Anne.

Evans. Od's plessed will, I will not be absence at the grace. [*Exeunt Shallow and Evans.*]

Anne. Will't please your worship to come in, sir?

Slen. No, I thank you, forsooth, heartily; I am very well.

Anne. The dinner attends you, sir.

Slen. I am not a-hungry, I thank you, forsooth. [*To Simple*] Go, sirrah, for all you are my man, go wait upon my cousin Shallow. [*Exit Simple.*] A Justice of

230. content] *F;* contempt *Theobald.* 232. fall] *F;* faul' *Hanmer;* fault *Collier.* 233. 'ord] *F;* 'Ort *Rowe*[3]. 237. S.D.] *Rowe* (*after l. 236*)*; not in F.* 240. worships'] *Capell;* worships *F1;* Worship's *F4.* 243. S.D.] *As Rowe; not in F.* 247–8. *To Simple*] *New Camb.* (*as Steevens*[2]) *; not in F.* 249. S.D.] *Theobald; not in F.*

230. *content*] An editor is not entitled, with Theobald, to write jokes for Shakespeare, by supplying the proverb (Tilley F47) '(too much) familiarity breeds contempt'. It is, of course, quite possible that Shakespeare meant Slender to try to quote another proverb and get it wrong, as he certainly gets 'resolved' and 'resolutely' wrong in the following lines. He thereby catches for the minute Evans's disease, and Quickly's—for the sake of the laugh.

232. *fall*] mistake. *O.E.D.* does not seem to list this sense, but cf. modern 'slip'. Other editors suppose an elision ('faul''), a mispronunciation, or a compositor's misreading of 'falt'.

238.] Shallow's greeting, of course, is a cliché (Tilley S68).

245.] Slender's answer does make sense: there was a proverb 'Fresh air is ill for the diseased or wounded man' (Tilley A93) and he is thus denying the (unintended) implication that he ought to 'come in' because he is not well.

Peace sometime may be beholding to his friend for a man. I keep but three men and a boy yet, till my mother be dead: but what though, yet I live like a poor gentleman born.

Anne. I may not go in without your worship: they will not sit till you come.

Slen. I' faith, I'll eat nothing; I thank you as much as though I did.

Anne. I pray you, sir, walk in.

Slen. I had rather walk here, I thank you. I bruised my shin th' other day with playing at sword and dagger with a master of fence—three veneys for a dish of stewed prunes—and, by my troth, I cannot abide the smell of hot meat since. Why do your dogs bark so? Be there bears i' th' town?

Anne. I think there are, sir; I heard them talked of.

Slen. I love the sport well, but I shall as soon quarrel at it as any man in England. You are afraid if you see the bear loose, are you not?

Anne. Ay, indeed, sir.

252. though,] *F;* though? *Capell.* 264.] *Collier*[2] *adds 'Dogs bark'.*

252. *what though*] no matter; what if I do (frequent in Shakespeare).

260. *sword and dagger*] Hart, citing *Two Angry Women of Abingdon* and Harington's *Metamorphosis of Ajax*, shows that this method of fighting, or duelling, would seem to have been common among retainers rather than among gentlemen, so that once again Slender is giving himself away.

261. *master of fence*] proved and recognized master or 'professor' of fencing.

three veneys] i.e. the best of three bouts (French *venue*).

262. *stewed prunes*] A most inappropriate wager or trophy, for a dish of stewed prunes in the window was the sign or badge of a brothel (they seem to have been served inside the house as an aphrodisiac) and so came to be a synonym for a prostitute—as did 'hot meat'. Cf. *1H4*, III. iii. 127–8, *2H4*, II. iv. 156–9; this is also the innuendo in *Meas.*, II. i. 91ff. Slender seems unaware of it.

262–3.] The connection between the hurt shin and hot meat may be only the smell of blood or rawness of flesh—sufficient for Slender's 'mind'. Q hardly improves matters with a feeble pun on 'hot': 'I cannot abide the smell of hot meate / Nere since I broke my shin. Ile tel you how it came / By my troth. A Fencer and I plaid three venies / For a dish of stewd prunes and I with my ward / Defending my head he hot [hit, or hurt] my shin. Yes faith.' *New Cambridge*, e.g., incorporates in its text the words 'and I . . . shin', after 'prunes'. Sisson, *N.R.*, p.65, argues that, in a speech by Slender on such an occasion, 'no intelligibility is necessary or even desirable'.

266. *the sport*] the popular sport of bear-baiting.

Slen. That's meat and drink to me, now. I have seen Sackerson loose twenty times, and have taken him by the chain; but, I warrant you, the women have so cried and shrieked at it that it passed: but women, indeed, cannot abide 'em; they are very ill-favoured rough things.

Enter PAGE.

Page. Come, gentle Master Slender, come: we stay for you.

Slen. I'll eat nothing, I thank you, sir.

Page. By cock and pie, you shall not choose, sir: come, come.

Slen. Nay, pray you lead the way.

Page. Come on, sir.

Slen. Mistress Anne, yourself shall go first.

Anne. Not I, sir; pray you keep on.

Slen. Truly, I will not go first; truly, la, I will not do you that wrong.

Anne. I pray you, sir.

Slen. I'll rather be unmannerly than troublesome. You do yourself wrong, indeed, la! *Exeunt.*

275. S.D.] *Q; not in F.*

270. *That's . . . me*] Proverbial (Tilley M842); cf. *AYL.*, v. i. 11–12, 'It is meat and drink to me to see a clown'. In ll. 271–2 Slender may similarly be trying to adapt the proverbial boast of strength, that one could 'bind bears' (B134).

271. *Sackerson*] One of the most famous of the bears used for bear-baiting in Shakespeare's day.

273. *passed*] surpassed, was truly remarkable. Cf. l. 19 and IV. ii. 113 and notes.

275. *ill-favoured*] ugly.

279. *By cock and pie*] A euphemistic oath: 'cock' (*O.E.D. sb.*[8]) is a perversion of 'God' (via 'gock'); 'pie' (*O.E.D. sb.*[3]) 'a collection of rules, adopted in the pre-Reformation Church, to show how to deal . . . with the concurrence of more than one office on the same day'. Shallow uses the same oath in *2H4*, v. i. 1.

288.] Again Slender is only quoting a proverb (Tilley U15).

SCENE II

Enter EVANS *and* SIMPLE.

Evans. Go your ways, and ask of Doctor Caius' house which is the way; and there dwells one Mistress Quickly, which is in the manner of his nurse; or his dry nurse; or his cook; or his laundry; his washer, and his wringer.

Sim. Well, sir.

Evans. Nay, it is petter yet. Give her this letter; for it is a 'oman that altogether's acquaintance with Mistress Anne Page; and the letter is to desire and require her to solicit your master's desires, to Mistress Anne Page. I pray you be gone. I will make an end of my dinner; there's pippins and cheese to come. *Exeunt.*

SCENE III

Enter FALSTAFF, HOST, BARDOLPH, NYM, PISTOL, *and* ROBIN.

Fal. Mine host of the Garter!

Host. What says my bully rook? Speak scholarly and wisely.

Scene II

SCENE II] *F; Scene II. The lobby in* Page's *house Halliwell.* S.D.] *F; Enter sir* Hugh *and* Simple, *from dinner. Q.* 5. wringer] *Theobald;* Ringer *F.* 8. altogether's] *Steevens*[2], *conj. Tyrwhitt;* altogeathers *F.* 10. desires,] *F1;* desires *F3.* 12. cheese] *F;* seese *Dyce.*

Scene III

SCENE III] *F;* Scene VII. *Changes to the Garter-Inn. Pope; Scene III. A Room in the garter Inn. Capell.* S.D. *Robin*] *Rowe; Page F.* 2. rook] *As F; Rock Rowe*[1-2] *(throughout play)*; Rooke *Rowe*[3].

Scene II

3–4. *nurse . . . dry nurse*] Not Evans's error but apparently means housekeeper, for Caius also applies the word to Quickly at III. ii. 58.

4. *laundry*] i.e. laundress.

12. *pippins*] apples, as dessert.

cheese] The Welsh were traditionally very fond of cheese. Falstaff, in v. v. 82–3, fears that the 'Welsh fairy' will turn him into cheese and eat him. Cf. also II. ii. 292.

Scene III

2. *bully rook*] For 'bully' as a half-affectionate form of address (*O.E.D. sb.*[1] 1) cf. *MND.*, IV. ii. 19, 'O sweet bully Bottom!' (spoken by Flute) and

Fal. Truly, mine host, I must turn away some of my followers.

Host. Discard, bully Hercules, cashier: let them wag; trot, trot.

Fal. I sit at ten pounds a week.

Host. Thou'rt an emperor, Caesar, Keiser, and Pheazar. I will entertain Bardolph; he shall draw, he shall tap. Said I well, bully Hector?

Fal. Do so, good mine host.

Host. I have spoke; let him follow. [*To Bard.*] Let me see thee froth and lime. I am at a word; follow. *Exit.*

Fal. Bardolph, follow him. A tapster is a good trade; an old cloak makes a new jerkin; a withered serving-man a fresh tapster. Go; adieu.

9. Keiser] *F1; Kesar Q;* Keisar *F2.* Pheazar] *F; Phesser Q;* Pheezar *Steevens*[2]. 13. *To Bard.*] *Camb.; not in F.* 14. lime] *Q* (lyme)*;* liue *F1;* live *F2.* S.D.] *Q; not in F.*

Tp., v. i. 258, 'Coragio, bully-monster, coragio!' (Stephano to Caliban). Its use is a distinguishing mannerism of the Host, who repeats it in ll. 6 and 11. 'Rook', on the other hand, is better known as a term of disparagement but may be used by the Host with jocular irony (as is, probably, 'bully Hector' in l. 11. Others have seen a reference to the rook or castle in chess; and *New Cambridge* even suggested that it goes back to Falstaff's original name in the Henry IV plays, Oldcastle.

scholarly] Such references to Falstaff's learning are further evidence to *New Cambridge* of a source or earlier play in which the hero was a scholar; but they too may all be ironical or simply part of Ford's flattery, for example (cf. II. ii. 174).

6. *cashier*] See I. i. 160 and note.

wag] move, depart (*O.E.D. v.* 7).

8. *sit*] dwell here, have my lodging (*O.E.D. v.* 8).

9. *Keiser*] emperor (the regular, ME, form, until the language adopted the German 'Kaiser'; it is derived from 'Caesar'). Cf. *George-a-Greene the Pinner of Wakefield* (attributed to Robert Greene), v. i. (ed. Dickinson), where a shoemaker proclaims 'King or Kaisar, none shall pass this way, / Except King Edward'.

Pheazar] Q 'Phesser' is no help and may suggest that the reporter also did not know what it meant. Malone and Dyce explained it as 'one who pheezes', i.e. beats or frightens; most editors now accept Hart's conjecture that the Host means 'vizier' (Turkish viceroy). There may even be a quibble involving both.

10. *entertain*] employ, hire (*O.E.D. v.* II. 5. b). Cf. l. 51 and note.

10, 11. *draw, tap*] draw liquor (from the cask), serve as a tapster.

14. *froth and lime*] 'Froth' clearly means 'make the beer go further by serving it with plenty of froth on it'; and 'lime' (if the Q reading is correct) refers to a method of adulterating wine, by adding lime to remove any taste of sourness (cf. *1H4*, II. iv. 136–9). F 'liue' ('live'), however, also makes good sense: earn your living, by cheating the customers with the froth.

at a word] not inclined to waste words. Cf. I. i. 98 and *2H4*, III. ii. 319, 'I have spoke at a word'.

15–16. *an old . . . jerkin*] One of many

Bard. It is a life that I have desired: I will thrive.

Pist. O base Hungarian wight, wilt thou the spigot wield? *Exit Bardolph.*

Nym. He was gotten in drink: is not the humour conceited?

Fal. I am glad I am so acquit of this tinder-box: his thefts were too open; his filching was like an unskilful singer, he kept not time.

Nym. The good humour is to steal at a minute's rest.

Pist. 'Convey', the wise it call. 'Steal'! Foh, a fico for the phrase!

Fal. Well, sirs, I am almost out at heels.

Pist. Why, then, let kibes ensue.

19. Hungarian] *F;* gongarian *Q.* 20. S.D.] *As Q (before l. 19); not in F.* 26. minute's] *F, Q;* minim's *Collier*[2], *conj. Bennet Langton.*

forms of an old proverb (Tilley B607). A jerkin was a close-fitting short coat or jacket.

16–17. *a withered . . . tapster*] Falstaff completes his sentence by deliberately varying, or misquoting, another proverb, 'an old servingman a young beggar' (Tilley S255).

19–20.] 'Hungarian' seems to have been a term of general abuse. Tilley quotes a proverb (from the seventeenth century) 'He is hidebound, he is an Hungarian' (H810) and cites from Ray's *Collection of English Proverbs*, 1670, 'To be hide-bound, an Hungarian, a Curmudgeon'. Hart also gives good evidence for associating the word with the needy discarded soldiers returned from wars in Hungary; and there is sure to be a pun on 'hungry', as recorded elsewhere at this time in *O.E.D.*, with the implication that hunger often leads to theft. Steevens said he remembered a line in an old play, 'O base *Gongarian*, wilt thou the distaff wield?' but it has never been traced (Q reads 'O bace gongarian wight, wilt thou the spicket willd?'). The words may be one original verse line, or, as elsewhere, Pistol may be combining phrases from different sources.

21. *gotten in drink*] begotten while his parents were drunk—and therefore not a real man. Falstaff spells out this belief in *2H4*, IV. iii. 98–101. Some editors insert the line which replaces this in Q—'His minde is not heroick. And theres the humour of it'—which once again only labours the obvious.

21–2. *is . . . conceited?*] i.e. (presumably) is that not an ingenious application of the facts, or interpretation?

23. *tinder-box*] Bardolph—because of his red nose, but also, as the remainder of the speech makes clear, because he is inflammable, likely to cause trouble.

26. *minute's*] Since the phrase was, and is, common to indicate the shortest possible time, emendation to 'minim's', with *Rom.*, II. iv. 23, as the alleged parallel, is gratuitous, particularly as Q confirms the reading of F.

27. *fico*] fig (Spanish). Pistol uses it again ('figo') in *H5*, III. vi. 59, and indeed 'a fig for it' was a standard phrase (Tilley F210), often with an obscene gesture.

29. *out at heels*] with shoes worn through, and so poverty-stricken, penniless (Tilley H389).

30. *kibes*] *O.E.D.* explains 'kibe' as

Fal. There is no remedy: I must cony-catch; I must shift.

Pist. Young ravens must have food.

Fal. Which of you know Ford of this town?

Pist. I ken the wight: he is of substance good.

Fal. My honest lads, I will tell you what I am about.

Pist. Two yards, and more.

Fal. No quips now, Pistol. Indeed, I am in the waist two yards about, but I am now about no waste: I am about thrift. Briefly, I do mean to make love to Ford's wife. I spy entertainment in her: she discourses, she carves, she gives the leer of invitation; I can construe the action of her familiar style, and the

42. carves] *F;* craues *Q3.*

'a chapped or ulcerated chilblain, *esp.* one on the heel'; but Hart argues convincingly that most Elizabethans distinguished between chilblains and the sore heels, caused by inadequate covering, referred to here. (The three other uses of the word in Shakespeare do not decide the question.)

32. *shift*] Not necessarily 'cheat' but 'improvise', 'live on my wits': cf. *Ven.*, 690, 'Danger deviseth shifts; wit waits on fear', or *AYL.*, IV. i. 76–8, 'for lovers lacking—God warn us!—matter, the cleanliest shift is to kiss'.

33.] The line is at one and the same time a variation on a proverb—'small birds must have meat' (Tilley B397); a Biblical allusion—Job 38:41 and Psalms 147:9; and a reference to the reputation of the raven as an unprincipled bird of prey.

35. *ken the wight*] know the man (cf. l. 19). The words would probably have sounded archaic to the Elizabethan audience also; and again Pistol may be quoting from some old melodrama or poem.

41. *entertainment*] Not only, surely, willingness to listen but also pleasure, of various kinds. (Similarly, there must be a double meaning in 'familiar' in l. 43.)

42. *carves*] Most of the notes written on this word are misleading and cite imaginary or unhelpful parallels, such as *Err.*, II. ii. 119–20, and *LLL.*, V. ii. 323 (Biron's complaint, of Boyet, that ''A can carve too, and lisp; why, this is he / That kiss'd his hand away in courtesy'). It is debatable whether Vittoria's 'I did nothing to displease him [her husband], I carved to him at supper-time' (Webster's *White Devil*, I. ii. 123) means, as F. L. Lucas claims, that she made 'advances by signalling with the fingers—a sort of digitary ogle'; and there is doubtful support in the passage cited from Overbury's Character of 'A very very Woman' (*A Wife*, 1614): 'Her lightnesse gets her to swim at top of the Table, where her wry little finger, bewrayes *caruing*; her neighbours at the latter end, know they are welcome, and for that purpose shee quencheth her thirst' which Lucas takes to mean 'a sort of motion of the little finger backwards and forwards, not unlike carving, as the wineglass was raised to the lips'. That there is some kind of association between carving at table and making guests feel, properly or improperly, at home —and that it goes beyond the allotting of the choicest cuts—does seem certain. Cf. also *The Two Noble Kinsmen*, IV. iii. 90.

hardest voice of her behaviour, to be Englished rightly, is, 'I am Sir John Falstaff's'.

Pist. He hath studied her will, and translated her will— out of honesty into English.

Nym. The anchor is deep: will that humour pass?

Fal. Now, the report goes she has all the rule of her husband's purse; he hath a legion of angels.

Pist. As many devils entertain; and to her, boy, say I.

46. studied her will, and translated her will] *F;* studied her well, *Q;* study'd her well, and translated her well *Pope;* studied her will, and translated her well *Collier*[2]*;* studied her well and translated her will *Grant White;* studied her well and translated her ill *conj. Camb.* 48. anchor] *F;* authour *conj. Johnson;* angle *conj. Kinnear.* 50. he] *F;* She *Q.* a legion] *Rowe*[3]*;* a legend *F;* legians *Q.* 51. entertain] *F;* attend her *Q.*

44. *voice*] Baldwin (I. 569) sees a pun on the 'voices' (active and passive) of the verb 'to love' and also suggests 'a glancing pun' on 'action'–'active' in the previous line.

46. *will*] Emendation seems unnecessary although Whiter (p. 83) and Farmer noted that 'well'–'deep' (as in l. 48) was a Shakespearian image-link. Pistol surely means 'will', her intention or desire, possibly with a quibble on 'will' meaning 'carnal desire' and certainly with a pun on the legal will that has to be 'translated' into ordinary English to be understood.

47. *honesty*] chastity (a normal Elizabethan meaning).

48. *The anchor is deep*] Explanations of this crux are unconvincing, from Hart's suggestion of a pun on 'anchor', in the sense of 'anchoret' or 'hermit', to Kökeritz's argument (*R.E.S.*, 23, 1947) that the word meant is 'anker', a wine keg—a meaning that adds little (and the word is not found elsewhere before 1673). The natural interpretation is that just as a deep anchor normally holds firmly, so Falstaff's ideas are firm. There would be further point in Nym's phrase if it refers to the proverb (Tilley A240) 'An anchor that is ever in the water never learns to swim'—i.e. Falstaff may have had a long association with women but has learnt little about them (which would be a good follow-up to Pistol's comment).

50. *legion*] F's 'legend' may be right, if there was in fact confusion between the two words as *O.E.D.* implies (citing also 'a Legend of his Divels' from Mrs Behn's *Roundheads*, 1682). 'Legend' could mean e.g. a list (*O.E.D. sb.* 4), and a collection of saints' lives. 'Legion', however, seems preferable; not only was it commonly used in the sense of 'great number' (*O.E.D.* 3), derived from Mark 5:9, but also Falstaff is probably quoting Matthew 26:53 ('Thinkest thou that I cannot now pray to my Father, and he shall presently give me more than twelve legions of angels?'). Hence the pun on 'angels', gold coins stamped with the device of the archangel Michael and worth about ten shillings. The pun is repeated by Quickly, almost in reverse, at II. ii. 68–9; cf. also *Ado*, II. iii. 35.

51. *As many devils entertain*] Hart explains 'many bad people have many, or have the use of many, angels (i.e. money)'—which does some violence to the syntax; Schmidt, more convincingly, glosses 'entertain' as 'to take or keep in service'—a common meaning of the word (cf. l. 10 of this scene) and relevant if (as Warburton sup-

Nym. The humour rises; it is good. Humour me the angels.

Fal. I have writ me here a letter to her; and here another to Page's wife, who even now gave me good eyes too, examined my parts with most judicious œillades: sometimes the beam of her view gilded my foot, sometimes my portly belly.

Pist. Then did the sun on dunghill shine.

Nym. I thank thee for that humour.

Fal. O, she did so course o'er my exteriors with such a greedy intention that the appetite of her eye did seem to scorch me up like a burning-glass! Here's another letter to her; she bears the purse too: she is a region in Guiana, all gold and bounty. I will be cheaters to them both, and they shall be exchequers to me: they shall be my East and West Indies, and I will trade to them both. Go bear thou this letter to Mistress Page; and thou this to Mistress Ford: we will thrive, lads, we will thrive.

Pist. Shall I Sir Pandarus of Troy become,

56. œillades] *Hanmer, conj. Pope;* illiads *F;* eyliads *Johnson.* 59. *Pist.*] *F; Pist* [*Aside*] *Theobald.* 66. cheaters] *F;* cheater *Theobald.*

posed) Pistol is advising Falstaff to have as many devils on his side as Ford (or Mrs Ford) has angels on his (or hers).

to her, boy] The whole phrase is probably a hunting cry; certainly 'to her' is a regular expression of encouragement. Cf. III. iv. 36.

52, 54. *me*] Good examples of the 'ethic dative', which seems to be unusually frequent in Falstaff's speech in all three plays.

56. *œillades*] a significant look, especially an amorous one (French *œil* + *ade*). Regan tells Oswald that Goneril 'gave strong œillades and most speaking looks / To noble Edmund' (*Lr.*, IV. v. 25–6). Dennis, in *The Comical Gallant*, rendered it as 'Eye-lids'!

57. *gilded*] Falstaff is carrying on the metaphor of Mrs Page's eyes being like the rays ('beam') of the sun.

59.] Pistol is alluding to the proverb 'The sun is never the worse for shining on a dunghill' (Tilley S982).

62. *intention*] Perhaps a pun (1) import or aim; (2) intentness or thoroughness (*O.E.D.* 7b, 8—and cf. 'intentively', *Oth.*, I. iii. 155).

65. *Guiana*] Like the East and West Indies of l. 67, Guiana was to be the source of untold wealth to those who could exploit it. Shakespeare may well be thinking of Ralegh's 1595 voyage to find Eldorado.

66. *cheaters*] Yet another pun: 'cheater' was a common shorter form of 'escheater', an official of the Exchequer who supervised the 'escheats' or forfeited estates that came to the king. The same pun is in *Tit.*, V. i. 111.

71–2.] The lines are printed as verse in F and may well be a quotation. The meaning is: 'If I, who wear a sword and ought therefore to be a soldier, descend to being a mere pro-

And by my side wear steel? Then Lucifer take all!
Nym. I will run no base humour. Here, take the humour-letter; I will keep the haviour of reputation.
Fal. [*To Robin*] Hold, sirrah, bear you these letters tightly;
Sail like my pinnace to these golden shores.
Rogues, hence, avaunt, vanish like hailstones; go;
Trudge; plod away i' th' hoof; seek shelter, pack!
Falstaff will learn the honour of the age;
French thrift, you rogues—myself and skirted page.

Exeunt Falstaff and Robin.

Pist. Let vultures gripe thy guts, for gourd and fullam holds,
And high and low beguiles the rich and poor;

75. *To Robin*] *Theobald* (*after l. 76*); *not in F.* tightly] *F;* rightly *Q3.* 76. these] *F;* the *Q.* 78. i' th'] *F1* (ith'); oth' *F2.* 79. honour] *F;* humor *Q.* 80. S.D.] *Q* (*Exit Falstaffe, and the Boy.*); *not in F.* 81–2.] *Verse as Pope; prose F.*

curer, like Pandarus of Troy (who acted as go-between for Troilus and Cressida), then the devil may as well take charge of everything'.

74. *haviour*] deportment (*O.E.D.* 'haviour' or 'havour' 2). Cf. *Cym.*, III. iv. 9.

75. *sirrah*] Not used ironically, meaning 'Sir', but correctly used to the page as one over whom Falstaff has authority.

tightly] skilfully, carefully. This meaning of the word is common (cf. *Ant.*, IV. iv. 15), and the reading is confirmed by Q.

76–80.] Falstaff's transition to verse here is unexpected but not inexplicable. Again half-seriously speaking of his plan as if it were the equivalent of a romantic voyage in search of Eldorado, he adopts for the minute the manner of Pistol.

76. *pinnace*] a small light vessel often used as a tender, scout, or message-ship—whence perhaps its common figurative meanings (*O.E.D.* 3) of 'mistress' or 'prostitute' or (as Hart shows) 'bawd'.

78.] Tilley records a slightly later 'proverb' (H587) 'to beat it on the hoof' (travel the hard way) and this colloquial use of 'hoof' is still not rare—nor is 'pack' in the sense of 'be off' (cf. the far commoner 'send someone packing'). F2's 'oth'' is tempting but not necessary.

79. *honour*] Editors who accept Q's 'humor' assume that F's 'honour' is a misreading.

80. *French thrift*] Perhaps being waited on by fewer servants was—or was thought to be—the French custom (this has been argued with dubious success); or perhaps 'French thrift' was the equivalent of the modern 'Scottish thrift'.

skirted] Cf. I. i. 27 and note.

81. *Let . . . guts*] Perhaps, as Halliwell suggested, Pistol is parodying (or unintentionally ruining) Marlowe's *Tamburlaine*, II. vii. 48–50 (ed. U. M. Ellis-Fermor).

gourd and fullam] Each is explained by *O.E.D.* as a kind of false, or loaded, dice. Similarly 'high and low' in l. 82 are dice loaded to throw high or low numbers.

holds] wins the day, prevails.

82.] Pistol is now ringing the changes on the second verse of Psalm 49 (or perhaps a metrical version of it). Compare II. i. 110. Muir (pp. 14–15)

Tester I'll have in pouch when thou shalt lack,
Base Phrygian Turk!
Nym. I have operations which be humours of revenge.
Pist. Wilt thou revenge?
Nym. By welkin and her star!
Pist. With wit or steel?
Nym. With both the humours, I: I will discuss the humour of this love to Ford.
Pist. And I to Page shall eke unfold
How Falstaff, varlet vile,
His dove will prove, his gold will hold,
And his soft couch defile.
Nym. My humour shall not cool: I will incense Ford to deal with poison; I will possess him with yellowness, for the revolt of mine is dangerous. That is my true humour.

85.] *As one line, Pope;* I . . . opperations, / Which . . . reuenge *F.* operations] *F;* operations in my head *Q.* 87. star] *F;* stars *Collier*[2]. 89. discuss] *F;* disclose *Q.* 90. Ford] *F; Page Q.* 91. Page] *F; Foord Q.* 97. the] *F;* this *Pope.* mine] *F;* Mien *Theobald;* men *conj. Johnson;* mine anger *conj. Camb.;* mind *conj. Jackson.*

thinks that ll. 91–4 may similarly have begun from the metrical version of Psalm 50.

83. *Tester*] a small coin, originally a shilling, but by Shakespeare's day equal to sixpence.

84. *Phrygian Turk*] There are many parallels for 'Turk' as a term of abuse (originally as 'infidel' or 'savage'). Perhaps 'Phrygian' is attached as an intensive because the Phrygians were particularly war-like (cf. 'Phrygian mode' in music); or perhaps Pistol thinks of it because Pandarus is still in his mind (cf. 'Lord Pandarus of Phrygia', *Tw.N.*, III. i. 58).

85. *operations*] (Presumably) plans for action.

86–9. *Wilt . . . humours, I:*] Again it is possible that these should be printed as two verse lines.

89. *both the humours*] i.e. *my* wit and Ford's steel (sword).

discuss] make known, disclose (*O.E.D. v.* 5). Cf. IV. v. 2; the word is also used thus four times in *H5*.

90, 95. *Ford*] In fact, in II. i, Nym goes to Page, and Pistol goes to Ford; some editors therefore alter 'Ford' to 'Page' in both l. 90 and l. 95 and alter 'Page' in l. 91 to 'Ford'. But apparently Shakespeare changed his mind, for, as *New Cambridge* noted, Nym's speech (ll. 95–8) is more appropriate when spoken, as in F, about Ford; and presumably Pistol replies to Falstaff in l. 71 (before Nym does) because he is addressed first, being the intended messenger to Page.

93. *prove*] put to the test. Cf. *1H6*, II. ii. 58.

96. *yellowness*] jealousy (probably so called because the liver was thought to be the seat of the passions, and yellowness is the symptom of the known disease of the liver, jaundice).

97. *the revolt of mine*] (Presumably) this rebellion of mine against Falstaff; but *New Cambridge*, accepting the emendation 'mind', well compares

Pist. Thou art the Mars of Malcontents. I second thee; troop on. *Exeunt.*

SCENE IV

Enter MISTRESS QUICKLY *and* SIMPLE.

Quick. What, John Rugby! [*Enter* RUGBY.] I pray thee go to the casement and see if you can see my master, Master Doctor Caius, coming. If he do, i' faith, and find anybody in the house, here will be an old abusing of God's patience and the King's English.

Rug. I'll go watch.

Quick. Go; and we'll have a posset for 't soon at night, in faith, at the latter end of a sea-coal fire. [*Exit Rugby.*] An honest, willing, kind fellow, as ever servant shall come in house withal; and, I warrant you, no tell-

Scene IV

SCENE IV] *F;* Scene IX. *Changes to Dr.* Caius'*s house. Pope; Scene IV. A Room in Doctor* Caius' *House. Capell.* S.D.] *Q; Enter Mistris Quickly, Simple, Iohn Rugby, Doctor, Caius, Fenton. F; Enter Mistress* Quickly, Simple *and* John Rugby. *Rowe.* 1. S.D.] *Wheatley; not in F.* 8. S.D.] *Rowe (after l. 6); not in F; Rugby goes to the window New Camb.*

Gent., III. ii. 58–9, 'You are already Love's firm votary / And cannot soon revolt and change your mind'.

99. *Mars of Malcontents*] Although 'Malcontents' were most in theatrical fashion at the time of Marston's *Malcontent* (1600 or, more probably, 1604), the word was known much earlier. *O.E.D.* first finds it as a noun in 1581; and Nashe uses it often and as early as 1589 (e.g. in *The Anatomy of Absurdity*, I. 22). Shakespeare elsewhere applies it to a malcontent in love; but here it may have rather the significance of 'rebel' or 'dissentient from accepted opinion' (of which there are other instances). Mars is mentioned, of course, as the God of war.

Scene IV

4. *old*] excessive, great (*O.E.D. a.* I. 6).

5. *King's English*] A standard phrase (even in the days of the second Elizabeth) and therefore not a 'proof' that the play was revised in the reign of James I. In any case, there is a half-hearted attempt elsewhere to put the action of the play in the reign of Henry IV or Henry V: Fenton 'kept company with the wild Prince and Poins' (III. ii. 66–7)—even if certain references in v. v are inconsistent with this (see v. v. 47 and note).

7. *posset*] a drink, often used as a restorative, normally made by curdling hot milk with wine or ale, and sometimes spiced. In many ways it was the equivalent of the modern egg-flip 'laced' with brandy.

8. *sea-coal*] better-class coal brought by sea, most often from Newcastle on Tyne.

10. *withal*] This is the normal use of

tale nor no breed-bate. His worst fault is that he is given to prayer; he is something peevish that way; but nobody but has his fault; but let that pass. Peter Simple, you say your name is?

Sim. Ay, for fault of a better.

Quick. And Master Slender's your master?

Sim. Ay, forsooth.

Quick. Does he not wear a great round beard, like a glover's paring-knife?

Sim. No, forsooth: he hath but a little wee face, with a little yellow beard—a Cain-coloured beard.

Quick. A softly-sprighted man, is he not?

Sim. Ay, forsooth, but he is as tall a man of his hands as any is between this and his head: he hath fought with a warrener.

20. wee] *F* (wee-); whey- *Capell.* 21. Cain-coloured] *F* (Caine colourd); kane colored *Q;* Cane-colour'd *Rowe*[3].

the word as a substitute for 'with' 'esp. at the end of a relative clause or its equivalent' (*O.E.D.*); cf. II. i. 83.

11. *breed-bate*] maker of discord, mischief-maker. Poins is similarly allowed by Falstaff in *2H4*, II. iv. 273–4, to be one who 'breeds no bate with telling of discreet stories'.

12. *peevish*] silly, as in *1H6*, v. iii. 185, rather than 'obstinate', as often elsewhere.

13. *nobody . . . fault*] A popular saying (Tilley M116)—as is Simple's reply to her query (F106).

19. *glover's paring-knife*] The simile is rather startling, but Shakespeare should have known what such a knife looked like, for his father was a glover (one who worked in leather, not only to make gloves).

20. *wee*] Many editors print 'whey', under the influence of Q's version of Quickly's previous speech: 'I take it hee is somewhat a weakly man: / And he has as it were a whay coloured beard', and Kökeritz assumes that 'wee' is a dialectal pronunciation of 'whey'. Q's 'whay', however, is as likely as not a confused remembrance of the 'Cain-coloured beard' (which is also duly preserved in Q in Simple's reply). *Pace* Hart, *O.E.D.* has one example of 'wee' as an adjective meaning 'tiny' *c.* 1450; and Steevens cites two others from Elizabethan drama.

21. *Cain-coloured*] of the traditional colour of Cain's beard (red or reddish-yellow according to *O.E.D.*); similarly 'Judas-coloured' (red) is frequent (cf. *AYL.*, III. iv. 7–10).

22. *softly-sprighted*] 'soft' or meek in spirit.

23. *tall . . . hands*] 'Tall' meant valiant, but was often used ironically; 'of his hands', with his hands. For the complete phrase, cf. *Wint.*, v. ii. 177–8, 'I'll swear to the prince thou art a tall fellow of thy hands'.

24. *between . . . head*] Hart shows that the phrase was a cliché.

25. *warrener*] Simple, meaning to praise Slender, succeeds only in revealing that he was caught stealing rabbits. Keats preserved the full irony of the phrase when he wrote to Haydon on 8 April 1818 about Wordsworth, who had allegedly left town in a disgruntled mood: 'O that he had not fit

Quick. How say you?—O, I should remember him: does he not hold up his head, as it were, and strut in his gait?

Sim. Yes, indeed, does he.

Quick. Well, heaven send Anne Page no worse fortune! Tell Master Parson Evans I will do what I can for your master: Anne is a good girl, and I wish—

[*Enter* RUGBY.]

Rug. Out, alas, here comes my master.

Quick. We shall all be shent. Run in here, good young man; go into this closet; he will not stay long. (*Simple steps into the closet.*) What, John Rugby! John! What, John, I say! Go, John, go enquire for my master: I doubt he be not well, that he comes not home. [*Singing*] And down, down, adown-a, etc.

[*Enter* DOCTOR CAIUS.]

Caius. Vat is you sing? I do not like des toys. Pray you go and vetch me in my closet *une boitine verde*—a box, a

32. S.D.] *Rowe; not in F.* 33. *Rug.*] *F; Rugby* [*calls from the window*] *New Camb.* Out, alas,] *F* (Out alas:). 34. shent] *F*; shent. [*Exit Rugby*] *Wheatley.* 35–6. S.D.] *Q* (*He steps into the Counting-house*)*; not in F; Shuts Simple in the closet Rowe* (*before* 'he'). 39. *Singing*] *As Theobald; not in F.* *Enter Doctor Caius.*] *Rowe; not in F.* 40. des toys] *F* (des-toyes)*;* dese toys *Capell.* 41. *une boitine verde*] *Craig;* vnboyteene verd *F; un boitier verd Rowe;* un boitier vert *Camb.;* une boite en verde *Hart.*

with a Warrener that is din'd at Kingston's' (*Letters*, ed. Hyder E. Rollins, 1958, I. 265–6).

33. *Out, alas*] Cf. IV. v. 60. 'Out' is merely an intensifier in such phrases.

34. *shent*] Past participle of the verb 'shend', to reprove or scold; now only dialectal.

38. *doubt*] fear.

39. *And down . . .*] The refrain seems to have been used in more songs than one, but perhaps there was one favourite version and tune. Cf. *Ham.*, IV. v. 170–1.

40. *toys*] Either 'whims', 'caprices', or 'absurdities' (cf. *R3*, I. i. 60).

41. boitine verde] small green box. There are many difficulties in interpreting Caius' French as printed in F. Presumably Shakespeare would not have intended the Frenchman to speak unidiomatically, but Shakespeare himself may not have progressed beyond 'schoolboy French' (see l. 49 and note). Apparently too some of the F spelling is phonetic rather than 'standard'. An editor can but leave it much as it is, 'correcting' only what he assumes to be scribal or compositorial error (as clearly in l. 46). 'Boitine', if it is what Shakespeare intended, is perfectly intelligible but may have been his own

green-a box. Do intend vat I speak? A green-a box.

Quick. Ay, forsooth; I'll fetch it you. [*Aside*] I am glad he went not in himself: if he had found the young man, he would have been horn-mad.

Caius. Fe, fe, fe, fe, ma foi, il fait fort chaud. Je m'en vais voir à la court la grande affaire.

Quick. Is it this, sir?

Caius. Oui, mette le au mon pocket: dépêche, quickly. Vere is dat knave Rugby?

Quick. What, John Rugby! John!

Rug. Here, sir!

Caius. You are John Rugby, and you are Jack Rugby. Come, take-a your rapier, and come after my heel to the court.

43. Ay . . . I] *Prose as Capell;* I . . . you: / I . . . *F.* *Aside*] *Pope; not in F.* 46–7. *ma foi . . . affaire*] *This ed.; mai foy, il fait for ehando, Ie man voi a le Court la grand affaires F; ma foi, Il fait fort chaud, je m'en va a la Cour—la grande Affaire Rowe*[1]*; ma foi Il fait fort chaud, je m'en vais à la Cour—la grande Affaire Rowe*[3]. 49–50.] *Prose as Pope; Ouy . . . quickly:* / Vere . . . *F.* 49. *mette*] *F; mettez Theobald.* *dépêche*] *Rowe (Depêch); de-peech F; depêchez Theobald.* 51.] *Wheatley adds 'Re-enter Rugby'.*

invention (*boîte* + the diminutive *ine* regularly attached to nouns and adjectives).

42. *intend*] Caius must mean 'attend', unless, as Bowers suggests, he is anglicizing the French *entendre*, to hear.

45. *horn-mad*] beside himself with anger, like a horned beast in the breeding season, ready to attack anything. The phrase is proverbial (Tilley H628) Cf. III. v. 140–2 (where even more clearly the phrase takes on the other association, of a cuckolded husband mad with jealousy) and *Err.*, II. i. 57–9: '*Dromio.* Why, mistress, sure my master is horn-mad. / *Adriana.* Horn-mad, thou villain! *Dromio.* I mean not cuckold-mad; / But sure, he is stark mad.'

46. chaud] F1 prints Caius' French in italic, presumably because the words were written in the 'Italian' hand; and *ehando*, followed by Ff 2–4, is probably a misreading of *chaude* in that script (indeed the word in F1 can easily be misread as *chaudo*).

46–7. m'en vais voir . . . affaire] This reading, postulating a F omission because of the similarity in appearance of 'vais' and 'voir', seems more likely than Rowe's ellipsis, which has been generally adopted. F's 'Court' is supported by Eliot's *Ortho-Epia Gallica*, which has 'Venez à la Court' (though elsewhere 'cour'); and J. W. Lever (*Shakespeare Survey* 6, 1953, 79–90) has suggested that Eliot left his mark on Shakespeare's French in other places.

49. pocket] If Shakespeare intended Caius to lapse into English, as he does with 'quickly', then strictly the word should be printed in roman. (Both are italic in F.) Possibly, however, Shakespeare's own French failed, as it seems to have failed again in ll. 57–8.

53. *Jack*] See note on l. 102.

Rug. 'Tis ready, sir, here in the porch.

Caius. By my trot, I tarry too long. Od's me, *que ai je oublié*? Dere is some simples in my closet dat I vill not for the varld I shall leave behind.

Quick. Ay me, he'll find the young man there, and be mad!

Caius. *O diable, diable*! Vat is in my closet? Villainy, *larron*! [*Pulling Simple out*] Rugby, my rapier!

Quick. Good master, be content.

Caius. Wherefore shall I be content-a?

Quick. The young man is an honest man.

Caius. What shall de honest man do in my closet? Dere is no honest man dat shall come in my closet.

Quick. I beseech you, be not so phlegmatic. Hear the truth of it: he came of an errand to me from Parson Hugh.

Caius. Vell?

Sim. Ay, forsooth; to desire her to—

Quick. Peace, I pray you.

Caius. Peace-a your tongue. [*To Simple*] Speak-a your tale.

Sim. To desire this honest gentlewoman, your maid, to speak a good word to Mistress Anne Page for my master in the way of marriage.

Quick. This is all, indeed, la, but I'll ne'er put my finger in the fire, and need not.

57–8. *que . . . oublié*?] *F* (*que ay ie oublie*:); *Qu'ay je oublié? Warburton; Qu'ay 'oubliè? Johnson.* 62–3.] *Prose as Pope;* O . . . Clossett? / Villanie . . . *F.* 62. Villainy] *F;* Villaine *Q3.* 63. *larron*] *Rowe;* La-roone *F.* S.D.] *As Theobald; not in F.* 75. *To Simple*] *This ed., as Steevens; not in F.*

57. *Od's me*] Another elliptical oath, formed (probably) from 'God save me'.

58. *simples*] medicines made from single ingredients, especially herbs or plants—but the audience, of course, knows of another kind of Simple in the closet.

63. larron] French for thief (though *O.E.D.* cites one earlier example suggesting that French *larron* may already have been anglicized). By 'villainy' Caius possibly means 'villain'; cf. II. iii. 15.

69. *phlegmatic*] No doubt Quickly means the opposite, choleric, for predominant phlegm was supposed to make for coldness or dullness.

80–1. *I'll . . . need not*] Quickly is citing a proverb (Tilley F230) that may be paraphrased 'there's no sense in getting one's fingers burnt if one doesn't have to'. Her theory hardly corresponds with her practice.

Caius. Sir Hugh send-a you? Rugby, ballow me some paper. Tarry you a little-a while. *Writes.*

Quick. [*Aside to Simple*] I am glad he is so quiet: if he had been throughly moved, you should have heard him so loud and so melancholy. But notwithstanding, man, I'll do you your master what good I can; and the very yea and the no is, the French doctor, my master—I may call him my master, look you, for I keep his house; and I wash, wring, brew, bake, scour, dress meat and drink, make the beds, and do all myself—

Sim. [*Aside to Quickly*] 'Tis a great charge to come under one body's hand.

Quick. [*Aside to Simple*] Are you avised o' that? You shall find it a great charge; and to be up early and down late; but notwithstanding—to tell you in your ear; I would have no words of it—my master himself is in love with Mistress Anne Page; but notwithstanding that, I know Anne's mind—that's neither here nor there.

Caius. You jack'nape, give-a this letter to Sir Hugh; by

82. ballow] *F; baillez Theobald;* baille *Camb.* 83. S.D.] *Q* (*The Doctor writes*)*; not in F.* 84, 93, 95. S.D.] *Camb.; not in F.* 87. you] *F1* (yoe)*;* for *F2; omitted by Capell.* 90. wring] *Rowe*[3]*;* ring *F.* 100. that,] *Rowe;* that *F.*

82. *ballow*] The emendations 'baillez' and 'baille' are implausible: a scribe or compositor could hardly have misread thus in either script. 'Ballow' must be an anglicized form of French *bailler*, to bring (Eliot, C1^{v}, has 'Baille moy vne chemise blanche', translated as 'Giue me a cleane shirt'; cf. *O.E.D.* 'bail' *v.*[1]) or Caius' attempt to find an equivalent. (The only other occurrence of 'ballow' in Shakespeare and, probably, in Elizabethan literature is in F *Lr.*, IV. vi. 247, and would seem to be irrelevant: Edgar, speaking in dialect as a 'peasant', uses it as a noun to mean, apparently, cudgel.)

86. *melancholy*] Quickly doesn't mean 'melancholy'; and when she does mean it (in l. 147) the best she can do is 'allicholy'.

87. *you*] Another example of the construction described by Abbott (220) as 'representing the old dative'. It may even be paraphrased as 'since you ask me'.

93. *charge*] Sometimes explained as 'responsibility' (*O.E.D. sb.* II. 8[2]) but also, obviously, 'burden' in the sense of 'weight' (*sb.* I. 1). This and the following line form the first *double entendre* of a series; and the Q reporter, remembering the trend but not the detail, invented his own indecencies.

95. *avised*] aware, informed—though *O.E.D.* cites this line under 'advised' *ppl.a.* 1. 'having considered' (cf. I. i. 150 and note).

100–1. *that's . . . there*] Yet another ready-made phrase (Tilley H438).

102. *jack'nape*] The regular form is

gar, it is a shallenge. I will cut his troat in de Park, and I will teach a scurvy jack-a-nape priest to meddle or make. You may be gone; it is not good you tarry here. By gar, I will cut all his two stones; by gar, he shall not have a stone to throw at his dog. [*Exit Simple.*]

Quick. Alas, he speaks but for his friend.

Caius. It is no matter-a ver dat: do not you tell-a me dat I shall have Anne Page for myself? By gar, I vill kill de Jack-priest; and I have appointed mine host of de Jarteer to measure our weapon. By gar, I will myself have Anne Page.

Quick. Sir, the maid loves you, and all shall be well. We must give folks leave to prate: what the good year!

Caius. Rugby, come to the court with me.—[*To Quickly*] By gar, if I have not Anne Page, I shall turn your head out of my door.—Follow my heels, Rugby.

Quick. You shall have An—[*Exeunt Caius and Rugby*]—

108. S.D.] *Rowe; not in F.* 113. Jarteer] *F1;* Garter *F4; Jartere Rowe; Jarterre Theobald; Jarretière Collier.* 116. good year] *Capell;* good-ier *F;* goujeres *Hanmer;* goujere *Johnson.* 117–18. *To Quickly*] *As Wheatley; not in F.* 121. S.D.] *Chambers, as conj. Daniel; not in F; after l. 120 Rowe.*

'jackanapes', meaning 'monkey' and so 'fool', 'idiot'. (Cf. IV. iv. 67 and note.) *O.E.D.* suggests that the original term was Jack Napes, perhaps a playful name for a tame ape. 'Jack' was a general term of abuse, for a male, as in l. 53 and in 'Jack priest' in l. 112, with the further point that 'Sir John' was the traditional name for a priest in popular tales.

105. *meddle or make*] The proverb 'I will neither meddle nor make' (Tilley M852) is alluded to several times in Shakespeare.

107–8.] This, of course, is another proverb (Tilley S880); and the pun on 'stone'–'testicle' is obvious enough.

113.] *Jarteer*] Garter: Caius is possibly conflating the Fr. *jarretière.*

to measure our weapon] i.e. to act as my second. (The seconds in a duel measured the weapons to make sure that there was no unfair advantage.)

115.] Once again Quickly is relying on folk wisdom: 'All shall be well and Jack shall have Jill' (Tilley A164); and her next phrase is another cliché.

116. *what the good year*] Another more or less meaningless asseveration. (Quickly uses it again in *2H4*, II. iv. 64.) It was apparently equivalent to 'what the devil'.

121.] F makes the jest clear by italicizing 'An' and printing with a hyphen or dash ('*An*—fooles head') and spelling 'An' throughout the speech, exceptionally. Caius goes out believing that Quickly has said 'You shall have Anne'; then she adds the proverbial 'fool's head of your own' (Tilley F519).

fool's head of your own. No, I know Anne's mind for that; never a woman in Windsor knows more of Anne's mind than I do, nor can do more than I do with her, I thank heaven.

Fent. [*Within*] Who's within there, hoa?

Quick. Who's there, I trow? Come near the house, I pray you.

[*Enter* FENTON.]

Fent. How now, good woman, how dost thou?

Quick. The better that it pleases your good worship to ask.

Fent. What news? How does pretty Mistress Anne?

Quick. In truth, sir, and she is pretty, and honest, and gentle, and one that is your friend—I can tell you that by the way, I praise heaven for it.

Fent. Shall I do any good, think'st thou? Shall I not lose my suit?

Quick. Troth, sir, all is in His hands above; but notwithstanding, Master Fenton, I'll be sworn on a book she loves you. Have not your worship a wart above your eye?

Fent. Yes, marry, have I; what of that?

Quick. Well, thereby hangs a tale. Good faith, it is such another Nan; but, I detest, an honest maid as ever broke bread; we had an hour's talk of that wart— I shall never laugh but in that maid's company!—

126. *Within*] *Rowe; not in F.* 127. I trow] *F* (I troa); trow *conj. Hart.* 128. S.D.] *As Rowe; not in F.*

126–7. *hoa . . . trow*] Perhaps Quickly completes a rhyme here (F spells 'hoa', 'troa'). 'I trow' (rather than 'trow') is unusual in the sense of 'I wonder' rather than 'I believe', but it is used again in II. i. 61.

127. *near*] Hart gives good reason for believing that 'near' often meant 'in' or 'into', citing, e.g., III. iii. 138.

133. *honest*] virtuous.

140. *Have*] The verb takes the second person according to the general sense ('you') rather than strict syntax (the third person, 'your worship').

143. *thereby hangs a tale*] Another 'proverb' (Tilley T48) or cliché, still in popular use.

143–4. *such another Nan*] so remarkable a Nan. The comparable modern idiom would probably be 'such a Nan' or 'such a one' (cf. *Troil.*, I. ii. 282, where Pandarus says to Cressida 'You are such a woman!').

144. *detest*] Quickly means 'protest'.

144–5. *an honest . . . bread*] Yet another 'proverb' (Tilley M68).

but, indeed, she is given too much to allicholy and musing; but for you—well—go to.

Fent. Well, I shall see her to-day. Hold, there's money for thee: let me have thy voice in my behalf; if thou seest her before me, commend me.

Quick. Will I? I' faith, that we will; and I will tell your worship more of the wart the next time we have confidence; and of other wooers.

Fent. Well, farewell; I am in great haste now.

Quick. Farewell to your worship. [*Exit Fenton.*] Truly, an honest gentleman—but Anne loves him not; for I know Anne's mind as well as another does.—Out upon't, what have I forgot? *Exit.*

152. we] *F* (wee); I *Hanmer.* 156. S.D.] *Rowe* (*after l. 155*); *not in F.*

147. *allicholy*] i.e. melancholy.

148. *go to*] An expression of impatience (here feigned).

153–4. *have confidence*] confer *or* confide in each other.

ACT II

SCENE I

Enter MISTRESS PAGE, *with a letter.*

Mrs. Page. What, have I scaped love-letters in the holiday-time of my beauty, and am I now a subject for them? Let me see. [*Reads.*]

'Ask me no reason why I love you, for though Love use Reason for his precisian, he admits him not for his counsellor. You are not young, no more am I; go to, then, there's sympathy. You are merry, so am I; ha, ha, then, there's more sympathy. You love sack, and so do I; would you desire better sympathy? Let it suffice thee, Mistress Page—at the least, if the love of soldier can suffice—that I love thee. I will not say pity me—'tis not a soldier-like phrase—but I say, love me. By me,

Thine own true knight,

ACT II

Scene I

ACT II SCENE I] *F;* Act II. Scene 1. *Before* Page'*s house. Pope.* S.D.] *Rowe; Enter Mistris* Page, *Mistris* Ford, *Master* Page, *Master* Ford, Pistoll, Nim, Quickly, Host, Shallow. *F; Enter Mistresse* Page, *reading of a Letter. Q.* 1. I] *Q3; not in F.* 3. *Reads*] *Capell; not in F.* 5. precisian] *F;* physician *Collier*[2], *conj. Johnson.* 11. soldier] *F1;* a soldier *F3.* 13–19. By me . . . FALSTAFF.] *As Capell; By me . . . night: / Or . . . might, / For . . . Falstaffe. F; By . . . Knight, / By . . . night, / Or . . . light, / With . . . might, / For . . .* Falstaff. *Johnson.*

1–2. *holiday-time*] hey-day. 'Holiday' seems to have had the happiest associations for Shakespeare: cf. III. ii. 62 and note.

5. *precisian*] puritanical (or puritan) guide in religious or spiritual matters —as opposed to a sympathetic 'counsellor'. Proverb lore had it that 'Love is without reason' (Tilley L517).

6. *counsellor*] confidant, one who can be trusted not to take a merely formal view of a problem. Falstaff is thus telling Mrs Page not to be concerned that Reason might puritanically be against their liaison, and he proceeds to enumerate such arguments for that liaison as the more sympathetic confidant could give.

8. *sack*] wine from Spain or the Canaries, often but not always white; sometimes equated with sherry.

By day or night,
Or any kind of light,
With all his might
For thee to fight,
JOHN FALSTAFF.'

What a Herod of Jewry is this? O wicked, wicked world: one that is well-nigh worn to pieces with age to show himself a young gallant! What an unweighed behaviour hath this Flemish drunkard picked—with the devil's name—out of my conversation, that he dares in this manner assay me? Why, he hath not been thrice in my company! What should I say to him? I was then frugal of my mirth. Heaven forgive me! Why, I'll exhibit a bill in the parliament for the putting down of men. How shall I be revenged on

20–31.] *Prose as Pope;* What . . . world: / One . . . age / To . . . *F* (*thereafter as prose but beginning each line with a capital letter until* 'of men'); What . . . World! / One . . . Age, / To . . . unwayed / Behaviour . . . pickt, / *then prose. Rowe.* 22. an unweighed] *F1* (an vnwaied); unwayed *F3;* one unweigh'd *Capell.* 24. with] *F1;* I' th' *F3.* 27–8. mirth. Heaven forgive me!] *Kittredge;* mirth: (heauen forgiue mee:) *F;* mirth—heav'n forgive me—*Johnson.* 29. men] *F;* fat men *Theobald;* Mum *Hanmer.*

20–31.] The setting-out of these lines in F is quite likely to be the fault of the transcriber, Ralph Crane, who in *Demetrius and Enanthe* and *The Witch* sometimes writes prose out thus in separate lines. The compositor would think that verse was indicated and would start setting them accordingly, until he decided, after 'putting down' (l. 29), that the divisions into lines were meaningless. *New Cambridge*'s early theory that 'at this point the "copy" was written in short lengths, which suggests players' parts' is both implausible and unnecessary.

20. *Herod*] The allusion is probably to the miracle plays, in which Herod was traditionally loud-mouthed and thus absurd as well as evil.

Jewry] Judaea, 'the form . . . in the Liturgy and all the Bibles except the Genevan' (Noble, p. 271).

22. *unweighed*] Either 'unconsidered', 'unbalanced' (*O.E.D.* 'weigh' *v.*[1] II. 11) or 'light' (III). This is the only time Shakespeare uses the word, but cf. Lucio's description of the Duke in *Meas.*, III. ii. 147–8, as 'a very superficial, ignorant, unweighing fellow'.

23. *Flemish*] The inhabitants of the Low Countries—and, of course, the Danes—were alleged to be often drunk.

24. *with the devil's name*] Presumably, 'with the help of the devil' or (as F3 took it, printing 'i' th'') 'acting in the name of the devil'.

conversation] conduct, or, perhaps, 'social relationship with him' (Coriolanus, in North's Plutarch, was 'churlishe, uncivill, and unfit for any mans conversation'—Bullough, v. 506).

26–7. *What should I say to him?*] What did he expect me to say to him?

28. *exhibit*] submit, introduce (*O.E.D.* 'exhibit' *v.* II. 5. a).

29. *putting down*] suppression (but

him? For revenged I will be, as sure as his guts are made of puddings.

Enter Mistress Ford.

Mrs. Ford. Mistress Page! Trust me, I was going to your house.

Mrs. Page. And, trust me, I was coming to you. You look very ill.

Mrs. Ford. Nay, I'll ne'er believe that; I have to show to the contrary.

Mrs. Page. Faith, but you do, in my mind.

Mrs. Ford. Well, I do, then; yet, I say, I could show you to the contrary. O Mistress Page, give me some counsel!

Mrs. Page. What's the matter, woman?

Mrs. Ford. O woman, if it were not for one trifling respect, I could come to such honour!

Mrs. Page. Hang the trifle, woman, take the honour. What is it? Dispense with trifles—what is it?

Mrs. Ford. If I would but go to hell for an eternal moment or so, I could be knighted.

Mrs. Page. What? Thou liest! Sir Alice Ford? These knights will hack; and so thou shouldst not alter the article of thy gentry.

31. S.D.] *Q; not in F.* 50. will hack] *F;* will lack *Warburton;* we'll hack *conj. Johnson.*

there may be a *double entendre*—which would make Theobald's emendation even sillier).

30–1. *guts . . . puddings*] Close to tautology: 'pudding' is defined by *O.E.D.* (*sb.* i. 1) as 'the stomach or one of the entrails of a pig, sheep, or other animal, stuffed with . . . minced meat . . ., etc. . . .; a kind of sausage', and the plural 'puddings' normally meant 'guts'.

36. *have*] have something (i.e. the letter).

48. *moment*] Hart argued that 'moment' could mean any period of time—and thereby spoilt the joke.

50. *hack*] No clear explanation of the word has ever been given, although from iv. i. 57, in a scene where nearly every phrase spoken by Quickly involves a *double entendre*, it would seem to mean 'associate with loose women'. Cf. *O.E.D.* 'hack' *v.*[3] 1 *trans*, 'to put to indiscriminate or promiscuous use'; and *LLL.*, iii. i. 33, where 'hackney'—of which 'hack' is often used as an abbreviation—apparently means 'whore' (*O.E.D. sb.* 4). Mistress Page (who has just read a letter from Sir John) is thus saying that knights can be expected to behave promiscuously. The argument that there is some

Mrs. Ford. We burn daylight. Here, read, read; perceive how I might be knighted. I shall think the worse of fat men as long as I have an eye to make difference of men's liking; and yet he would not swear, praised women's modesty, and gave such orderly and well-behaved reproof to all uncomeliness that I would have sworn his disposition would have gone to the truth of his words; but they do no more adhere and keep place together than the hundred Psalms to the tune of 'Greensleeves'. What tempest, I trow, threw this whale, with so many tuns of oil in his belly, ashore at Windsor? How shall I be revenged on him? I think the best way were to entertain him with hope till the wicked fire of lust have melted him in his own grease. Did you ever hear the like?

Mrs. Page. Letter for letter, but that the name of Page and Ford differs! To thy great comfort in this

55. praised] *Theobald;* praise *F.* 60. place] *F;* pace *Rann, conj. Mason.* hundred Psalms] *F;* hundredth Psalm *Rowe.* 61. trow] *Rowe;* troa *F.*

reference to Essex's lavish conferring of knighthoods during the Cadiz voyage is far-fetched.

51. *article of thy gentry*] matter of your rank (*O.E.D.* 'article' *sb.* IV. 10. b, and 'gentry' 1).

52. *burn daylight*] Proverbial for 'waste time' (Tilley D123), as in *Rom.*, I. iv. 43.

55. *liking*] bodily condition (*O.E.D.* 6), as in *1H4*, III. iii. 6.

55–9. *and yet . . . words*] Hart and *New Cambridge* suspect the passage to be a 'fossil' from an old play, since the description hardly fits the normal Falstaff. It would not be the only time, however, that Falstaff has pretended to admire virtue.

57. *uncomeliness*] improper behaviour (cf. *O.E.D.* 'comeliness' 2).

58. *gone to*] gone along with, accorded with.

59. *adhere*] agree, go together (*O.E.D.* 4).

60. *hundred*] Rowe's emendation 'hundredth' has won general acceptance, and *New Cambridge* defends it on the ground that 'hundred' was a common sixteenth-century spelling of 'hundredth'. But the emendation partly spoils the joke, for—as Hart pointed out—the hundredth psalm is in fact one of praise, 'Make a joyful noise unto the Lord, all ye lands'. There is even less likelihood of all hundred (or so) psalms being sung or fitted to the lively tune of 'Greensleeves'.

61. *'Greensleeves'*] A popular love song, to the tune of which many words were later set. It is in 6/8 time. The music is given, with words written to it by Sir Philip Sidney, in Bruce Pattison's *Music and Poetry of the English Renaissance*, 1948, p. 175.

trow] wonder. Cf. I. iv. 127 and note.

62. *tuns*] casks (not necessarily of fixed capacity, 252 old wine-gallons).

65–6. *the wicked fire . . . grease*] An adaptation of a proverb ('frying or stewing in one's own grease', Tilley G433) that also lies behind the very different III. v. 105.

mystery of ill opinions, here's the twin-brother of thy letter; but let thine inherit first, for I protest mine never shall. I warrant he hath a thousand of these letters, writ with blank space for different names—sure, more—and these are of the second edition. He will print them, out of doubt; for he cares not what he puts into the press, when he would put us two: I had rather be a giantess, and lie under Mount Pelion. Well, I will find you twenty lascivious turtles ere one chaste man.

Mrs. Ford. Why, this is the very same: the very hand, the very words. What doth he think of us?

Mrs. Page. Nay, I know not: it makes me almost ready to wrangle with mine own honesty. I'll entertain myself like one that I am not acquainted withal; for, sure, unless he know some strain in me that I know not myself, he would never have boarded me in this fury.

Mrs. Ford. 'Boarding' call you it? I'll be sure to keep him above deck.

Mrs. Page. So will I: if he come under my hatches, I'll never to sea again. Let's be revenged on him: let's appoint him a meeting, give him a show of comfort in his suit, and lead him on with a fine-baited delay

84. strain] *F;* stain *Pope.*

69. *ill opinions*] i.e. the bad opinion of her that Falstaff seems to have formed for no apparent reason.

70. *inherit*] come into possession (of a legacy or gift—here Falstaff's offer of the 'knighthood'). Mrs Page is jocularly resigning any claim that her letter may be the older of 'twins' and thus entitled to the 'inheritance'.

77. *Pelion*] The giants Otus and Ephialtes, in an attempt to climb to heaven and defeat the gods, tried to pile Mt Ossa on Mt Olympus, and Mt Pelion on top of Ossa. Legend also said that the Titans were buried under these mountains. The fate of Falstaff's mistress would be comparable.

78. *turtles*] turtledoves, proverbial for their faithfulness.

82. *wrangle . . . honesty*] quarrel with, or act in a way contrary to, my own virtue. 'Honesty' is used again, in the same sense, in l. 96.

entertain] treat *or* think of.

84. *strain*] quality or tendency (a sense not unknown today).

85. *boarded*] accosted, approached. It is a nautical metaphor, from the original sense of coming alongside another ship (not necessarily to attack it). Mrs Ford and Mrs Page then carry on the metaphor in its other common, sexual, senses.

92. *fine-baited delay*] delay during which tempting bait will be dangled in front of him—an admirable description of the tactics they do adopt.

till he hath pawned his horses to mine host of the Garter.

Mrs. Ford. Nay, I will consent to act any villainy against him that may not sully the chariness of our honesty. O that my husband saw this letter; it would give eternal food to his jealousy.

Mrs. Page. Why, look where he comes; and my good man too. He's as far from jealousy as I am from giving him cause; and that, I hope, is an unmeasurable distance.

Mrs. Ford. You are the happier woman.

Mrs. Page. Let's consult together against this greasy knight. Come hither. [*They stand back.*]

Enter FORD, [*with*] PISTOL, *and* PAGE, [*with*] NYM.

Ford. Well, I hope it be not so.

Pist. Hope is a curtal dog in some affairs:
Sir John affects thy wife.

Ford. Why, sir, my wife is not young.

Pist. He woos both high and low, both rich and poor,
Both young and old, one with another, Ford;
He loves the gallimaufry: Ford, perpend.

99–100. good man] *F;* goodman *Bowers.* 105. *They stand back*] *Theobald* (*They retire*) ; *not in F.* *Enter . . . Nym*] *Rowe* (*as Q*) ; *not in F.* 110–12.] *Verse as Pope; prose F.* 112. the] *F1;* thy *F2.*

93–4. *pawned . . . Garter*] This first mention of horses, and of the Host's concern with them, presumably as post-horses, has received much comment because of loose ends later in the play (see Introduction, pp. xlvii ff.). In themselves, however, the words create no problem. Falstaff is known to be in need of money; the wives will lead him on till he has even less and has to pawn his horses to pay for his food and lodging. In the long run the horses are 'arrested' because of his debt to Ford–Brook (v. v. 115–16).

96. *chariness*] scrupulous integrity (*O.E.D.* 2; cf. 'chary' 4, 5), often applied as here to a woman's honour.

99–100. *good man*] So F; but the word 'goodman' (husband) may be intended, as in III. ii. 22.

107–8.] Again it is difficult to know whether Pistol's first words are a complete verse line from some lost play. He is bound to be quoting single phrases, at least.

107. *curtal*] with docked tail (and therefore less good for hunting, because of loss of balance).

108. *affects*] aims at or (less probably) loves.

110.] Another Biblical quotation (Psalms 49: 2).

112. *gallimaufry*] Strictly a cooking term, meaning hotchpotch; thus 'variety', 'mixture'. Cf. *Wint.*, IV. iv. 335–6.

perpend] consider (cf. 'perpend, my

Ford. Love my wife?
Pist. With liver burning hot. Prevent,
Or go thou, like Sir Actæon he,
With Ringwood at thy heels.
O, odious is the name!
Ford. What name, sir?
Pist. The horn, I say. Farewell.
Take heed; have open eye; for thieves do foot by night:
Take heed, ere summer comes, or cuckoo-birds do sing.
—Away, Sir Corporal Nym!—Believe it, Page, he
speaks sense. *Exit.*

114–17.] *This ed.;* With . . . preuent: / Or . . . with / Ring-wood . . . name. *F; as prose, Pope;* With . . . go thou / Like . . . heels: / O . . . name! *Capell.* 121. do sing] *F;* affright *Theobald.* 122–3.] *As Theobald;* Away sir Corporall *Nim*: / Beleeue it (*Page*) he speakes sence. *F; Page* belieue him what he ses. Away sir Corporall Nym. *Q;* Away, Sir corporal. / *Nym.* Believe . . . sense. *conj. Johnson;* Away, sir corporal Nym. / *Nym.* Believe . . . sense. *Collier.* 123. *Exit*] *Q; not in F.*

princess, and give ear', *Tw.N.*, v. i. 307–8).

114–16.] Again, the status and division of Pistol's lines are doubtful. The division adopted in the text perhaps makes better verse of them than does the usual setting out.

114. *liver burning hot*] Another allusion to the liver as the supposed seat of the passions.

114–15. *prevent, Or*] anticipate (the danger), and get in first lest.

115–16. *Sir Actæon . . . heels*] Perhaps 'Sir' is used by Pistol because he is quoting from some old play or poem, or because he is implying his own familiarity with the characters of mythology (cf. 'Sir Corporal Nym' in l. 122). (It was not uncommon, however, to add 'Sir' to the names of characters from classical myth and legend. Cf. 'Sir Diomed' in *Troil.*, IV. v. 88.) Actæon, either because he happened to see the naked Diana bathing or because he boasted that he was a better hunter than the goddess, was chased and killed by his own hunting dogs. 'Ringwood' was a popular name for a hound, and one of Actæon's dogs had already been called 'Ringwood' not only in Golding's translation of Ovid but also in the song 'New Mad Tom of Bedlam'. (See Baldwin II. 430–2.) Since as a stag Actæon had horns, the Elizabethans seem to have turned him also into a symbol of cuckoldry: hence his name is 'odious' (l. 117). Cf. III. ii. 38–9, where both self-satisfied rashness and cuckoldry are involved in the allusion.

121. *ere . . . sing*] The cuckoo is associated with warm weather (there is still 'competition' each year in England to report the first cuckoo of spring) and because of its habit of leaving other birds to hatch its eggs, it gave its name to the cuckold, the deceived husband, on whom, so to speak, the cuckoo's trick has been played.

122–3.] The Q version of Pistol's words lends support to the F reading and tells against most emendations. Pistol cannot go without assuring Page that what Nym has already told him or has still to tell him is just as true as what he, Pistol, has told Ford.

Ford. [*Aside*] I will be patient; I will find out this.

Nym. [*To Page*] And this is true; I like not the humour of lying. He hath wronged me in some humours. I should have borne the humoured letter to her; but I have a sword, and it shall bite upon my necessity. He loves your wife; there's the short and the long. My name is Corporal Nym; I speak, and I avouch; 'tis true: my name is Nym, and Falstaff loves your wife. Adieu. I love not the humour of bread and cheese. Adieu. *Exit.*

Page. The 'humour' of it, quoth 'a! Here's a fellow frights English out of his wits.

Ford. I will seek out Falstaff.

Page. I never heard such a drawling, affecting rogue.

124. *Aside*] *As Capell; not in F.* 125. *To Page*] *As Hanmer; not in F.* 130–2. My . . . wife] *Prose as F;* My . . . avouch; / 'Tis . . . wife *New Camb.* 130. avouch; 'tis] *F;* auouch tis *Q.* 133. cheese. Adieu.] *F;* cheese: / And theres the humor of it. *Q;* cheese; and there's the humour of it. Adieu. *Capell.* *Exit*] *Q; not in F.* 134. The 'humour' of it] *This ed.;* The humour of it *F; The humour of it Capell;* (*aside*) 'The humour of it' *Dyce.* 135. English] *F;* humor *Q.* 136, 138, 141.] *As asides, Capell.* 137. *Page*] *F; Page* (*aside*) *Dyce.* drawling, affecting] *F* (drawling-affecting).

128. *bite*] For 'bite' used of the stroke of a sword reaching its mark, cf. *Lr.*, v. iii. 276–7, 'I have seen the day, with my good biting falchion / I would have made them skip'.

upon my necessity] when I need it.

129. *the short and the long*] Hart shows that this is the normal earlier form of our 'the long and the short of it'. Cf. II. ii. 56. (Tilley's citations, L419, give further evidence.)

132–3. *bread and cheese*] Earlier editors explained this, on good authority, as the proverbial description of the hard fare Nym had been forced to accept as Falstaff's retainer. *New Cambridge*, however, citing *O.E.D.*'s other mention of bread and cheese 'as a child's name for the young leaves of the cuckoo-bread plant', sees an allusion to Page's fate as the eating of cuckoo-bread if he does not take Nym's advice. Perhaps both meanings are there.

133.] Editors who include the Q phrase 'And theres the humor of it' do so because they think it necessary if sense is to be made of Page's next line. They themselves are assuming, however, that Page quotes four of Nym's words, whereas he may be quoting only one. 'There's the humour of it' does not occur anywhere in F *Wiv.*; it is Nym's favourite phrase in *H5* and probably gets into Q *Wiv.* by confusion of memory. See Introduction, pp. xxi–xxii.

134–41.] These lines are not necessarily 'asides' in the ordinary sense, but neither Ford nor Page listens to what the other is saying.

135. *his*] its.

137. *drawling, affecting*] Shakespeare does not use 'drawling' elsewhere, and *O.E.D.*, taking it to refer to the lengthening of sounds 'in an indolent or affected manner' and so to 'speaking slowly', cites no earlier example. 'Affecting', however, is common in the sense of trying to be impressive,

Ford. If I do find it—well.

Page. I will not believe such a Cataian, though the priest o' th' town commended him for a true man.

Ford. 'Twas a good sensible fellow—well.

Page. How now, Meg?

[*Mistress Page and Mistress Ford come forward.*]

Mrs. Page. Whither go you, George? Hark you.

Mrs. Ford. How now, sweet Frank, why art thou melancholy?

Ford. I melancholy? I am not melancholy. Get you home, go.

Mrs. Ford. Faith, thou hast some crotchets in thy head now. Will you go, Mistress Page?

Mrs. Page. Have with you. You'll come to dinner, George? [*Aside to Mistress Ford*] Look who comes yonder: she shall be our messenger to this paltry knight.

Mrs. Ford. [*Aside to Mistress Page*] Trust me, I thought on her: she'll fit it.

[*Enter* MISTRESS QUICKLY.]

Mrs. Page. You are come to see my daughter Anne?

Quick. Ay, forsooth; and, I pray, how does good Mistress Anne?

139. *Page*] *F; Page* (*aside*) *Dyce.* 142. S.D.] *Theobald* (*after l. 141*); *not in F;* Page *and* Ford *meeting their wives. Pope.* 146–7.] *Prose as Pope;* I . . . not melancholy: / Get . . . *F.* 148–9. head now. Will] *Hanmer;* head, / Now: will *F1;* head. Now: will *F3.* 151. *Aside . . . Ford*] *Johnson; not in F.* 154. *Aside . . . Page*] *As Capell; not in F.* 155. S.D.] *Rowe* (*after l. 153*); *not in F.*

'putting on airs', affected. There is a close parallel to the thought of the whole line in Mercutio's disgust with Tybalt in *Rom.*, II. iv. 30–1, 'The pox of such antic, lisping, affecting fantasticoes; these new tuners of accents'.

139. *Cataian*] Cathaian or Chinese—apparently noted for boasting and falsehood (Hart cites a relevant passage from William Watreman's translation *The Fardle of Facions,* 1555). Sir Toby, however, is not thinking of either boasting or lying when he applies the term to Olivia (not in her presence) in *Tw.N.*, II. iii. 80.

140. *priest o' th' town*] The modern idiom would be 'parish priest'.

148. *crotchets . . . head*] absurd ideas. The phrase is proverbial (Tilley C843).

150. *Have with you*] I am coming (used again in ll. 210 and 220).

Mrs. Page. Go in with us and see; we have an hour's talk with you.

Exeunt Mistress Page, Mistress Ford, and Mistress Quickly.

Page. How now, Master Ford?

Ford. You heard what this knave told me, did you not?

Page. Yes; and you heard what the other told me?

Ford. Do you think there is truth in them?

Page. Hang 'em, slaves: I do not think the knight would offer it. But these that accuse him in his intent towards our wives are a yoke of his discarded men: very rogues, now they be out of service.

Ford. Were they his men?

Page. Marry, were they.

Ford. I like it never the better for that. Does he lie at the Garter?

Page. Ay, marry, does he. If he should intend this voyage toward my wife, I would turn her loose to him, and what he gets more of her than sharp words, let it lie on my head.

Ford. I do not misdoubt my wife; but I would be loath to turn them together; a man may be too confident; I would have nothing lie on my head; I cannot be thus satisfied.

Page. Look where my ranting host of the Garter comes; there is either liquor in his pate or money in his purse when he looks so merrily.

Enter HOST.

159. we have] *F;* we would have *Hudson*[2], *conj. Walker;* we'd have *Craig.* 160. S.D.] *Q; not in F.* 171–2.] *Prose as Pope;* I . . . that, / Do's . . . *F.* 181. ranting] *F;* ramping *Q.* 183. *Enter Host*] *Dyce; not in F; after l. 184, Collier; Enter Host and Shallow Q (before l. 181); Enter Host, Shallow, and Slender Harness (after l. 184).*

166. *offer it*] attempt it, presume so far. Cf. *Troil.*, II. iii. 67–8, 'Agamemnon is a fool to offer to command Achilles'.

167. *yoke*] pair, brace.

174. *voyage*] The image is used again, of an attempt to seduce, in *Cym.*, I. iv. 171–3: Posthumus, making his wager on Imogen's virtue, says to Iachimo, 'If you make your voyage upon her and give me directly to understand you have prevailed, I am no further your enemy'.

176. *lie on my head*] be my responsibility or blame—but Ford in l. 179 twists it to mean 'wear the horns of cuckoldry'.

How now, mine host?

Host. How now, bully rook? Thou'rt a gentleman.— Cavaliero Justice, I say!

Enter SHALLOW.

Shal. I follow, mine host, I follow. Good even and twenty, good Master Page! Master Page, will you go with us? We have sport in hand.

Host. Tell him, Cavaliero Justice; tell him, bully rook.

Shal. Sir, there is a fray to be fought between Sir Hugh the Welsh priest and Caius the French doctor.

Ford. Good mine host o' th' Garter, a word with you.

Drawing him aside.

Host. What say'st thou, my bully rook?

Shal. [*To Page*] Will you go with us to behold it? My merry host hath had the measuring of their weapons, and, I think, hath appointed them contrary places; for, believe me, I hear the parson is no jester. Hark, I will tell you what our sport shall be. [*They converse apart.*]

Host. Hast thou no suit against my knight, my guest cavalier?

186. S.D. *Enter Shallow*] *Collier*[2]*; not in F.* 193. S.D.] *Capell; not in F;* Ford *and the Host talkes. Q; They go a little aside. Johnson* (*after l. 194*). 195. *To Page*] *Johnson; not in F.* 200. S.D.] *Capell; not in F.* 202. cavalier] *F* (-Caualeire); -cavaleiro *Kittredge.*

186. *Cavaliero*] From the earlier meaning of '(Spanish) knight on horseback', it came to mean, in Dr Johnson's dictionary definition, 'a gay sprightly military man' or 'gallant' and is used ironically in that sense here and at II. iii. 70 and in *2H4*, v. iii. 62.

187–8. *Good even and twenty*] Good afternoon, many times over. 'Twenty' seems to have been used to indicate any reasonably large number; 'even' meant any time after noon. The time of the action, however, must be early morning, because the Host and his party are on the way to the 'duel' from which they all return to interrupt Falstaff's first assignation with Mrs Ford, between ten and eleven (a.m.). The 'error' here gives ammunition to those who argue that Shakespeare was carelessly taking over unaltered some parts of the 'earlier' play he was 'revising'; but there is an identical problem in *Measure for Measure* where Lucio, at IV. iii. 154, says 'Good even' to the Duke and Isabella only thirty-eight lines after the Duke has said 'Good morning' to Isabella. One wonders whether 'good even' may not have meant 'good day'. In any case, there are other instances of time confusion in Shakespeare.

195–7. *My merry host . . . weapons*] See I. iv. 113 and note.

Ford. None, I protest; but I'll give you a pottle of burnt sack to give me recourse to him, and tell him my name is Brook—only for a jest.

Host. My hand, bully; thou shalt have egress and regress—said I well?—and thy name shall be Brook. It is a merry knight. —Will you go, Anheers?

Shal. Have with you, mine host.

Page. I have heard the Frenchman hath good skill in his rapier.

203. *Ford*] *Q; Shal.* (*Shallow*) *F.* 205. Brook] *Q* (*Brooke, throughout play; here misprinted* '*Rrooke*'); *Broome F* (*throughout play*). 209. Anheers] *As F;* myn-heers *Hanmer, conj. Theobald;* on here *Collier, conj. Theobald;* on, heris *Warburton;* on, hearts *Steevens*[3], *conj. Heath;* on, heers *Knight;* on, sirs *Halliwell;* Minheers *Grant White;* Ameers *New Camb., conj. Hart.*

203. Ford] The F attribution of the speech to Shallow must be wrong, in view of the subsequent action involving Ford in disguise. *New Cambridge* claims that the Host's previous question is 'pointless as addressed to Ford' —but it would certainly be pointless addressed to Shallow, for the Host has already been appointed 'umpire' to hear the dispute between him and Falstaff (I. i. 124–8). It is far simpler to assume that the Host is replying to Ford's opening remarks to him, asking for his help in approaching Falstaff (and Falstaff must be the Host's 'knight', his 'guest cavalier').

pottle] half a gallon, or a vessel containing half a gallon.

203–4. *burnt sack*] Generally explained as heated or mulled wine, but one wonders whether, in view of the Elizabethan fondness for sugaring liquor, it may not mean rather wine to which burnt sugar has been added.

205. *Brook*] For this name, following Q, as against F's 'Broome', see Introduction, pp. xxxiv–xxxv.

206–7. *egress and regress*] Legal terms, not used strictly but meaning 'the freedom or opportunity to come and go'.

209. *Anheers*] No fully satisfactory emendation or explanation has been proposed. That the F reading ('Anheires') is a form of a non-extant but then understood word is suggested both by the fact that the later seventeenth-century Folios did not attempt to emend (except in the spelling) and by the occurrence in *1H4*, II. i. 85, of what may well be the same word: Gadshill asserts that he keeps company not with 'sixpennie strikers' and such riff-raff, 'but with nobilitie, & tranquilitie, Burgomasters & great Oneyres' (Qo and, subst., Q1; the later Qq and F1 read 'Oneyers'). The required word, because of the association with 'Burgomasters', is thus probably an anglicization of the Dutch *heer* (or possibly German *herr*). 'Minheers' (for 'mynheers') would fit if one could believe not only (with Grant White and Sisson) that it could have been misread as 'An-heires' but also (which is far less likely) that it could have been misread as 'Oneyres' ('mynheers' is found by Dyce as early as the 1647 Fletcher Folio, in *The Beggar's Bush*). Indeed 'Myne Heire' occurs, as a term of address, in the Crane manuscript of *Sir John Van Olden Barnavelt* (B.M. Add. MS. 18653) and does not look in the least like 'An-Heire', 'On-Heire', or 'Oneyre'. 'Amheeres' (for 'ameers' or 'emirs', the Turkish title) is more likely to have been misread as 'an-

Shal. Tut, sir, I could have told you more. In these times you stand on distance, your passes, stoccadoes, and I know not what. 'Tis the heart, Master Page, 'tis here, 'tis here. I have seen the time, with my long sword I would have made you four tall fellows skip like rats.

Host. Here, boys, here, here; shall we wag?

Page. Have with you. I had rather hear them scold than fight. [*Exeunt Host, Shallow, and Page.*]

Ford. Though Page be a secure fool, and stands so firmly on his wife's frailty, yet I cannot put off my opinion so easily: she was in his company at Page's house; and what they made there, I know not. Well, I will look further into 't, and I have a disguise to sound Falstaff. If I find her honest, I lose not my labour; if she be otherwise, 'tis labour well bestowed. *Exit.*

220. hear] *F;* have *Hanmer.* than] *F* (then)*;* than see them *Collier*[2]. 221. S.D.] *Rowe; not in F.* 223. frailty] *F;* fealty *Theobald*[2], *conj. Theobald*[1]*;* fidelity *Collier*[2]. 229. *Exit*] *Rowe; Exeunt F.*

heires' but perhaps fits less easily into the *1H4* context.

214. *stand on*] rely on, abide by the accepted practice concerning.

distance] the distance between the duellists (which would determine the 'passes' or thrusts used).

214–15. *stoccadoes*] Another technical term for thrusts in fencing. The whole sentence is like Mercutio's scornful account of Tybalt's text-book fencing, in *Rom.*, II. iv. 21–9: 'He fights as you sing prick-song, keeps time, distance, and proportion . . . ah, the immortal passado! the punto reverso! the hai!'

216–17. *I have seen the time . . . I*] The phrase seems to have been a favourite with Shakespeare, as given to old men recalling their alleged youthful prowess; cf. Capulet, in *Rom.*, I. v. 23–4, and *Lr.*, v. iii. 276–7. A great part of the comedy of Shallow in *2H4* (III. ii) comes from such 'memories' of his 'mad' youth.

217. *long sword*] Shallow is probably contrasting the heavier sword of his day (Q reads 'two hand sword') with the lighter modern rapier of l. 212.

you] Almost equivalent to 'for you'. Cf. I. iv. 87 and note. (Harness, misunderstanding the phrase, brought Slender on stage that Shallow might have four men to address.)

tall] (allegedly) valiant.

219. *wag*] go, as in I. iii. 6.

222. *secure*] rashly over-confident. So York calls to Bolingbroke, whom he thinks in danger, 'Open the door, secure, fool-hardy king' (*R2*, v. iii. 43) and the Ghost tells Hamlet how he was murdered when 'Upon my secure hour thy uncle stole' (*Ham.*, I. v. 61).

222–3. *stands . . . frailty*] relies so much on what is really his wife's frailty, believing it to be otherwise. Theobald's emendation 'fealty' is quite unnecessary.

225. *made*] did (or created).

227. *lose*] waste (*O.E.D. v.*[1] 6). 'To lose one's labour' is a common idiom —as in *Love's Labour's Lost.*

SCENE II

Enter FALSTAFF *and* PISTOL.

Fal. I will not lend thee a penny.

Pist. Why, then the world's mine oyster, which I with sword will open.

Fal. Not a penny. I have been content, sir, you should lay my countenance to pawn; I have grated upon my good friends for three reprieves for you and your coach-fellow Nym—or else you had looked through the grate, like a geminy of baboons; I am damned in hell for swearing to gentlemen my friends you were good soldiers and tall fellows; and when Mistress Bridget lost the handle of her fan, I took 't upon mine honour thou hadst it not.

Pist. Didst not thou share? Hadst thou not fifteen pence?

Fal. Reason, you rogue, reason: think'st thou I'll en-

Scene II

SCENE II] *F; Scene* VII. *The* Garter-Inn. *Pope; Scene II. A Room in the garter Inn. Capell.* S.D.] *Q; Enter* Falstaffe, Pistoll, Robin, Quickly, Bardolffe, Ford. *F.* 2–3.] *Prose as F;* Why . . . oyster, / Which . . . *Steevens*[3]*;* I will retort the sum in equipage *Q.* 7. coach-fellow] *F;* couch-fellow *Theobald.*

2–3.] It is difficult to find any justification for tacking on to this speech, as some editors do, the line that replaces it in Q and is presumably the best the reporter could do to recall the original. (*New Cambridge* even uses the Q line to *open* the scene.) There is no difficulty in the F text: Pistol replies that if Falstaff will lend him nothing he will have to use his sword to extract money from an unwilling—and rotten—world; he is adapting the proverbial 'open an oyster with a dagger' (Tilley M777), where the dagger implies keeping one's distance because of the smell.

5. *countenance*] reputation, position, standing (*O.E.D. sb.* III. 9, 10). Falstaff has, in short, allowed Pistol to trade on his, Falstaff's, name.

grated upon] The metaphor was common and is self-explanatory; it corresponds to the modern colloquial 'made myself a nuisance to'.

7. *coach-fellow*] a horse yoked with another to draw a carriage; hence, a companion. Shakespeare uses 'yoke-fellow' in the same sense in *Lr.*, III. vi. 39, and 'yoke-fellows' in *H5*, II. iii. 56.

8. *the grate*] i.e. prison-bars.

geminy] pair, of twins; Latin *gemini*, plural of *geminus*, the name also given to the constellation Castor and Pollux.

10. *tall*] brave.

11. *handle of her fan*] Such handles were often made of precious metal, pearl, or ivory.

11–12. *took 't upon mine honour*] gave my word of honour (that).

14. *Reason . . . reason*] i.e. and it is reasonable enough (that I should have shared in the spoils, since I risked damnation by lying about the matter).

danger my soul gratis? At a word, hang no more about me; I am no gibbet for you. Go—a short knife and a throng!—to your manor of Pickt-hatch, go! You'll not bear a letter for me, you rogue? You stand upon your honour? Why, thou unconfinable baseness, it is as much as I can do to keep the terms of my honour precise: I, I, I myself sometimes, leaving the fear of heaven on the left hand, and hiding mine honour in my necessity, am fain to shuffle, to hedge, and to lurch; and yet you, rogue, will ensconce your rags, your cat-a-mountain looks, your red-lattice phrases, and your bold beating oaths, under the shelter of your honour! You will not do it, you?

Pist. I do relent: what would thou more of man?

17. throng!] *F* (throng,); thong, *Pope*. 21. I, I, I] *F; I Pope;* I, ay, I *Grant White;* Ay, ay, I *New Camb.* 22. heaven] *F;* God *Q*. 26. bold beating] *F* (bold-beating-); bold-bearing *conj. Warburton;* bull-baiting *Hanmer;* bowl-beating *conj. New Camb.* 28. relent] *F;* recant *Q*.

15–16. *hang no more about me*] It is not clear whether the verb is used intransitively, 'be an encumbrance on me no longer' (*O.E.D. v.* II. 14. e and 15), with a pun on the other sense (Pistol is destined for a gibbet, but Falstaff is not it), or transitively, 'fasten no more crimes or responsibility on me', as one hangs a felon on a gibbet.

16–17. *a short knife and a throng*] Presumably, using your short knife for cutting purses in a convenient crowd—and no doubt there is a linking of the idea of *picking* purses and '*Pickt*-hatch', a disreputable part of London where there would certainly be no 'manors'.

19. *unconfinable*] limitless, infinite.

23–4. *shuffle . . . hedge . . . lurch*] All three words are used colloquially or as thieves' jargon and they are more or less synonymous: 'shuffle', cheat; 'hedge', use devious methods (as in *Troil.*, III. iii. 158, where to 'hedge aside from the direct forthright' is to abandon honour, which 'travels in a strait so narrow, / Where one but goes abreast'); 'lurch', pilfer, steal (*O.E.D. v.*[1] 3) rather than 'remain in or about a place furtively' (*O.E.D. v.*[1] 1, citing this line).

24. *ensconce*] hide, shelter, or protect (particularly within or behind a fortification). Cf. III. iii. 82.

25. *cat-a-mountain*] Variously used of the leopard, panther, tiger-cat, or wild cat, and probably applied to Pistol because of his lawlessness and (perhaps) his moustaches, which remind Falstaff of the feline's whiskers.

red-lattice] i.e. tavern or ale-house, which normally had red-painted lattice instead of glass windows. Cf. *2H4*, II. ii. 85–9.

26. *bold beating*] The phrase has caused difficulty, probably only because of the F hyphens (which may be easily explained as the responsibility of Ralph Crane, who often thus linked adjectives, and adjectives and nouns). Johnson well compared 'beating' with 'thwacking' or 'swinging' as intensives.

28. *relent*] give way (*O.E.D. v.*[1] 2. b).

[*Enter* ROBIN.]

Rob. Sir, here's a woman would speak with you.

Fal. Let her approach.

Enter MISTRESS QUICKLY.

Quick. Give your worship good morrow.

Fal. Good morrow, goodwife.

Quick. Not so, and't please your worship.

Fal. Good maid, then.

Quick. I'll be sworn—as my mother was, the first hour I was born.

Fal. I do believe the swearer. What with me?

Quick. Shall I vouchsafe your worship a word or two?

Fal. Two thousand, fair woman, and I'll vouchsafe thee the hearing.

Quick. There is one Mistress Ford, sir—I pray come a little nearer this ways—I myself dwell with Master Doctor Caius—

Fal. Well, on; Mistress Ford, you say—

Quick. Your worship says very true.—I pray your worship come a little nearer this ways.

Fal. I warrant thee, nobody hears. Mine own people, mine own people.

Quick. Are they so? Heaven bless them, and make them his servants!

Fal. Well, Mistress Ford—what of her?

28. *Enter Robin*] *Rowe; not in F.* 30. S.D.] *Q; not in F.* 32. goodwife] *F1* (good-wife); good wife *F4.* 35–6.] *Prose as Pope;* Ile be sworne, / As . . . borne. *F.* 44. on; Mistress] *F;* one Mistress *Halliwell, conj. Douce.* 49. Heaven] *F;* God *Q.*

32. *goodwife*] A civil form of address to the mistress of a house. Cf. 'goodman', III. ii. 22.

33. *and't*] if it.

35. *I'll be sworn*] I'll swear to that (as in III. iii. 25)—and Quickly proceeds with a delightful 'Freudian' conflation of the proverbs 'as good a maid as her mother' and 'as innocent as a new-born babe' (Tilley M14, B4). Hudson must be the only reader of the play to deduce that Quickly is 'a maiden' (p. 212).

38. *vouchsafe*] grant to, or bestow on—obviously not the word Quickly means, for she is asking for the favour.

42. *ways*] This is the genitive of 'way', used in such adverbial expressions as 'come this ways' and 'go thy ways' (l. 133).

49–50. *Heaven . . . servants*] An example of expurgation. See Introduction, pp. xxxv–xxxvi.

Quick. Why, sir, she's a good creature.—Lord, Lord, your worship's a wanton! Well, heaven forgive you and all of us, I pray!

Fal. Mistress Ford; come, Mistress Ford.

Quick. Marry, this is the short and the long of it; you have brought her into such a canaries as 'tis wonderful. The best courtier of them all, when the court lay at Windsor, could never have brought her to such a canary. Yet there has been knights, and lords, and gentlemen, with their coaches—I warrant you, coach after coach, letter after letter, gift after gift—smelling so sweetly, all musk, and so rushling, I warrant you, in silk and gold, and in such alligant terms, and in such wine and sugar of the best and the fairest, that would have won any woman's heart; and, I warrant you, they could never get an eye-wink of her; I had myself twenty angels given me this morning; but I defy all angels—in any such sort, as they say—but in the way of honesty; and, I warrant you, they could never get her so much as sip on a cup with the proudest of them all, and yet there has been earls, nay, which is more, pensioners, but, I warrant you, all is one with her.

65. in such wine] *F;* such wine *Hanmer.* 69. this] *F;* of a *Collier*[2].

57. *canaries*] Presumably, quandary (Steevens, 1778). Quickly perhaps associates such a state of confusion either with the dance called a canary or with canary wine (see III. ii. 81–3 and notes).

58–9. *when the court lay at Windsor*] The phrase may be no more than an attempt to add local colour. The notes of Hart and *New Cambridge*, e.g., see difficulty or topical reference when probably none exists.

60. *has*] Quickly is always likely to be muddled, but this use of the 'quasi-singular' before the plural subject is normal (Abbott 335).

63. *rushling*] Quickly's version of 'rustling', perhaps by conflation with rushes moving in the wind.

64. *alligant*] An attempt at either 'elegant' or 'eloquent'.

69. *defy*] deny, reject.

angels] gold coins. See I. iii. 50 and note.

73. *pensioners*] gentlemen of the royal bodyguard within the palace, noted for their colourful uniforms (cf. *MND.*, II. i. 8–11)—but of course they would not be superior to earls. There were also royal 'pensioners', 'Knights of Windsor', who in return for £18 per annum and clothes were required to attend the Chapel twice a day and pray for the monarch (see a note in McKerrow's edition of Nashe, III. 348). If perchance Quickly is thinking of them, she is even more confused.

Fal. But what says she to me? Be brief, my good she-Mercury.

Quick. Marry, she hath received your letter; for the which she thanks you a thousand times; and she gives you to notify that her husband will be absence from his house between ten and eleven.

Fal. Ten and eleven.

Quick. Ay, forsooth; and then you may come and see the picture, she says, that you wot of; Master Ford, her husband, will be from home. Alas, the sweet woman leads an ill life with him: he's a very jealousy man; she leads a very frampold life with him, good heart.

Fal. Ten and eleven. Woman, commend me to her; I will not fail her.

Quick. Why, you say well. But I have another messenger to your worship: Mistress Page hath her hearty commendations to you too; and let me tell you in your ear, she's as fartuous a civil modest wife, and one, I tell you, that will not miss you morning nor evening prayer, as any is in Windsor, whoe'er be the other; and she bade me tell your worship that her husband is seldom from home, but she hopes there will come a time. I never knew a woman so dote upon a man; surely, I think you have charms, la; yes, in truth.

Fal. Not I, I assure thee; setting the attraction of my good parts aside, I have no other charms.

Quick. Blessing on your heart for 't!

Fal. But I pray thee tell me this: has Ford's wife and

75–6. *she-Mercury*] Mercury (Hermes) was the messenger of the gods.

79. *gives you to notify*] Perhaps further confusion, between 'notifies' and 'gives you notice'; but 'notify' could mean 'take note of' or 'observe' (*O.E.D.* 1).

83. *wot*] know—a (false) new formation from the preterite of 'wit'. Not archaic then, and used often by Shakespeare.

86. *frampold*] disagreeable because of his ill-temper, peevish. The derivation is unknown but Wright (under 'frampald') records forms of the word in many dialects.

92. *fartuous*] Quickly's unfortunate version of 'virtuous'.

93. *miss you*] Another example of the 'ethic dative' (Abbott 220).

98, 101. *charms*] enchantments—meaning magic charms.

101. *parts*] qualities (and often used also for appearance, good looks).

102. *Blessing . . . for 't*] i.e. God's blessing (Tilley G266).

Page's wife acquainted each other how they love me?

Quick. That were a jest indeed! They have not so little grace, I hope; that were a trick indeed! But Mistress Page would desire you to send her your little page, of all loves: her husband has a marvellous infection to the little page; and, truly, Master Page is an honest man. Never a wife in Windsor leads a better life than she does; do what she will, say what she will, take all, pay all, go to bed when she list, rise when she list, all is as she will; and, truly, she deserves it; for if there be a kind woman in Windsor, she is one. You must send her your page, no remedy.

Fal. Why, I will.

Quick. Nay, but do so, then, and, look you, he may come and go between you both; and in any case have a nay-word, that you may know one another's mind, and the boy never need to understand anything; for 'tis not good that children should know any wickedness: old folks, you know, have discretion, as they say, and know the world.

Fal. Fare thee well; commend me to them both. There's my purse; I am yet thy debtor. Boy, go along with this woman. [*Exeunt Mistress Quickly and Robin.*] This news distracts me.

Pist. This punk is one of Cupid's carriers.

128. S.D.] *As Rowe* (*after* 'distracts me'); *not in F.* 130. *Pist.*] *F; Pist.* [*aside*] *Kittredge.* punk] *F* (Puncke); pink *Warburton.*

109. *of all loves*] The nearest equivalent is 'for love's sake' but the Elizabethan phrase is more emphatic. Hermia uses it in *MND.*, II. ii. 154, when calling in alarm to Lysander whom she had thought to be near her: 'Speak, of all loves! I swoon almost with fear'.

110. *infection to*] Quickly's attempt at 'affection for' or 'attraction to'.

113. *take all, pay all*] Another ready-made phrase (Tilley A203).

117. *no remedy*] A common phrase, of the same meaning as the modern 'it can't be helped'.

121. *nay-word*] password (as also in v. ii. 5).

130–2.] There is no corresponding speech in Q; and Hart and *New Cambridge* regard the lines as an addition or afterthought, to make a connection with *H5*, where Pistol is married to Quickly. *New Cambridge* has to add, however, that 'Pistol would hardly call his future wife a "punk"'—and therefore accepts the

Clap on more sails, pursue; up with your fights;
Give fire; she is my prize, or ocean whelm them all!
[*Exit.*]

Fal. Say'st thou so, old Jack? Go thy ways; I'll make more of thy old body than I have done. Will they yet look after thee? Wilt thou, after the expense of so much money, be now a gainer? Good body, I thank thee. Let them say 'tis grossly done; so it be fairly done, no matter.

Enter BARDOLPH.

Bard. Sir John, there's one Master Brook below would fain speak with you, and be acquainted with you; and hath sent your worship a morning's draught of sack.

Fal. Brook is his name?

Bard. Ay, sir.

Fal. Call him in. [*Exit Bardolph.*] Such Brooks are welcome to me, that o'erflows such liquor. Ah, ha, Mistress Ford and Mistress Page, have I encompassed you? Go to; via!

132. *Exit*] *Rowe; not in F.* 138. S.D.] *Q; not in F.* 145. S.D.] *Theobald; not in F.* 146. o'erflows] *F;* o'erflow with *Pope;* o'er-flow *Capell.*

emendation 'pink'. There need be no connection with *H5* at all; and the Pistol of *H4* was quite capable of chasing any punk.

130. *punk*] Walter Whiter pointed out (p. 224) that women (good or bad)—sailing ships formed a Shakespearian image-link, as in *Troil.*, I. i. 103–7 and three passages in *Rom.* This neither supports nor rules out the emendation: 'pink', if accepted, would be the word used for a small sailing ship.

carriers] go-betweens.

131. *fights*] protective screens used on warships going into battle.

132. *whelm*] overturn, or submerge (*O.E.D. v.* 2, 4).

133. *Say'st thou so?*] Falstaff is ruminating, not commenting on Pistol's words, to which he pays no attention.

Go thy ways] See l. 42 and note.

133–4. *make more of*] think more highly of.

145–6. *Such Brooks . . . liquor*] These lines afford evidence that when Shakespeare wrote the play Ford's pseudonym was 'Brook'; 'Such Broomes . . .' is meaningless.

146. *o'erflows*] The third person plural in -s (Abbot 333).

147–8. *encompassed*] Explained by *O.E.D.* (*v.* 5), citing only this line, as 'got round' (which is plausible); by Schmidt as 'come by' (comparing 'compass' in such uses as 'Things out of hope are compass'd oft with venturing', *Ven.*, 567; cf. also *Gent.*, II. iv. 214).

148. *Go to*] Normally an exclamation of impatience and therefore perhaps means here 'hurry up! on with it!'.

via] An exclamation of encourage-

Enter [BARDOLPH, *and*] FORD *in disguise.*

Ford. Bless you, sir.

Fal. And you, sir. Would you speak with me?

Ford. I make bold to press with so little preparation upon you.

Fal. You're welcome. What's your will?—Give us leave, drawer. [*Exit Bardolph.*]

Ford. Sir, I am a gentleman that have spent much; my name is Brook.

Fal. Good Master Brook, I desire more acquaintance of you.

Ford. Good Sir John, I sue for yours: not to charge you, for I must let you understand I think myself in better plight for a lender than you are—the which hath something emboldened me to this unseasoned intrusion; for they say, if money go before, all ways do lie open.

Fal. Money is a good soldier, sir, and will on.

Ford. Troth, and I have a bag of money here troubles me; if you will help to bear it, Sir John, take all, or half, for easing me of the carriage.

Fal. Sir, I know not how I may deserve to be your porter.

Ford. I will tell you, sir, if you will give me the hearing.

Fal. Speak, good Master Brook, I shall be glad to be your servant.

Ford. Sir, I hear you are a scholar—I will be brief with you—and you have been a man long known to me, though I had never so good means as desire to make myself acquainted with you. I shall discover a thing to you, wherein I must very much lay open mine

148. S.D.] *As Theobald; not in F; Enter* Foord *disguised like* Brooke. *Q.* 154. S.D.] *Theobald; not in F.* 167–8. all, or half,] *F;* half, or all, *Collier*[2].

ment (from the Italian but used as 'French' by the Dauphin in *H5*, IV. ii. 4). Cf. *3H6*, II. i. 182.

153–4. *Give us leave*] please leave us to ourselves.

159. *charge*] put a load upon, and so, figuratively, put to expense.

162. *unseasoned*] unseasonable.

163–4. *if money . . . open*] As Ford indicates, a popular maxim (Tilley M1050).

174. *scholar*] See I. iii. 2 note.

177. *discover*] reveal (a normal Elizabethan meaning).

own imperfection; but, good Sir John, as you have one eye upon my follies, as you hear them unfolded, turn another into the register of your own, that I may pass with a reproof the easier, sith you yourself know how easy it is to be such an offender.

Fal. Very well, sir; proceed.

Ford. There is a gentlewoman in this town—her husband's name is Ford.

Fal. Well, sir.

Ford. I have long loved her and, I protest to you, bestowed much on her; followed her with a doting observance; engrossed opportunities to meet her; fee'd every slight occasion that could but niggardly give me sight of her; not only bought many presents to give her, but have given largely to many to know what she would have given: briefly, I have pursued her as love hath pursued me; which hath been on the wing of all occasions. But whatsoever I have merited, either in my mind or in my means, meed I am sure I have received none, unless experience be a jewel, that I have purchased at an infinite rate and that hath taught me to say this:

Love like a shadow flies when substance love pursues;
Pursuing that that flies, and flying what pursues.

199. jewel, that] *F1;* Jewel that *F4;* Jewel *Rowe;* jewel. That *New Camb.*

181. *register*] In the sense (still familiar) of catalogue. Ford is perhaps adapting the proverb 'He that speaks ill of another let him first think of himself' (Tilley I27).

182. *sith*] since (OE *siððan*). The word was going out of use and is probably meant to add to the quaint formality of Ford's manner of speech in his role as Brook.

190. *observance*] deference, dutiful attention (as in *AYL.*, v. ii. 102, 104; and *Troil.*, I. iii. 31).

engrossed] Probably 'collected' (as in *Ant.*, III. vii. 37) rather than 'monopolized' (as explained by Onions, comparing *Rom.*, v. iii. 115, 'engrossing death').

191. *fee'd*] paid for, purchased.

194. *would have given*] would wish to be given.

197. *meed*] recompense or reward.

201–2. Love . . . pursues] The inverted commas preceding each of these lines in F are a regular Elizabethan method of drawing attention to an epigrammatic or proverbial pronouncement. (Tilley lists this proverb in the form 'Love, like a shadow, flies one following and pursues one fleeing'—L518.)

201. substance] i.e. money—with, of course, a quibble based on the wider meaning of 'substance' in the proverbial 'shadow and substance' antithesis.

Fal. Have you received no promise of satisfaction at her hands?

Ford. Never.

Fal. Have you importuned her to such a purpose?

Ford. Never.

Fal. Of what quality was your love, then?

Ford. Like a fair house built on another man's ground, so that I have lost my edifice by mistaking the place where I erected it.

Fal. To what purpose have you unfolded this to me?

Ford. When I have told you that, I have told you all. Some say that though she appear honest to me, yet in other places she enlargeth her mirth so far that there is shrewd construction made of her. Now, Sir John, here is the heart of my purpose: you are a gentleman of excellent breeding, admirable discourse, of great admittance, authentic in your place and person, generally allowed for your many warlike, court-like, and learned preparations.

Fal. O sir!

Ford. Believe it, for you know it. There is money; spend it, spend it, spend more; spend all I have, only give

209–11.] In law, any building erected on ground that was not one's own property belonged to the owner of the ground and this was recognized in the proverb (Tilley G470) 'Who builds upon another's ground loses both mortar and stones'. This makes less convincing, though it does not rule out, Roy F. Montgomery's theory that there is a reference here to the problem of Burbage's Theatre, which stood on ground the lease of which expired in April 1597. (Later, in 1598–9, it was surreptitiously pulled down and the timbers used to build the Globe on the Bankside.—*Shakespeare Quarterly*, v, 1954, 207–8.) Whiter (p. 224) found the comparison of love to a mansion that was (but was not necessarily thought to be) in danger of destruction in, e.g., *Troil.*, IV. ii. 109–11; *Rom.*, III. ii. 26–7; and *Gent.*, V. iv. 7–12.

215. *enlargeth her mirth*] gives free rein to her natural love of merriment.

216. *shrewd*] malicious (a frequent Shakespearian use).

219. *admittance*] Almost equivalent to 'admissibility' (*O.E.D.* 2): Falstaff is readily admitted to the best of homes.

authentic] entitled to respect (*O.E.D.* 1).

220. *generally allowed*] universally accepted or approved.

221. *preparations*] Presumably a stilted use of the word to mean equipment, in the sense of natural endowments, or, as *O.E.D.* suggests (*sb.* 4), 'a personal capacity gained by previous instruction or training; an accomplishment'.

me so much of your time in exchange of it as to lay an amiable siege to the honesty of this Ford's wife. Use your art of wooing; win her to consent to you; if any man may, you may as soon as any.

Fal. Would it apply well to the vehemency of your affection that I should win what you would enjoy? Methinks you prescribe to yourself very preposterously.

Ford. O, understand my drift: she dwells so securely on the excellency of her honour that the folly of my soul dares not present itself; she is too bright to be looked against. Now, could I come to her with any detection in my hand, my desires had instance and argument to commend themselves; I could drive her then from the ward of her purity, her reputation, her marriage-vow, and a thousand other her defences which now are too too strongly embattled against me. What say you to 't, Sir John?

Fal. Master Brook, I will first make bold with your money; next, give me your hand; and last, as I am a gentleman, you shall, if you will, enjoy Ford's wife.

Ford. O good sir!

Fal. I say you shall.

Ford. Want no money, Sir John; you shall want none.

Fal. Want no Mistress Ford, Master Brook; you shall want none. I shall be with her, I may tell you, by her own appointment; even as you came in to me, her assistant, or go-between, parted from me: I say

225. exchange] *F* (enchange). 235. soul] *F; suit Collier*[2]. 252. assistant] *F;* spokes mate *Q*.

226. *amiable*] of love, amorous.

229. *apply well to*] be consistent with.

233. *dwells so securely*] relies so confidently (but again in 'securely' there is the suggestion of false confidence; cf. II. i. 222).

234. *folly*] wantonness—as often in Shakespeare; cf. III. ii. 31.

236. *looked against*] looked at or into—as one is unable to look directly at the sun.

237. *had*] would have (a subjunctive).

instance] evidence.

239. *ward*] Generally explained as 'posture of defence in fencing' but is also often used of a fortress or stronghold, or parts of them.

240. *other her*] An example of the transposition of the unemphatic possessive pronoun (Abbott 13).

241. *too too*] The repetition lends emphasis; cf. *Ham.*, I. ii. 129.

I shall be with her between ten and eleven; for at that time the jealous rascally knave her husband will be forth. Come you to me at night, you shall know how I speed.

Ford. I am blest in your acquaintance. Do you know Ford, sir?

Fal. Hang him, poor cuckoldly knave, I know him not. Yet I wrong him to call him poor: they say the jealous wittolly knave hath masses of money, for the which his wife seems to me well-favoured. I will use her as the key of the cuckoldly rogue's coffer, and there's my harvest-home.

Ford. I would you knew Ford, sir, that you might avoid him if you saw him.

Fal. Hang him, mechanical salt-butter rogue! I will stare him out of his wits; I will awe him with my cudgel: it shall hang like a meteor o'er the cuckold's horns. Master Brook, thou shalt know I will predominate over the peasant, and thou shalt lie with his wife. Come to me soon at night. Ford's a knave, and I will aggravate his style; thou, Master Brook,

259. cuckoldly] *F; cuckally Q1; cuckoldy Q3.* 263. cuckoldly] *F1; cuckally Q; Cuckold- F2.*

255. *at night*] A natural enough instruction, which would not be worthy of comment except that it again gives ammunition to those who postulate 'revision', since Brook in fact returns the following morning.

256. *speed*] fare.

261. *wittolly*] The adjective—not used elsewhere by Shakespeare—is formed from 'wittol', a husband who is complaisant about being cuckolded (and it too is found in Shakespeare only in this scene, l. 288).

262. *well-favoured*] good-looking, and so, more generally, attractive.

264. *harvest-home*] A splendid image: the festival to celebrate the bringing home of the corn.

267. *mechanical*] vulgar—a secondary or derived meaning from the original one of 'engaged in manual or other inferior labour' (as Bottom and his friends in *MND.*, III. ii. 9–10, are to Puck 'rude mechanicals, / That work for bread upon Athenian stalls').

salt-butter] The best explanation is Hart's: salt-butter, particularly that imported from Flanders, was considered inferior and would be eaten only if one could afford no better. He quotes from Nashe's *Pierce Penniless* (1592) a contemptuous reference to one who pretends to social standing though in fact living all year with only 'salt butter and Holland cheese in his chamber'.

268. *stare*] For a possible second meaning, see note on v. v. 160.

273. *aggravate his style*] 'Aggravate' had both its modern meaning of 'make worse' and that of 'increase' ('to aggravate thy store' in *Sonn.*, cxlvi. 10). Fal-

shalt know him for knave and cuckold. Come to me soon at night. *Exit.*

Ford. What a damned Epicurean rascal is this? My heart is ready to crack with impatience. Who says this is improvident jealousy? My wife hath sent to him, the hour is fixed, the match is made. Would any man have thought this? See the hell of having a false woman: my bed shall be abused, my coffers ransacked, my reputation gnawn at, and I shall not only receive this villainous wrong, but stand under the adoption of abominable terms, and by him that does me this wrong. Terms! Names! Amaimon sounds well; Lucifer, well; Barbason, well: yet they are devils' additions, the names of fiends. But cuckold? Wittol? Cuckold! The devil himself hath not such a name. Page is an ass, a secure ass: he will trust his wife, he will not be jealous. I will rather trust a Fleming with my butter, Parson Hugh the Welshman with my cheese, an Irishman with my aqua-vitæ bottle, or a thief to walk my ambling

275. S.D.] *Q; not in F.* 285. this] *F;* the *Rowe*[2]. 288. cuckold? Wittol? Cuckold!] *This ed.;* Cuckold, Wittoll, Cuckold? *F;* Cuckold, Wittol-Cuckold! *Rowe*[1]*;* Cuckold, Wittol, Cuckold! *Rowe*[3].

staff probably means both, and is thinking of the horns which he will add to Ford's attainments or title.

276. *Epicurean*] pleasure-loving, and so, sensual.

283. *stand under*] run the risk of, or have to submit to.

284. *the adoption of*] being 'christened' with (*O.E.D.* 'adopt' 7).

abominable] exciting disgust (probably a stronger adjective then).

285–6. *Amaimon . . . Lucifer . . . Barbason*] All these 'additions' or names of devils are recorded elsewhere, the first two, notably, in *1H4*, II. iv. 370–3 (where Falstaff is ridiculing Glendower) and the third in *H5*, II. i. 57–8 (where Nym defies Pistol: 'I am not Barbason; you cannot conjure me'). J. H. Walter has suggested, however, that 'Barbason' may be Shakespeare's conflation of the demon Barbas with the French knight Barbason whom he had read about in Holinshed.

288. *Wittol*] See note on l. 261.

290–1. *I will . . . butter*] As in l. 267, the reference derives from the scorn directed at those who live on a weak diet of butter (instead of meat), in the alleged manner of the inhabitants of the Low Countries.

292. *Welshman . . . cheese*] The Welshman's proverbial fondness for cheese is ridiculed also at I. ii. 11–12 and v. v. 82–3.

293. *aqua-vitæ*] Lit. water of life and since 1547, at the latest, commonly applied to strong spirits. The Irish were said to be too fond of these—particularly of their own whisky, usquebaugh (the name of which also means 'water of life').

293–4. *ambling gelding*] Properly

gelding, than my wife with herself. Then she plots, then she ruminates, then she devises; and what they think in their hearts they may effect, they will break their hearts but they will effect. Heaven be praised for my jealousy!—Eleven o'clock the hour: I will prevent this, detect my wife, be revenged on Falstaff, and laugh at Page. I will about it; better three hours too soon than a minute too late. Fie, fie, fie; cuckold, cuckold, cuckold! *Exit.*

SCENE III

Enter CAIUS *and* RUGBY.

Caius. Jack Rugby!

Rug. Sir?

Caius. Vat is the clock, Jack?

Rug. 'Tis past the hour, sir, that Sir Hugh promised to meet.

Caius. By gar, he has save his soul, dat he is no come; he has pray his Pible well, dat he is no come; by gar, Jack Rugby, he is dead already, if he be come.

Rug. He is wise, sir: he knew your worship would kill him if he came.

Caius. By gar, de herring is no dead so as I vill kill him.

297. Heaven] *F;* God *Q.*

Scene III

SCENE III] *F;* Scene XI. *Windsor-Park. Pope; Scene III. Field near Windsor. Knight.* S.D.] *Rowe (as Q); Enter Caius, Rugby, Page, Shallow, Slender, Host. F.* 11. is . . . him] *F;* be not so dead as I shall make him *Q.*

a gelding with a comfortable trot or canter but it seems to have become the standard term for a riding horse.

298. *Eleven . . . hour*] Ford is not, of course, stating the time, but saying over to himself the (approximate) time of Falstaff's appointment with Mistress Ford—nor is his 'better *three* hours too soon' a statement of how early he intends to be.

300–1. *better . . . late*] Proverbial (Tilley H745).

Scene III

11. *no dead so as*] not as dead as he will be when. 'Dead as a herring' was a stock phrase even then (Tilley H446).

Take your rapier, Jack; I vill tell you how I vill kill him.

Rug. Alas, sir, I cannot fence.

Caius. Villainy, take your rapier.

Rug. Forbear; here's company.

Enter HOST, SHALLOW, SLENDER, *and* PAGE.

Host. Bless thee, bully Doctor.

Shal. Save you, Master Doctor Caius.

Page. Now, good Master Doctor.

Slen. Give you good morrow, sir.

Caius. Vat be all you, one, two, tree, four, come for?

Host. To see thee fight, to see thee foin, to see thee traverse, to see thee here, to see thee there, to see thee pass thy punto, thy stock, thy reverse, thy distance, thy montant. Is he dead, my Ethiopian? Is he dead, my Francisco? Ha, bully? What says my Æsculapius? My Galen? My heart of elder? Ha, is he dead, bully stale? Is he dead?

15. Villainy] *F;* Villan-a *Johnson;* Villain *Dyce*². 16. S.D.] *Q; not in F.* 24. punto] *Q;* puncto *F.* 26. Francisco] *F;* francoyes *Q.* 27. Galen] *Rowe; Galien F;* gallon *Q1; Gallen Q3.* 28. bully stale] *F* (bully-Stale); bullies taile *Q.*

15. *villainy*] Caius' form of 'villain', as at I. iv. 62.

22. *foin*] lunge—often used of the tactical pass that keeps the opponent at a distance (as probably in *Lr.*, IV. vi. 251) rather than of a home thrust (as Quickly probably misuses it in *2H4*, II. i. 17). Doll no doubt gives it a second meaning in *2H4*, II. iv. 252.

23. *traverse*] Another fencing and also military term, of movement from side to side.

24. *punto*] direct thrust. F's 'puncto' is not necessarily wrong, but 'punto' seems to be the normal form and is used e.g. in the 'good Quarto', Q2, of *Rom.*, II. iv. 27. The Host is ridiculing Caius' knowledge of the technical jargon of fencing much as Mercutio ridicules Tybalt's. Similarly it is the pretentious Bobadill who knows all the terms in Jonson's *Every Man in His Humour*: 'your *Punto*, your *Reuerso*, your *Stoccata*, your *Imbroccata*, your *Passada*, your *Montanto*' (IV. vii. 77–9).

stock] Anglicized form and abbreviation of *astoccata* or *stoccado*. Cf. II. i. 214–15 and note.

reverse] The 'punto reverso' of *Rom.*, II. iv. 27—a back-handed stroke.

25. *distance*] (knowledge of) the correct distance from one's opponent.

montant] upward thrust ('montanto').

Ethiopian] blackamoor, as in Jeremiah, 13:23. Caius is apparently dark, or black-bearded, as Frenchmen are sometimes alleged to be today.

26. *Francisco*] That the reporter of Q took this to mean 'Frenchman', as it probably does, is shown by Q's 'francoyes'.

27. *Æsculapius*] The god of medicine, under his Roman name.

Galen] The famous Greek physician of the second century A.D.

heart of elder] 'Heart of oak' would

Caius. By gar, he is de coward Jack priest of de vorld; he is not show his face.

Host. Thou art a Castalian-king-Urinal: Hector of Greece, my boy!

Caius. I pray you bear witness that me have stay six or seven, two, tree hours for him, and he is no come.

Shal. He is the wiser man, Master Doctor: he is a curer of souls, and you a curer of bodies; if you should fight, you go against the hair of your professions. Is it not true, Master Page?

Page. Master Shallow, you have yourself been a great fighter, though now a man of peace.

31. Castalian-king-Urinal:] *F* (Castalion-king-Vrinall:); castallian king vrinall. *Q*; Cardalion, king Urinal, *Hanmer*; *Castillian*, king urinal; *Capell*; Castilian king, Urinal! *Steevens*[2], *conj. Farmer*; Castilian king-Urinal *Hudson*; Castilian King Urinal *Sisson*. 34. two, tree] *F* (two tree).

be a compliment to a man's bravery; 'heart of elder' is just the opposite, for the elder is a low tree, the wood of which is often spongy, and it had other derogatory implications as 'Judas' tree', the one on which he hanged himself. The Host takes the justifiable risk of assuming that Caius will not follow this inflated and allusive language.

28. *bully stale*] In effect, this is the Host's equivalent of 'Master Doctor'. For 'bully' see note on I. iii. 2; 'stale' is probably used in the sense of 'urine' (*O.E.D. sb.*[5]) and is a reference to the practice of diagnosing by analysing it (cf. *2H4*, I. ii. 1–6). Conceivably, however, there is a quibble on other meanings of 'stale'—e.g. stuffed bird used as a decoy or a dupe (*O.E.D. sb.*[3] 1, 5) or laughing stock (cf. Nashe's jibe at those who become 'the scoffe of a Scholler and the stale of a Courtier', I. 35). Q's amusing reading 'bullies taile' is significant as showing that the reporter or his scribe wrote down what he *heard*.

29. *Jack priest*] Used before at I. iv. 112; see note on I. iv. 102 and cf. l. 59 below.

31–2.] The Host becomes ever more grandiloquent, and impossible to paraphrase. The image of 'stale' (l. 28) is carried on in 'urinal', but it is by no means certain which words have the function of nouns and which of adjectives, as the collations show. If the Host says 'king-urinal' (i.e. king of urinals), then his 'Castalian' (for 'Castilian') is a pejorative adjective natural in the days of the feared Spanish invasion; if he says 'Castalian-king urinal', then it would mean the urinal used by the hated Philip II of Castile. And it is quite possible that the three words form a compound adjective qualifying 'Hector of Greece' in, of course, the most ironic way. Hart's argument for reading 'Castalian' (F 'Castalion') rather than 'Castilian' is sound: there may well be, as he suggests, a further atrocious quibble on the water from the Castalian spring. (Hanmer's explanation that the Host meant to say 'Cœur de lion' is unconvincing.)

37. *against the hair*] i.e. against the proper function—a proverbial image (Tilley H18) from rubbing an animal's fur the wrong way. Cf. also 'against the grain'.

Shal. Bodykins, Master Page, though I now be old, and of the Peace, if I see a sword out, my finger itches to make one. Though we are justices, and doctors, and churchmen, Master Page, we have some salt of our youth in us; we are the sons of women, Master Page.

Page. 'Tis true, Master Shallow.

Shal. It will be found so, Master Page. Master Doctor Caius, I am come to fetch you home. I am sworn of the Peace; you have showed yourself a wise physician, and Sir Hugh hath shown himself a wise and patient churchman; you must go with me, Master Doctor.

Host. Pardon, guest Justice.—A word, Mounseur Mock-water.

Caius. Mock-vater? Vat is dat?

Host. Mock-water, in our English tongue, is valour, bully.

Caius. By gar, then, I have as much mock-vater as de Englishman. Scurvy Jack-dog priest! By gar, me vill cut his ears.

Host. He will clapper-claw thee tightly, bully.

Caius. Clapper-de-claw? Vat is dat?

53. A word] *Q; a Ff;* ah! *Hanmer.* 53–4. Mock-water] *F, Q;* Muck-water *Steevens*[3], *conj. Farmer;* Make-water *Sisson, conj. Cartwright.*

41. *Bodykins*] by God's dear body ('bodykin' is the familiar or affectionate diminutive). Cf. 'Od's heartlings' in III. iv. 56. Shallow's over-frequent use of the term of address 'Master Page' is also to be noted as giving an undignified and even puerile tone to his speech.

42–3. *to make one*] The modern colloquial equivalent would be 'to be in it'.

44. *salt*] strength or 'drive' (*O.E.D. sb.*[1] 3. b).

53. *guest Justice*] The Host must mean that Shallow, like Falstaff, is a paying guest in his inn, the Garter; he similarly calls Shallow 'Master guest' in l. 69.

Mounseur] 'Mounseer' was perhaps the common anglicized form, often used mockingly, but the Host may be allowed his own variation as F gives it.

53–4. *Mock-water*] The listed emendations will show that the phrase has caused trouble. What is clear is that the 'stale–urinal' image is being continued, with a quibble on 'make water'—one sign of the opposite of valour. Whether there is some further reference to the analysis of urine is uncertain.

59. *Jack-dog*] a mongrel, *or* a male dog, not castrated; see I. iv. 102 and note.

61. *clapper-claw*] drub, thrash, as in *Troil.*, v. iv. 1, where it is used derisively by Thersites.

tightly] soundly. Cf. I. iii. 75 and note.

Host. That is, he will make thee amends.

Caius. By gar, me do look he shall clapper-de-claw me, for, by gar, me vill have it.

Host. And I will provoke him to 't, or let him wag.

Caius. Me tank you for dat.

Host. And, moreover, bully—[*To the others, aside*] But first, Master guest, and Master Page, and eke Cavaliero Slender, go you through the town to Frogmore.

Page. Sir Hugh is there, is he?

Host. He is there. See what humour he is in; and I will bring the doctor about by the fields. Will it do well?

Shal. We will do it.

Page, Shal., and Slen. Adieu, good Master Doctor.

[*Exeunt Page, Shallow, and Slender.*]

Caius. By gar, me vill kill de priest, for he speak for a jack-an-ape to Anne Page.

Host. Let him die; sheathe thy impatience; throw cold water on thy choler; go about the fields with me through Frogmore, I will bring thee where Mistress Anne Page is, at a farm-house a-feasting; and thou shalt woo her. Cried game; said I well?

Caius. By gar, me dank you vor dat; by gar, I love you; and I shall procure-a you de good guest: de earl, de knight, de lords, de gentlemen, my patients.

68. S.D.] *As Capell; not in F.* 76. *Page, Shal., and Slen.*] *Malone; All. F; Page. Slen. Capell.* S.D.] *Rowe; not in F; Exit all but the Host and Doctor. Q.* 80–1. go . . . Frogmore] *F;* com go with me / Through the fields to *Frogmore*, and *Q.* 83. her. Cried game;] *F* (her: Cride-game,); hir cried game: *Q;* her Cride-game; *Rowe;* her. Cry'd game, *Pope;* her. Try'd Game; *Theobald;* her. Cry aim, *Warburton;* her. Cried I aim? *Halliwell, conj. Douce;* her. Cried, Game? *Keightley;* her. Cried game? *Sisson.*

66. *wag*] Normally means 'depart', as in I. iii. 6 and II. i. 219 and l. 90 below, but the Host probably means here something more like 'run for his life'.

71. *Frogmore*] Then a small village—on the opposite side of Windsor from where Caius has been sent for the duel.

80. *go*] i.e. if you go. Alternatively the F comma after 'Frogmore' may be replaced by a semi-colon.

83. *Cried game*] Q confirms the F reading; 'cry aim'—as in III. ii. 40—is therefore irrelevant. 'Cried game' must be a hunting cry, equivalent to 'the hunt is up': the game has been located and the chase is on. And Caius assumes that Evans is the 'game', not realizing that he himself is too. (By 1702 the phrase was apparently no longer current: Dennis omits it from his version of the play.)

Host. For the which I will be thy adversary toward Anne Page. Said I well?
Caius. By gar, 'tis good; vell said.
Host. Let us wag, then.
Caius. Come at my heels, Jack Rugby. *Exeunt*

87. *adversary*] Caius, again misled, thinks that the word means something like 'advocate', instead of the opposite. (Q confirms the reading.)

ACT III

SCENE I

Enter EVANS *and* SIMPLE.

Evans. I pray you now, good Master Slender's serving-man, and friend Simple by your name, which way have you looked for Master Caius, that calls himself Doctor of Physic?

Sim. Marry, sir, the Pitty-ward, the Park-ward, every way; Old Windsor way, and every way but the town way.

Evans. I most fehemently desire you you will also look that way.

Sim. I will, sir. [*Going aside.*]

Evans. Pless my soul, how full of chollors I am, and trempling of mind: I shall be glad if he have de-

ACT III

Scene I

ACT III SCENE I] *F;* Act III. Scene I. Frogmore *near* Windsor. *Pope; Act III. Scene I. Fields near* Frogmore. *Capell.* S.D.] *Q; Enter Euans, Simple, Page, Shallow, Slender, Host, Caius, Rugby. F.* 5. Pitty-ward] *Dyce;* pittie-ward *F1;* pitty-wary *F2;* pitty-way *conj. Mason;* city-ward *Capell;* petty-ward *Collier*[1]*;* pit-way *Collier*[2]*;* Petty-ward *Halliwell.* Park-ward] *F;* park-way *Collier*[2]. 10. S.D.] *This ed.; not in F; Retiring / Collier; Exit / Camb.*

5. *the Pitty-ward*] Emendations vary from 'Petty-ward' (meaning towards Windsor Little or 'Petty' Park) to 'Pity-ward' (meaning towards the pietà and so the church of the Blessed Virgin in Windsor) to 'pit-ward' (meaning towards the saw-pit mentioned in v. iii. 13). The first is the most plausible, but emendation may be unnecessary: F's 'pittie' may be an alternative spelling of 'petty' (from French *petit*) and may indicate the common pronunciation.

the Park-ward] in the direction of Windsor Great Park.

6. *Old Windsor way*] in the direction of Old Windsor, two or three miles from the Windsor of Shakespeare's day and ours.

11. *chollors*] i.e. choler or bile, which was supposed to cause quick temper (so Fluellen is 'valiant, / And, touch'd with choler, hot as gunpowder', *H5*, IV. vii. 187–8)—but Evans, as usual, seems to be confused and to mean 'sadness' or 'agitation'.

ceived me. How melancholies I am! I will knog his urinals about his knave's costard when I have good opportunities for the 'ork. Pless my soul!

[*Singing*] To shallow rivers, to whose falls
Melodious birds sings madrigals;
There will we make our peds of roses,
And a thousand fragrant posies.
To shallow—

Mercy on me! I have a great dispositions to cry.—

[*Singing*] Melodious birds sing madrigals—
Whenas I sat in Pabylon—
And a thousand vagram posies.
To shallow, etc.

Sim. Yonder he is coming, this way, Sir Hugh.

16, 22, 28. Singing] *As Pope* (*Sings, being afraid—in l. 16*)*; not in F.* 16–25, 28.] *Verse as Pope; italicized but continuous in F.* 26. *Sim.*] *F; Sim.* [*Coming forward*] *Collier; Enter Simple. Sim. Camb.*

13. *knog*] knock, rather than knot, but perhaps both.

14. *urinals*] Evans may have confused with the name of the glass vessel used in the medical examination of urine the associated word 'testicles'. His phrase is repeated at l. 81 (where Q has 'knock').

costard] The name of a large apple, applied in derision to the head (cf. the modern colloquial 'nut').

16–25.] To keep up his spirits, Evans sings snatches of Marlowe's famous lyric, 'Come live with me and be my love', which was probably sung to an old tune (perhaps the one later printed in William Corkine's *Second Book of Airs*, 1612). Although the words were not published until 1599, they presumably became popular, with the music, during Marlowe's lifetime; Chapman seems to take knowledge of them for granted when he has a variation on them in *The Blind Beggar of Alexandria* (1596), ix. 24ff. There are variant texts, but a standard version of the relevant lines (from stanzas 2 and 3) is: 'And we will sit upon the rocks, / Seeing the shepherds feed their flocks / By shallow rivers to whose falls / Melodious birds sing madrigals. // And I will make thee beds of roses, / And a thousand fragrant posies'. Mixed with Marlowe, however, is the first line of a metrical version of Psalm 137 (better known in the form 'By the rivers of Babylon, there we sat down, yea, we wept, when we remembered Zion'). The link in Evans's mind may be sadness (many madrigals were sad), the rivers, and even trees, for the next verse of the Psalm is 'We hanged our harps upon the willows in the midst thereof'. Peter J. Seng (*The Vocal Songs in the Plays of Shakespeare*, Cambridge, Mass., 1967, p. 164) asks whether Evans may not have sung Marlowe's words to the tune of the psalm, but in Q the words mixed up with Marlowe's lines are 'There dwelt a man in *Babylon*'—words from an old ballad that is similarly begun by Sir Toby in *Tw.N.*, II. iii. 84. The Q reporter remembered both that the parson was giving himself away by singing an 'indelicate' love lyric and that the lyric was confused with another song, but he apparently had no recollection of any psalm tune.

26. *he*] i.e., presumably, Caius

Evans. He's welcome.—
[*Singing*] To shallow rivers, to whose falls—
Heaven prosper the right!—What weapons is he?

Sim. No weapons, sir. There comes my master, Master Shallow, and another gentleman; from Frogmore, over the stile, this way.

Evans. Pray you, give me my gown, or else keep it in your arms.

Enter PAGE, SHALLOW, *and* SLENDER.

Shal. How now, Master Parson? Good morrow, good Sir Hugh. Keep a gamester from the dice, and a good student from his book, and it is wonderful.

Slen. Ah, sweet Anne Page!

Page. Save you, good Sir Hugh.

Evans. Pless you from His mercy sake, all of you.

Shal. What, the sword and the word? Do you study them both, Master Parson?

Page. And youthful still, in your doublet and hose this raw rheumatic day?

Evans. There is reasons and causes for it.

Page. We are come to you to do a good office, Master Parson.

Evans. Fery well: what is it?

Page. Yonder is a most reverend gentleman, who, belike

34. S.D.] *Q; not in F1; Enter All. F2.* 38, 66, 105.] *Marked 'Aside' Camb.* 41–2.] *Prose as Pope;* What? . . . Word? / Doe . . . *F.* 49. who, belike] *F* (who (belike)).

coming with Rugby and the Host from 'the fields' on the roundabout way to Frogmore, as planned in II. iii. 73–4 and 80–1, although the first to enter are Page, Shallow, and Slender, coming from 'the town' and Frogmore (II. iii. 70–1).

37. *book*] Apparently Evans is reading a book as he waits, and Shallow (see l. 41 and note) assumes that it is the Bible; but conceivably, as *New Cambridge* suggests, it is the book from which Evans was quoting or singing the Marlowe. Shallow is adapting some such proverb as Tilley's F351, 'Keep flax from fire and youth from gaming'.

40. *from His mercy sake*] Evans is probably thinking of Psalms 6:4 ('Oh save me for thy mercies' sake') but again has his constructions mixed. (Q reads 'God plesse you all from his mercies sake' and perhaps Shakespeare did write 'God . . .', but the phrase is clear enough without the additional word.)

41. *the word*] Shallow means 'the word of God' (see note on l. 37) but specific allusion to Ephesians 6:17 seems improbable.

having received wrong by some person, is at most odds with his own gravity and patience that ever you saw.

Shal. I have lived fourscore years and upward; I never heard a man of his place, gravity, and learning so wide of his own respect.

Evans. What is he?

Page. I think you know him: Master Doctor Caius, the renowned French physician.

Evans. Got's will and His passion of my heart, I had as lief you would tell me of a mess of porridge.

Page. Why?

Evans. He has no more knowledge in Hibocrates and Galen, and he is a knave besides: a cowardly knave as you would desires to be acquainted withal.

Page. I warrant you, he's the man should fight with him.

Slen. O sweet Anne Page!

Shal. It appears so by his weapons. Keep them asunder; here comes Doctor Caius.

Enter HOST, CAIUS [*and* RUGBY].

Page. Nay, good Master Parson, keep in your weapon.

Shal. So do you, good Master Doctor.

Host. Disarm them, and let them question; let them keep their limbs whole, and hack our English.

59. His passion] *F;* his—Passion *Staunton.* 68. S.D.] *Rowe (after l. 66); not in F1; Enter Doctor and the Host, they offer to fight. Q (after l. 66); Enter Caius. F2 (after l. 66).* 71–2.] *F; Host.* Disarme, let them question. / *Shal.* Let them keep their limbs hole, and hack our English. *Q.*

53. *fourscore*] Some commentators gravely point out that this would make Shallow some twenty years older than he 'was' in *2H4*—*if* the figure is meant to be exact.

55. *wide of his own respect*] Generally explained as 'far from' or even 'indifferent to' his own 'reputation'—but may rather mean 'different from his normal, true, quality or nature'.

60. *mess of porridge*] Evans may have meant to refer to the 'mess (dish) of pottage' for which, as the story is told in the Geneva Bible, Esau sold his birthright (in any case the word 'porridge' is an altered form of 'pottage'). Sisson, *N.R.*, p. 11, saw in F's 'porredge' a dialectal form—but Ralph Crane uses the spelling elsewhere and it probably comes from his transcript here.

62. *Hibocrates*] Hippocrates, the most famous physician of ancient Greece.

65. *he's . . . him*] i.e. Evans is the man whom Caius expects to fight.

71. *question*] argue.

Caius. I pray you let-a me speak a word with your ear. Verefore vill you not meet-a me?

Evans. [*Aside to Caius*] Pray you use your patience. [*Aloud*] In good time.

Caius. By gar, you are de coward; de Jack dog; John ape.

Evans. [*Aside to Caius*] Pray you let us not be laughing-stocks to other men's humours; I desire you in friendship, and I will one way or other make you amends. [*Aloud*] I will knog your urinal about your knave's cogscomb.

Caius. *Diable*! Jack Rugby, mine host de Jarteer, have I not stay for him to kill him? Have I not, at de place I did appoint?

Evans. As I am a Christians soul, now, look you, this is the place appointed. I'll be judgement by mine host of the Garter.

Host. Peace, I say, Gallia and Gaul, French and Welsh, soul-curer and body-curer.

Caius. Ay, dat is very good, excellant.

Host. Peace, I say; hear mine host of the Garter. Am I politic? Am I subtle? Am I a Machiavel? Shall I lose my doctor? No, he gives me the potions and the motions. Shall I lose my parson? My priest? My Sir Hugh? No, he gives me the proverbs and

75. *Aside to Caius*] *Camb.; not in F.* 75–6. patience. In] *Johnson;* patience in *F.* 76. *Aloud*] *Bowers; not in F.* 78, 81. S.D.] *Staunton; not in F.* 81. urinal] *F;* vrinalls *Q.* 82. cogscomb] *F;* cockcomes, for missing your meetings and appointments *Q;* cogs-comb, for missing your meetings and appointments *Pope.* 89. Gallia and Gaul] *F;* gawle and gawlia *Q; Gallia* and *Wallia Hanmer;* Gwallia and Gaul *Rann, conj. Farmer;* Gallia and Guallia *Collier.* 92–3. Peace . . . Shall] *Prose as Pope;* Peace, . . . Garter, / Am . . . Machiuell? / Shall *F.* 93. a Machiavel] *F* (a Machiuell), *Rowe*[3]*;* Matchauil *Q.*

77. *Jack dog; John ape*] See notes on I. iv. 102 and II. iii. 29, 59.

81–2.] See ll. 13–14 and notes. 'Cogscomb' is Evans's form of 'cockscomb', another colloquial term for the head. As the collations indicate, some editors add here Q's 'for missing your meetings and appointments'—which only spells out the obvious.

89. *Gallia and Gaul*] Wales (French *Galles*) and France.

91. *excellant*] The F spelling, used only here, probably means that Caius uses the French pronunciation.

93. *Machiavel*] i.e. perfect intriguer. Machiavelli, as author of *The Prince*, was understood, or misunderstood, by the Elizabethans to be advocating the doctrine of the end justifying the means (the so-called 'policy': hence the Host's 'Am I politic?'). The Machiavel, or Machiavillian (the pun was conscious), became a stock character in Elizabethan drama.

the no-verbs. Give me thy hand, terrestrial, so; give me thy hand, celestial, so. Boys of art, I have deceived you both: I have directed you to wrong places; your hearts are mighty, your skins are whole, and let burnt sack be the issue. Come, lay their swords to pawn. Follow me, lads of peace; follow, follow, follow. *Exit.*

Shal. Trust me, a mad host. Follow, gentlemen, follow.

Slen. O sweet Anne Page! [*Exeunt Shallow, Slender, and Page.*]

Caius. Ha, do I perceive dat? Have you make-a de sot of us, ha, ha?

Evans. This is well; he has made us his vlouting-stog. I desire you that we may be friends; and let us knog our prains together to be revenge on this same scall, scurvy, cogging companion, the host of the Garter.

Caius. By gar, with all my heart. He promise to bring me where is Anne Page; by gar, he deceive me too.

97–8. Give . . . Boys] *As Theobald;* Giue me thy hand (Celestiall) so: Boyes *F;* Giue me thy hand terestiall, / So giue me thy hand celestiall: / So boyes *Q.* 102. lads] *Q;* Lad *F.* 103. *Exit*] *Q; not in F.* 105. S.D.] *This ed.; not in F; Ex.* Shal. Slen. Page *and* Host. *Rowe; Exeunt* Host, Page, *&c. Capell.*

97. *no-verbs*] i.e. tells me, in his capacity as parson, what I must not do.

Give . . . terrestrial] The Q phrase must be included here; the bad text retains what the scribe or compositor of F dropped by accident. The Q reporter could hardly have invented so neat a phrase, and the F 'Celestiall' (addressed to Parson Evans) has no point without the balance of 'terrestrial' (addressed to Caius in the parallel phrase). The antithesis of 'body-curer' and 'soul-curer' of l. 90 is continued.

98. *art*] learning.

101. *burnt sack*] See II. i. 203–4 and note.

issue] outcome, the *only* result.

102. *to pawn*] i.e. because they will not be needed for fighting.

102–3. *Follow . . . follow*] Hart conjectures that 'follow, follow, follow' was the cry used by constables raising the 'hue and cry'.

106. *sot*] fool, idiot.

108. *vlouting-stog*] i.e. flouting-stock, something or somebody to be mocked (cf. 'laughing-stock'). Evans uses the word again to the Host at IV. v. 75—where he is taking the vengeance he 'adumbrates' here.

110. *knog*] knock (in the sense of 'join').

111. *scall*] Another form of 'scald': affected with the scall, a scabby disease of the scalp, and so used, as is 'scurvy' (and 'lousy') to mean 'contemptible'.

cogging] cheating, deceitful (cf. III. iii. 42 and *Oth.*, IV. ii. 132).

companion] Used contemptuously, as often in Shakespeare: rogue, villain.

Evans. Well, I will smite his noddles. Pray you follow. [*Exeunt.*]

SCENE II

[*Enter*] MISTRESS PAGE [*following*] ROBIN.

Mrs. Page. Nay, keep your way, little gallant; you were wont to be a follower, but now you are a leader. Whether had you rather lead mine eyes, or eye your master's heels?

Rob. I had rather, forsooth, go before you like a man than follow him like a dwarf.

Mrs. Page. O, you are a flattering boy: now I see you'll be a courtier.

[*Enter* FORD.]

Ford. Well met, Mistress Page. Whither go you?

Mrs. Page. Truly, sir, to see your wife. Is she at home?

Ford. Ay, and as idle as she may hang together, for want of company. I think, if your husbands were dead, you two would marry.

Mrs. Page. Be sure of that—two other husbands.

Ford. Where had you this pretty weathercock?

116. S.D.] *Pope; not in F; Exit omnes Q.*

Scene II

SCENE II] *F;* Scene IV. *The Street. Pope;* Scene, *The Street, in* Windsor. *Theobald.* S.D.] *This ed.; Mist. Page, Robin, Ford, Page, Shallow, Slender, Host, Euans, Caius. F; Enter Mistress* Page *and* Robin. *Rowe.* 8. S.D.] *Rowe; not in F.* 12. company] *F;* your company *Collier*[2].

116. *noddles*] 'Noddle' is another colloquialism for 'head', but the plural is Evans's own.

Scene II

1. *keep your way*] keep going, go on (as in *Ado*, I. i. 144).

11. *may hang together*] can manage to be while still surviving (a common saying). Schmidt compares *Wint.*, II. ii. 21–3, where, to Paulina's question 'How fares our gracious lady?', Emilia replies 'As well as one so great and so forlorn / May hold together'.

15. *weathercock*] The allusion is probably to the feathers Robin wears in his cap: weathercocks often had a pennon (cf. *LLL.*, IV. i. 96–7). Hart and some other editors see an allusion to gaudy dress and compare 'Jack-a-lent' in III. iii. 23.

Mrs. Page. I cannot tell what the dickens his name is my husband had him of.—What do you call your knight's name, sirrah?

Rob. Sir John Falstaff.

Ford. Sir John Falstaff?

Mrs. Page. He, he; I can never hit on's name. There is such a league between my goodman and he! Is your wife at home indeed?

Ford. Indeed she is.

Mrs. Page. By your leave, sir; I am sick till I see her.

[*Exeunt Mistress Page and Robin.*]

Ford. Has Page any brains? Hath he any eyes? Hath he any thinking? Sure, they sleep: he hath no use of them. Why, this boy will carry a letter twenty mile as easy as a cannon will shoot point-blank twelve score. He pieces out his wife's inclination; he gives her folly motion and advantage: and now she's going to my wife, and Falstaff's boy with her. A man may hear this shower sing in the wind. And Falstaff's boy with her! Good plots! They are laid; and our revolted wives share damnation together. Well, I will take him, then torture my wife, pluck the

22. goodman] *F1; good man F4.* 25. S.D.] *Rowe; not in F.*

16. *what the dickens*] An interesting example of a phrase that has not altered its colloquial status in nearly four hundred years. The derivation is uncertain.

18. *sirrah*] The common form of address to a boy not old enough to be called 'Master'.

22. *league*] i.e. of friendship. Intriguing is not implied.

goodman] husband.

29–30. *point-blank twelve score*] with direct aim in a horizontal line at a distance of twelve score (240) yards or, perhaps, paces—as contrasted with shooting an *arrow* accurately at this distance, the usual phrase for an exceptional feat (as in *2H4*, III. ii. 51–2).

30. *pieces out*] actually increases the scope of ('piece' in Shakespeare often means 'enlarge' or 'add to'; cf., particularly, *Ant.*, I. v. 44–6).

31. *folly*] wantonness—as in II. ii. 234 and, e.g., *Lucr.*, 556.

motion] instigation, or provocation (*O.E.D. sb.* 9).

advantage] favourable opportunity (*O.E.D. sb.* 4, 5).

32–3. *A man . . . wind*] i.e. trouble may be anticipated, as a storm may sometimes be heard coming before it is felt.

35. *revolted*] i.e. revolted from virtue, faithless, as in *Troil.*, V. ii. 186. The exact meaning is perhaps clearest from the Friar's philosophizing, *Rom.*, II. iii. 19–20: 'Nor aught so good but strain'd from that fair use / Revolts from true birth, stumbling on abuse'.

36. *torture*] Perhaps only in the more general sense of 'torment' (*O.E.D. v.* 2).

borrowed veil of modesty from the so-seeming Mistress Page, divulge Page himself for a secure and wilful Actæon; and to these violent proceedings all my neighbours shall cry aim. [*Clock strikes.*] The clock gives me my cue, and my assurance bids me search: there I shall find Falstaff. I shall be rather praised for this than mocked, for it is as positive as the earth is firm that Falstaff is there. I will go.

Enter PAGE, SHALLOW, SLENDER, HOST, EVANS, CAIUS [*and* RUGBY].

Shal., Page, etc. Well met, Master Ford.

Ford. [*Aside*] Trust me, a good knot.—[*Aloud*] I have good cheer at home, and I pray you all go with me.

Shal. I must excuse myself, Master Ford.

Slen. And so must I, sir: we have appointed to dine with Mistress Anne, and I would not break with her for more money than I'll speak of.

Shal. We have lingered about a match between Anne Page and my cousin Slender, and this day we shall have our answer.

Slen. I hope I have your good will, father Page.

Page. You have, Master Slender, I stand wholly for you.

40. S.D.] *As Capell* (*Clock heard*)*; not in F.* 41. cue] *F* (Qu), *Rowe*[3]. 44. *Enter . . . Caius*] *As Q; not in F.* *and Rugby*] *Malone; not in F or Q.* 46. *Aside*] *This ed.; not in F.* *Aloud*] *This ed.; not in F.* 49–51.] *Prose as Pope;* And . . . Sir, / We . . . *Anne,* / And . . . mony / Then . . . of. *F.*

38. *divulge*] reveal, proclaim openly (*O.E.D. v.* 1. b, 2).

secure] foolishly confident (as in II. ii. 233).

39. *Actæon*] For Actæon as prototype of the cuckold, see note on II. i. 115.

40. *cry aim*] applaud the accuracy of my aim (the phrase, originally used by the spectator applauding the archer's skill, had much the same force as the modern 'well played!' or even 'hear, hear!').

46. *knot*] IV. ii. 108 and several other Shakespearian uses (particularly *Tim.*, III. vi. 99, 'You knot of mouth-friends!') suggest that the word was often used pejoratively or ironically, like the modern 'gang'. If it is so used here, Page's first words must be an 'aside'.

50. *break with her*] break my word to her, or even break faith with her: cf. *Cor.*, IV. vi. 47–8.

52. *lingered about*] Unless it means 'hankered after' (*O.E.D.* 'linger' *v.* 8), probably means, in effect, 'considered as possible, without reaching any conclusion', 'left open the possibility of'; the closest parallel would be *1H6*, IV. iv. 19, where it is said that Talbot, 'in advantage lingering, looks for rescue'.

56. *stand . . . for*] support.

But my wife, Master Doctor, is for you altogether.

Caius. Ay, be-gar, and de maid is love-a me: my nursh-a Quickly tell me so mush.

Host. What say you to young Master Fenton? He capers, he dances, he has eyes of youth; he writes verses, he speaks holiday, he smells April and May. He will carry 't, he will carry 't; 'tis in his buttons he will carry 't.

Page. Not by my consent, I promise you. The gentleman is of no having: he kept company with the wild Prince and Poins. He is of too high a region; he knows too much. No, he shall not knit a knot in his fortunes with the finger of my substance; if he take her, let him take her simply: the wealth I have waits on my consent, and my consent goes not that way.

63. buttons he] *This ed.*; buttons, he *F*; betmes he *Q*; buttons; he *Steevens*; talons —he *conj. New Camb.*; fortunes, he *Sisson*.

58. *nursh-a*] Presumably, housekeeper; cf. I. ii. 3–4 and note.

60. *capers*] is able to make extravagant leaps when dancing—a sign, in the eyes of the Host, of masculinity and joy in living.

62. *speaks holiday*] speaks with the gaiety appropriate to a holiday; cf. from *AYL*. 'holiday foolery', I. iii. 14, and Rosalind's 'Come, woo me, woo me, for now I am in a holiday humour and like enough to consent', IV. i. 68–70.

smells April and May] has all the freshness of spring.

63. *carry 't*] succeed, prevail (a common expression, sometimes in the fuller form 'carry it away'; not unlike the modern 'carry it off'); cf. I. i. 217.

'tis in his buttons he] It is perhaps defence of a kind for the F text that the May-buttons image sequence is found also in *The Two Noble Kinsmen*, III. i, 'O Queene Emilia, / Fresher then May, sweeter / Then hir gold Buttons on the bowes . . .' (noted in another context by Kenneth Muir, in *Shakespeare Survey* 11, 52–3)—where 'buttons' means buds or blossoms. Q's 'he wil cary it, he will carit, / Tis in his betmes he will carite' is no help, except for the evidence that the phrase was spoken on the stage without a pause after 'buttons' or 'betmes' and understood to mean 'it is obvious (in some way) that he will win'. Perhaps 'buttons' does mean 'buds' and the image is of the flower that is yet to open but whose colour and character are already determined; more probably the phrase is parallel to 'it is written in his face that . . .'.

66. *having*] substance, means.

66–7. *he kept . . . Poins*] For this obvious attempt to make a link with the Henry IV plays, see Introduction, p. lii, and cf. III. iv. 8, and note on V. v. 103 S.D.

67. *region*] i.e. social sphere.

68–9. *shall . . . substance*] shall not use my wealth to save his own fortunes, as one ties a knot in a rope or a piece of string to prevent its fraying further. It is just possible that the phrase was suggested by the parallelism of the proverb 'he has tied a knot with his tongue that he can't untie with all his teeth' (Tilley K167), as Hart thought.

70. *simply*] as she is, without a dowry.

Ford. I beseech you heartily, some of you go home with me to dinner; besides your cheer, you shall have sport: I will show you a monster. Master Doctor, you shall go; so shall you, Master Page, and you, Sir Hugh.

Shal. Well, fare you well: we shall have the freer wooing at Master Page's. *Exeunt Shallow and Slender.*

Caius. Go home, John Rugby; I come anon. [*Exit Rugby.*]

Host. Farewell, my hearts; I will to my honest knight Falstaff, and drink canary with him. *Exit.*

Ford. [*Aside*] I think I shall drink in pipe-wine first with him; I'll make him dance.—Will you go, gentles?

All. Have with you to see this monster. *Exeunt.*

SCENE III

Enter MISTRESS FORD *and* MISTRESS PAGE.

Mrs. Ford. What, John! What, Robert!

Mrs. Page. Quickly, quickly, is the buck-basket—

77–8.] *Prose as Pope;* Well, . . . well: / We . . . *F.* 78. S.D.] *Q; not in F.* 79. *Exit Rugby*] *Capell; not in F.* 81. *Exit*] *Q; not in F.* 82. *Aside*] *Johnson; not in F.*

Scene III

SCENE III] *F;* Scene VII. *Ford's* House. *Pope.* S.D.] *Capell; Enter M. Ford, M. Page, Seruants, Robin, Falstaffe, Ford, Page, Caius, Euans. F; Enter Mistresse Ford, with two of her men, and a great buck basket. Q; Enter Mistress* Ford, *Mistress* Page, *and Servants with a Basket. Rowe.*

74. *show you a monster*] Hart has a good note on the popularity of monsters at fairs etc., and well compares Trinculo's wish that he could display Caliban in England: 'Not a holiday fool there but would give a piece of silver: there would this monster make a man; any strange beast there makes a man' (*Tp.*, II. ii. 30–3).

81. *canary*] wine from the Canaries (which was very popular)—but 'canary' was also the name of a dance; hence Ford's pun in ll. 82–3.

82. *drink in*] drink, or drink up (with relish).

pipe-wine] wine from the 'pipe' or cask—but there is a pun on 'pipe' in the sense of the musical instrument, played for the 'dance' (l. 83).

84. *Have with you*] we are coming.

Scene III

2. *buck-basket*] clothes-basket, basket for dirty clothes. 'Bucking' was the process of washing in lye (as a bleach) but also (as early as the fourteenth century) had the wider meaning of washing or soaking clothes (*O.E.D.* 'buck' *v.*[1] 1); 'buck', perhaps originally the tub in which the clothes soaked in

Mrs. Ford. I warrant. What, Robin, I say!

[*Enter* JOHN *and* ROBERT *with a basket.*]

Mrs. Page. Come, come, come.

Mrs. Ford. Here, set it down.

Mrs. Page. Give your men the charge; we must be brief.

Mrs. Ford. Marry, as I told you before, John and Robert, be ready here hard by in the brew-house, and when I suddenly call you, come forth, and, without any pause or staggering, take this basket on your shoulders. That done, trudge with it in all haste, and carry it among the whitsters in Datchet Mead, and there empty it in the muddy ditch close by the Thames side.

Mrs. Page. You will do it?

Mrs. Ford. I ha' told them over and over; they lack no direction.—Be gone, and come when you are called.

[*Exeunt John and Robert.*]

Mrs. Page. Here comes little Robin.

[*Enter* ROBIN.]

Mrs. Ford. How now, my eyas-musket, what news with you?

3. Robin] *F;* Robert *Bowers.* S.D.] *This ed.; not in F; Enter Servants with a basket Capell.* 12. Datchet Mead] *As Rowe; Dotchet* Mead *F1; Dutchet-*Mead *F4.* 17. *Exeunt John and Robert*] *As Johnson; not in F; Exit Seruant Q.* 18. *Enter Robin*] *Rowe; not in F.*

the lye, was later used of the clothes waiting to be so treated or washed ('buck' *sb.*[3] 3). Washing clothes in rivers is still, of course, common, particularly in the East.

3. *I warrant*] I'm sure of it.

Robin] Probably not the boy given to Page and his wife by Falstaff (although he enters at l. 18) but the servant of the Fords who is called 'Robert' in l. 1.

8. *brew-house*] outhouse used for brewing liquor, privately.

10. *staggering*] wavering, hesitating (*O.E.D.* 'stagger' *v.* 1. 2—and cf. *Meas.*, I. ii. 169).

12. *whitsters*] professional bleachers. In Q, in a badly reported version of this scene, Mistress Ford tells the servants to explain, if they are asked, that they are carrying the basket 'to the Launderers'.

Datchet Mead] the 'mead' or meadow between Windsor Little Park and the Thames.

19. *eyas-musket*] fledgling sparrow-hawk. The 'musket' was the male of the sparrow-hawk; 'eyas' (originally 'nyas') a young hawk taken from the nest or one incompletely trained. Cf. the famous reference to the children's acting companies as 'little eyases' in

Rob. My master, Sir John, is come in at your back door, Mistress Ford, and requests your company.

Mrs. Page. You little Jack-a-Lent, have you been true to us?

Rob. Ay, I'll be sworn. My master knows not of your being here, and hath threatened to put me into everlasting liberty if I tell you of it; for he swears he'll turn me away.

Mrs. Page. Thou'rt a good boy: this secrecy of thine shall be a tailor to thee, and shall make thee a new doublet and hose.—I'll go hide me.

Mrs. Ford. Do so.—Go tell thy master I am alone. [*Exit Robin.*] Mistress Page, remember you your cue.

Mrs. Page. I warrant thee; if I do not act it, hiss me.

Mrs. Ford. Go to, then: we'll use this unwholesome humidity, this gross watery pumpion; we'll teach him to know turtles from jays. [*Exit Mistress Page.*]

Enter FALSTAFF.

Fal. Have I caught thee, my heavenly jewel? Why, now let me die, for I have lived long enough: this is the period of my ambition. O this blessed hour!

32–3. *Exit Robin*] *Rowe (after l. 33); not in F.* 33. cue] *F (Qu), Rowe*[3]. 37. *Exit Mistress Page*] *Rowe (after l. 34); not in F.* *Enter Falstaff*] *Q; not in F.* 38. thee] *F; not in Q.*

competition with adults, *Ham.*, II. ii. 355.

23. *Jack-a-lent*] brightly dressed puppet, like the later 'Guy', set up by children in Lent as a butt at which to throw stones. Here the emphasis is probably on the bright colours of the dress (though *O.E.D.* takes it to be on the insignificance); at v. v. 128 it is on the function of the puppet as the equivalent of a coconut shy.

36. *pumpion*] Or 'pompion', the earlier form of the now commoner word 'pumpkin'.

37. *turtles from jays*] turtle-doves (proverbial for their faithfulness—cf. II. i. 78) from jays (notorious for their bright plumage—and the term was thus applied to 'made-up' women and even, as here, to immoral women or prostitutes).

38. *Have . . . jewel?*] The words are a quotation, incongruous in Falstaff's mouth, from a song in Sir Philip Sidney's romantic sonnet-sequence *Astrophel and Stella*. 'Thee' is not in the original (and Q omits it, as do some editors) but, as Hart well says, 'when a quotation is made in conversation, it is commonly altered to suit circumstances'. It is hardly likely that Falstaff burst into song with this line, although a musical setting of the Sidney poem has been found and printed by John P. Cutts (*Shakespeare Quarterly*, XI, 1960, 89–92).

40. *period*] conclusion; aim and end.

Mrs. Ford. O sweet Sir John!

Fal. Mistress Ford, I cannot cog, I cannot prate, Mistress Ford. Now shall I sin in my wish: I would thy husband were dead; I'll speak it before the best lord: I would make thee my lady.

Mrs. Ford. I your lady, Sir John? Alas, I should be a pitiful lady.

Fal. Let the court of France show me such another. I see how thine eye would emulate the diamond: thou hast the right arched beauty of the brow that becomes the ship-tire, the tire-valiant, or any tire of Venetian admittance.

Mrs. Ford. A plain kerchief, Sir John: my brows become nothing else, nor that well neither.

Fal. Thou art a tyrant to say so; thou wouldst make an absolute courtier, and the firm fixture of thy foot would give an excellent motion to thy gait in a semicircled farthingale. I see what thou wert if Fortune

51. tire-valiant] *F* (Tyre-valiant); tire vellet *Q;* tire-volant *conj. Steevens;* tire-velvet *conj. Tollet.* 53–4.] *Prose as Pope;* A . . . *Iohn*: / My . . . neither. *F.* 55. Thou . . . tyrant] *F;* By the Lord thou art a traitor *Q.* 58–9. I . . . friend] *This ed.;* I see what thou wert if Fortune thy foe, were not Nature thy friend *F1;* I see what thou wert if Fortune thy foe were not, Nature thy friend *F2;* I see what thou wert, if fortune thy foe were not, nature is thy friend *Pope;* I see what thou wert, if fortune thy foe, were but nature thy friend *conj. Staunton;* I see what thou wert, if Fortune thy foe were, not Nature, thy friend *Alexander.*

42. *cog*] Either 'lie' (cf. III. i. 111) or 'fawn', 'wheedle' (*O.E.D.* v.[3] 5).

51. *ship-tire*] elaborate head-dress in the form of a ship (or, perhaps, the sails of one). Falstaff is not making this up: such head-dresses were worn.

tire-valiant] No other use of this word has been recorded; the meaning is generally assumed to be 'fanciful' or 'extreme' head-dress, taking 'valiant' as an intensive adjective. In view of the possible reference to sails in 'ship-tire', is there perhaps a kind of concealed pun on 'valiant'–'gallant'–'top-gallant'?

51–2. *of Venetian admittance*] acceptable, or in fashion, in Venice. Italian fashions were eagerly imitated and were often elaborate.

53. *become*] suit.

55. *tyrant*] *New Cambridge* is surely right in rejecting Q's 'traitor' on the ground that there is a pun on 'tire'.

56. *absolute*] consummate, perfect.

fixture] placing (an apparently rare use, for which no parallel has been found; Falstaff is speaking in would-be formal language).

57–8. *semicircled farthingale*] The farthingale, or petticoat stretched over whalebone hoops, could take many different shapes; the semicircular one Falstaff is thinking of projected in a semicircle at the back but was flat at the front.

58–9. *I see . . . friend*] Staunton was perhaps the first editor to understand these words but, paradoxically, he (thy foe) were—not Nature—thy friend. Come, thou canst not hide it.

Mrs. Ford. Believe me, there's no such thing in me.

Fal. What made me love thee? Let that persuade thee there's something extraordinary in thee. Come, I cannot cog and say thou art this and that, like a many of these lisping hawthorn-buds that come like women in men's apparel, and smell like Bucklersbury in simple time; I cannot; but I love thee, none but thee; and thou deserv'st it.

Mrs. Ford. Do not betray me, sir. I fear you love Mistress Page.

Fal. Thou mightst as well say I love to walk by the Counter-gate, which is as hateful to me as the reek of a lime-kill.

62–3. thee there's] *As Q1* (thee / Ther's); thee. Ther's *F;* thee: ther's *Q3;* thee, there's *Theobald*[2]. 73. lime-kill] *F, Q;* lime-kiln *Rowe.*

wished to emend them; Peter Alexander showed how they could be retained and be punctuated satisfactorily. (See *Shakespeare Survey*, 5, 3.) Falstaff is flattering Mistress Ford: Nature, he insists, *is* her friend (she is beautiful) but Fortune is as yet her foe (she is a citizen's wife, not Falstaff's 'Lady'), and he can imagine how distinguished she would be if she had Fortune as well as Nature on her side. (Staunton's paraphrase is: 'I see what you would be if Fortune were as bountiful to you as Nature has been'.) 'Fortune (thy foe)' would be recognized immediately by an Elizabethan audience as a variation on 'Fortune my foe', the name of a popular tune to which many different sets of words were wr'tten. There is a similar allusion in *H5*, III. vi. 41.

62–3. *thee there's*] F's punctuation is possible but Q's makes rather better sense and is adopted, from a fairly well reported speech, as giving what was presumably spoken on the stage.

65. *hawthorn-buds*] The budding of the hawthorn is associated with the coming of spring and fine weather for the shepherd in *MND.*, I. i. 185; and in *3H6*, II. v. 42–3, the king thinks of the hawthorn bush as giving 'sweeter shade / To shepherds looking on their silly sheep' than canopies give to worried kings. Perhaps, then, Falstaff chooses the term as a contemptuous description of perfumed wooers not only because of the spring associations (cf. the Host's description of Fenton in III. ii. 60–2) but also because of a latent connection with the 'complaining' amorous shepherds of pastoral literature.

66–7. *Bucklersbury*] The street in the City of London where, *inter alia*, herbs were sold.

67. *simple time*] summer, when the simples or herbs used for medicinal purposes (cf. I. iv. 58 and note) were collected and sold.

71–2. *the Counter-gate*] the gate of the Counter, or prison for debtors, in the City, of which a Falstaff may be thought to have had special fear. Elizabethan prisons were notorious also for the foul stench that came from them; the Counter is therefore in Falstaff's mind the very opposite of the

Mrs. Ford. Well, heaven knows how I love you, and you shall one day find it.

Fal. Keep in that mind: I'll deserve it.

Mrs. Ford. Nay, I must tell you, so you do; or else I could not be in that mind.

[*Enter* ROBIN.]

Rob. Mistress Ford, Mistress Ford! Here's Mistress Page at the door, sweating and blowing, and looking wildly, and would needs speak with you presently.

Fal. She shall not see me: I will ensconce me behind the arras.

Mrs. Ford. Pray you do so; she's a very tattling woman.

Falstaff hides behind the arras.

[*Enter* MISTRESS PAGE.]

What's the matter? How now?

Mrs. Page. O Mistress Ford, what have you done? You're shamed, you're overthrown, you're undone for ever!

Mrs. Ford. What's the matter, good Mistress Page?

Mrs. Page. O well-a-day, Mistress Ford, having an honest man to your husband, to give him such cause of suspicion!

Mrs. Ford. What cause of suspicion?

Mrs. Page. What cause of suspicion? Out upon you: how am I mistook in you!

74–5. *Prose as F3;* Well . . . you, / And . . . *F1.* 77–8.] *Prose as F3;* Nay . . . doe; / Or . . . *F1.* 78. *Enter Robin*] *As Capell; not in F.* 79. *Rob.*] *F1; Within. / Rob. F2.* 84. *Falstaff . . . arras*] *As Q; not in F;* Falstaff *hides himself Theobald.* *Enter Mistress Page*] *F2; not in F1; Enter Mistress* Page, *and* Robin *Malone.* 86–8.] *Prose as F3;* O . . . done? / You'r sham'd, y'are ouerthrowne, y'are vndone for euer. *F.*

nearby Bucklersbury, fragrant with sweet-smelling herbs.

73. *lime-kill*] The now obsolete dialectal form 'kill' (for 'kiln') is confirmed by Q.

81. *presently*] immediately.

82. *ensconce*] hide (as in II. ii. 24).

83. *arras*] curtain of woven tapestry, hung in front of walls. It does not necessarily follow from the action here that there was an arras on the Elizabethan stage, in front of the (hypothetical) inner stage or against the rear wall; if there were no arras, a pillar or any other available hiding-place would have served.

Mrs. Ford. Why, alas, what's the matter?

Mrs. Page. Your husband's coming hither, woman, with all the officers in Windsor, to search for a gentleman that he says is here now in the house, by your consent, to take an ill advantage of his absence. You are undone.

Mrs. Ford. 'Tis not so, I hope.

Mrs. Page. Pray heaven it be not so, that you have such a man here—but 'tis most certain your husband's coming, with half Windsor at his heels, to search for such a one, I come before to tell you. If you know yourself clear, why, I am glad of it; but if you have a friend here, convey, convey him out. Be not amazed, call all your senses to you, defend your reputation, or bid farewell to your good life for ever.

Mrs. Ford. What shall I do? There is a gentleman, my dear friend; and I fear not mine own shame so much as his peril. I had rather than a thousand pound he were out of the house.

Mrs. Page. For shame, never stand 'you had rather' and 'you had rather': your husband's here at hand! Bethink you of some conveyance; in the house you cannot hide him. O, how have you deceived me! Look, here is a basket; if he be of any reasonable stature, he may creep in here; and throw foul linen upon him, as if it were going to bucking; or—it is whiting-time—send him by your two men to Datchet Mead.

Mrs. Ford. He's too big to go in there. What shall I do?

Fal. [*Coming forward*] Let me see 't, let me see 't, O, let me see 't! I'll in, I'll in. Follow your friend's counsel; I'll in.

Mrs. Page. What, Sir John Falstaff?—Are these your letters, knight?

125. *Coming forward*] *Camb.; not in F; Enter* Falstaff *Rowe; starting from his Concealment Capell.* 128–9. —Are . . . knight?] *F* (Are . . . Knight?); (*Aside.*) Fie sir *Iohn* is this your loue? Go too. *Q*; [*in his ear*] Are . . . knight? *New Camb.*

107. *clear*] innocent.

109. *amazed*] bewildered.

115. *stand*] Perhaps 'rely on' (cf. II. i. 214); perhaps 'waste time over'.

122. *whiting-time*] time for bleaching clothes; cf. 'whitsters' in l. 12.

Fal. I love thee; help me away. Let me creep in here. I'll never—

Gets into the basket; they cover him with 'foul linen'.

Mrs. Page. Help to cover your master, boy.—Call your men, Mistress Ford.—You dissembling knight!

Mrs. Ford. What, John! Robert! John!

[*Enter* JOHN *and* ROBERT.]

Go take up these clothes here quickly. Where's the cowl-staff? Look, how you drumble! Carry them to the laundress in Datchet Mead; quickly, come.

[*Enter* FORD, PAGE, CAIUS, *and* EVANS.]

Ford. Pray you come near: if I suspect without cause, why then make sport at me; then let me be your jest, I deserve it.—How now? Whither bear you this?

John. To the laundress, forsooth.

Mrs. Ford. Why, what have you to do whither they bear it? You were best meddle with buck-washing!

Ford. Buck? I would I could wash myself of the buck! Buck, buck, buck! Ay, buck; I warrant you, buck; and of the season too, it shall appear. [*Exeunt John, Robert, and Robin with the basket.*] Gentlemen, I have

130. I love thee] *F;* I loue thee, and none but thee *Q.* 131. S.D.] *As Rowe; not in F; Sir Iohn goes into the basket, they put cloathes ouer him, the two men carries it away: Foord meetes it, and all the rest, Page, Doctor, Priest, Slender, Shallow. Q.* 134. S.D.] *As Capell; not in F; Exit* Robin. *Re-enter Servants. Malone.* 137. S.D.] *Rowe; not in F.* 142. *John*] *This ed.; Ser. F.* 147–8. S.D.] *This ed.; not in F; Exeunt Servants with the Basket. Rowe.*

130. *love thee*] The additional words in Q, included by some editors, are probably the result of confusion with ll. 67–8.

136. *cowl-staff*] a wooden rod used to carry a 'cowl' (tub) or similar object; the staff was put through the two handles.

drumble] move sluggishly, lag (*O.E.D. v.*[1] 1). Wright found the word in Warwickshire, among other counties, but Nashe's uses of it, recorded by Hart, perhaps confirm that it was not necessarily dialectal.

143. *what have you to do*] what concern is it of yours.

145–7.] Ford is, of course, concerned with the other implications of 'buck'—the stag whose horns symbolize cuckoldry.

147. *of the season*] in season—perhaps with a further quibble: the buck is in season in the sense that it (Falstaff) is in such good (fat) condition; and perhaps, worse, the female he seeks is in season, ready for a mate.

dreamed to-night; I'll tell you my dream. Here, here, here be my keys; ascend my chambers; search, seek, find out. I'll warrant we'll unkennel the fox. Let me stop this way first. [*Locking the door*] So, now uncape.

Page. Good Master Ford, be contented; you wrong yourself too much.

Ford. True, Master Page.—Up, gentlemen, you shall see sport anon; follow me, gentlemen. [*Exit.*]

Evans. This is fery fantastical humours and jealousies.

Caius. By gar, 'tis no the fashion of France; it is not jealous in France.

Page. Nay, follow him, gentlemen; see the issue of his search. [*Exeunt Page, Caius, and Evans.*]

Mrs. Page. Is there not a double excellency in this?

Mrs. Ford. I know not which pleases me better, that my husband is deceived, or Sir John.

Mrs. Page. What a taking was he in when your husband asked who was in the basket!

152. S.D.] *Capell; not in F.* 153. uncape] *F;* uncouple *Hanmer;* uncope *New Camb.;* uncase *Sisson.* 157. *Exit*] *Capell; not in F.* 162. S.D.] *Capell; not in F; Exit omnes* (*after l. 158*) *Q; Exeunt* (*after l. 160*) *F2; Exeunt* (*after l. 160*). *Manent Mistress* Page *and Mistress* Ford (*after l. 162*) *Rowe.* 167. who] *F;* what *Harness.*

149. *to-night*] last night.

151. *unkennel*] unearth, uncover. Cf. *Ham.*, III. ii. 86.

153. *uncape*] If the F text is correct, 'uncape' presumably means 'uncover', but as a clothing, not a hunting, image. (Warburton said it meant 'dig out the fox'.) *New Cambridge's* emendation 'uncope' is based on the meaning of 'cope' as to tie or sew up the lips of a ferret to prevent its biting the rabbits it dislodges (as a greyhound is muzzled today); it also, however, would be odd used intransitively. Q's 'Ile . . . ferit him' in Ford's soliloquy at the end of III. v may be an attempt to recall either 'uncape' or 'unkennel the fox', neither of which is reproduced in the correct place.

156. *True*] Probably Ford agrees in the sense that too much wrong is done him; or perhaps he seems to agree with Page to placate him for the minute.

166. *taking*] state of overwhelming fear (as in *Lucr.*, 453)—though sometimes used of emotion in general.

166–7. *when . . . basket!*] In fact, Ford asked no such question, nor did he ask *what* was in the basket, as Falstaff alleges at III. v. 93–4. But it does not help at all to introduce from Q, as *New Cambridge* does, after 'How now?' in l. 140, Q's 'Who goes heare?' which obviously refers to the bearers of the basket. Hart's statement (in a note on III. v. 93–4) that 'in the Folio text the question is not asked. This is an oversight which the Quarto has right' is misleading; Q has only: 'How now who goes heare? whither goes this? / Whither goes it? set it downe.'

Mrs. Ford. I am half afraid he will have need of washing—so throwing him into the water will do him a benefit.

Mrs. Page. Hang him, dishonest rascal! I would all of the same strain were in the same distress.

Mrs. Ford. I think my husband hath some special suspicion of Falstaff's being here, for I never saw him so gross in his jealousy till now.

Mrs. Page. I will lay a plot to try that, and we will yet have more tricks with Falstaff: his dissolute disease will scarce obey this medicine.

Mrs. Ford. Shall we send that foolish carrion, Mistress Quickly, to him, and excuse his throwing into the water, and give him another hope, to betray him to another punishment?

Mrs. Page. We will do it: let him be sent for to-morrow eight o'clock to have amends.

[*Enter* FORD, PAGE, CAIUS, *and* EVANS.]

Ford. I cannot find him; maybe the knave bragged of that he could not compass.

Mrs. Page. [*Aside to Mrs. Ford*] Heard you that?

Mrs. Ford. You use me well, Master Ford, do you?

Ford. Ay, I do so.

Mrs. Ford. Heaven make you better than your thoughts!

Ford. Amen!

Mrs. Page. You do yourself mighty wrong, Master Ford.

Ford. Ay, ay; I must bear it.

179. foolish] *F2;* foolishion *F1.* 183–4. to-morrow eight] *F1;* to morrow by eight *F2.* 184. S.D.] *Capell; not in F; Enter all. Q; Re-enter* Ford, Page, *&c. Rowe; Re-enter* Ford, Page, *and the rest at a distance. Johnson.* 187. S.D.] *As Capell; not in F.* 189. Ay, I] *F* (I, I); Ay, ay, I *Rowe.* 190. you] *F;* me *conj. Capell* (*1783*). 193. Ay, ay; I] *F* (I, I: I).

168–9. *need of washing*] Not only because of the dirtiness of the clothes but also because of the physical results of his own fear.

176. *try*] test.

178. *obey*] i.e. respond to, be totally cured by.

179. *carrion*] From being applied to corrupted flesh, 'carrion' came to be a general term of contempt, particularly for a woman; so Capulet uses it, unforgivably, to Juliet, *Rom.*, III. v. 157.

186. *compass*] achieve.

Evans. If there be anypody in the house, and in the chambers, and in the coffers, and in the presses, heaven forgive my sins at the day of judgement!

Caius. By gar, nor I too: there is nobodies.

Page. Fie, fie, Master Ford, are you not ashamed? What spirit, what devil suggests this imagination? I would not ha' your distemper in this kind for the wealth of Windsor Castle.

Ford. 'Tis my fault, Master Page, I suffer for it.

Evans. You suffer for a pad conscience Your wife is as honest a 'omans as I will desires among five thousand, and five hundred too.

Caius. By gar, I see 'tis an honest woman.

Ford. Well, I promised you a dinner. Come, come, walk in the Park. I pray you pardon me; I will hereafter make known to you why I have done this. Come, wife, come, Mistress Page, I pray you pardon me; pray heartly pardon me.

Page. Let's go in, gentlemen—[*aside*] but, trust me, we'll mock him.—I do invite you to-morrow morning to my house to breakfast; after, we'll a-birding together—I have a fine hawk for the bush. Shall it be so?

Ford. Anything.

Evans. If there is one, I shall make two in the company.

Caius. If there be one or two, I shall make-a the turd.

Ford. Pray you go, Master Page. [*Exit, with Page*.]

200. the] *F* (*corrected*). 211. heartly] *F* (hartly). 212. *aside*] *This ed.; not in F.* 214. breakfast;] *F* (breakfast:); Breakfast, *Rowe*. 220. S.D.] *This ed., as New Camb.; not in F.*

195. *presses*] cupboards (a surviving meaning).

201. *Windsor Castle*] The reference is 'natural' from a citizen of Windsor but serves also to remind the audience of the supposed setting.

202. *fault*] misfortune (as in *Per.*, IV. ii. 79).

207–8. *walk in the Park*] i.e. until the promised dinner is ready.

211. *heartly*] heartily, sincerely.

212. *go in*] The direction is quite logical on the unlocalized Elizabethan stage, and they do go 'in' (away from the audience), not 'in' to the house.

214. *a-birding*] hunting small birds with sparrow-hawks. The hawk chased the smaller birds even from the bush in which they had taken shelter (hence l. 215) and then they could be shot. (In true falconry the falcon itself did the killing.)

Evans. I pray you now, remembrance to-morrow on the lousy knave mine host.

Caius. Dat is good, by gar; with all my heart!

Evans. A lousy knave, to have his gibes and his mockeries! *Exeunt.*

SCENE IV

Enter FENTON *and* ANNE PAGE.

Fent. I see I cannot get thy father's love;
Therefore no more turn me to him, sweet Nan.
Anne. Alas, how then?
Fent. Why, thou must be thyself.
He doth object I am too great of birth,
And that my state being gall'd with my expense,
I seek to heal it only by his wealth;
Besides these, other bars he lays before me—
My riots past, my wild societies—
And tells me 'tis a thing impossible
I should love thee but as a property.
Anne. Maybe he tells you true.
Fent. No, heaven so speed me in my time to come!
Albeit I will confess thy father's wealth
Was the first motive that I woo'd thee, Anne,
Yet, wooing thee, I found thee of more value

Scene IV

SCENE IV] *F; Scene* XII. *Changes to* Page'*s house. Pope; . . . Before Page's house Chambers.* S.D.] *As Rowe; Enter Fenton, Anne, Page, Shallow, Slender, Quickly, Page, Mist. Page. F.* 12. *Fent.*] *Q3; not in F.*

221–5.] Obviously Caius and Evans have 'knogged' their 'prains together' and have planned their revenge on the Host for the trick played on them over the duel, but the audience still does not know what form the vengeance is to take.

Scene IV

5. *state*] estate.

gall'd] Literally, chafed in such a way as to produce a sore, and so, metaphorically, seriously depleted.

8.] See Introduction, p. lii, and cf. III. ii. 66–7.

10. *property*] There may be one or two secondary meanings: stage property, and means to an end. Cf. IV. iv. 77 and *Cæs.* IV. i. 39–40.

12.] i.e. may heaven not favour me in future if his accusations are justified.

Than stamps in gold or sums in sealed bags;
And 'tis the very riches of thyself
That now I aim at.

Anne. Gentle Master Fenton,
Yet seek my father's love; still seek it, sir.
If opportunity and humblest suit
Cannot attain it, why then—hark you hither!
[*They converse apart.*]

[*Enter* SHALLOW, SLENDER, *and* MISTRESS QUICKLY.]

Shal. Break their talk, Mistress Quickly. My kinsman shall speak for himself.

Slen. I'll make a shaft or a bolt on 't. 'Slid, 'tis but venturing.

Shal. Be not dismayed.

Slen. No, she shall not dismay me: I care not for that, but that I am afeard.

Quick. [*To Anne*] Hark ye, Master Slender would speak a word with you.

Anne. I come to him. [*Aside*] This is my father's choice.
O, what a world of vile ill-favour'd faults
Looks handsome in three hundred pounds a year!

Quick. And how does good Master Fenton? Pray you, a word with you.

Shal. [*To Slender*] She's coming; to her, coz. O boy, thou hadst a father!

21. then—hark] *Theobald;* then harke *F.* *They converse apart*] *Capell, as Theobald; not in F.* *Enter . . . Quickly*] *Rowe; not in F.* 22–3.] *Prose as Pope;* Breake . . . *Quickly.* / My . . . *F.* 27–8.] *Prose as Pope;* No . . . me: / I . . . *F.* 29. *To Anne*] *This ed.; not in F.* 31. *Aside*] *As Capell; not in F; to Fenton New Camb.* 34–7.] *Prose as Pope;* And . . . *Fenton?* / Pray . . . with you. / *Shal.* Shee's . . . Coz: / O . . . *F.* 35.] *Capell adds 'drawing him aside'.* 36. S.D.] *This ed.; not in F.*

16. *stamps*] coins (on which a device has been stamped or impressed—*O.E.D.* 'stamp' *sb.* III. 15).

21.] *New Cambridge,* which rejects Capell's S.D. and prints the line without the dash, takes Anne to mean 'if all else fails come back to me'.

24. *I'll make . . . on 't*] The proverb (Tilley S264) derives from the contrast between the slim shaft of the true arrow (or even of the bow with which it was fired) and the shorter and thicker arrow known as the 'bolt' or 'quarrel' (used with the crossbow): 'do it one way or another'.

'Slid] by God's (eye)lid.

36. *to her, coz*] 'Coz' and 'cousin' (l. 42) meant 'kinsman' and not only 'cousin' in the modern sense; for 'to her', giving encouragement, cf. I. iii. 51 and note.

Slen. I had a father, Mistress Anne; my uncle can tell you good jests of him. Pray you, uncle, tell Mistress Anne the jest how my father stole two geese out of a pen, good uncle.

Shal. Mistress Anne, my cousin loves you.

Slen. Ay, that I do, as well as I love any woman in Gloucestershire.

Shal. He will maintain you like a gentlewoman.

Slen. Ay, that I will, come cut and long-tail, under the degree of a squire.

Shal. He will make you a hundred and fifty pounds jointure.

Anne. Good Master Shallow, let him woo for himself.

Shal. Marry, I thank you for it; I thank you for that good comfort. She calls you, coz; I'll leave you.

Anne. Now, Master Slender.

Slen. Now, good Mistress Anne.

Anne. What is your will?

Slen. My will? Od's heartlings, that's a pretty jest indeed! I ne'er made my will yet, I thank heaven: I am not such a sickly creature, I give heaven praise.

Anne. I mean, Master Slender, what would you with me?

Slen. Truly, for mine own part, I would little or nothing with you. Your father and my uncle hath made motions. If it be my luck, so; if not, happy man be his dole! They can tell you how things go, better than I can. You may ask your father; here he comes.

52.] *Collier*[2] *adds 'Stands back'.*

38. *uncle*] Slender probably does use the word in our sense; but see note on *Dramatis Personæ*, l. 4.

46. *come cut and long-tail*] Proverbial (Tilley C938) for 'no matter who or what is concerned' (since horses and dogs must fall into one of two classes, those with uncut and those with docked tails). A typical use is in *George-a-Greene* (attributed to Robert Greene), v. i, where George, having beaten all the shoemakers of Bradford, asks 'What, have you any more? / Call all your town forth, cut and long tail'.

under] Not 'beneath' but 'in accordance with' (*O.E.D. prep.* III).

56. *Od's heartlings*] by God's little heart—another mild oath.

62. *motions*] proposals.

62–3. *happy man be his dole*] Slender's speech is larded with clichés: this is another proverb (Tilley M158) meaning, roughly, 'good luck to any man who is successful' ('dole' in the sense of destiny, or lot—*O.E.D. sb.*[1] 4). Cf. *Shr.*, I. i. 144.

[*Enter* PAGE *and* MISTRESS PAGE.]

Page. Now, Master Slender; love him, daughter Anne.—
Why, how now, what does Master Fenton here?
You wrong me, sir, thus still to haunt my house.
I told you, sir, my daughter is disposed of.
Fent. Nay, Master Page, be not impatient.
Mrs. Page. Good Master Fenton, come not to my child.
Page. She is no match for you.
Fent. Sir, will you hear me?
Page. No, good Master Fenton.
Come, Master Shallow; come, son Slender; in.
Knowing my mind, you wrong me, Master Fenton.
[*Exeunt Page, Shallow, and Slender*.]
Quick. Speak to Mistress Page.
Fent. Good Mistress Page, for that I love your daughter
In such a righteous fashion as I do,
Perforce, against all checks, rebukes and manners,
I must advance the colours of my love,
And not retire. Let me have your good will.
Anne. Good mother, do not marry me to yond fool.
Mrs. Page. I mean it not; I seek you a better husband.
Quick. [*Aside*] That's my master, Master Doctor.
Anne. Alas, I had rather be set quick i' th' earth,
And bowl'd to death with turnips!
Mrs. Page. Come, trouble not yourself. Good Master Fenton,
I will not be your friend nor enemy.

64. S.D.] *Rowe; not in F*. 66. Fenton] *Q3; Fenter F*. 74. S.D.] *Rowe; not in F*. 83. *Aside*] *Bowers; not in F*. 86. yourself. Good] *Warburton* (your self; good); your selfe good *F*. 86–7.] *Arranged as Rowe*[3]; Come, . . . good M. / *Fenton*, . . . enemy: *F*.

66. *Fenton*] F's 'Fenter' is only a compositor's error, more probably from temporary conflation with 'Slender' than from misreading (although 'on' could easily be mistaken for 'er' in secretary hand).

78. *checks*] reproofs, censure.

79. *advance the colours*] A military metaphor: raising the flag as an indication of giving battle.

84–5. *set quick . . . turnips*] be fixed, alive, in the earth (up to the neck) and be killed by having turnips bowled at me. Anne's—and Shakespeare's—vivid imagining may have begun from a real, or mythical, treatment of madmen by burying them up to the neck in earth or worse (Hart cites some evidence for this), although Aaron's punishment in *Tit.* is to be 'set . . . breast-deep in earth' and starved to death.

My daughter will I question how she loves you,
And as I find her, so am I affected.
Till then, farewell, sir; she must needs go in;
Her father will be angry.

Fent. Farewell, gentle mistress; farewell, Nan.

[*Exeunt Mistress Page and Anne.*]

Quick. This is my doing now. 'Nay', said I, 'will you cast away your child on a fool, and a physician? Look on Master Fenton.' This is my doing.

Fent. I thank thee; and I pray thee, once to-night
Give my sweet Nan this ring. There's for thy pains.

Quick. Now heaven send thee good fortune! [*Exit Fenton.*] A kind heart he hath: a woman would run through fire and water for such a kind heart. But yet I would my master had Mistress Anne; or I would Master Slender had her; or, in sooth, I would Master Fenton had her. I will do what I can for them all three, for so I have promised, and I'll be as good as my word, but speciously for Master Fenton. Well, I must of another errand to Sir John Falstaff from my two mistresses; what a beast am I to slack it! *Exit.*

92. S.D.] *Rowe (after l. 91); not in F.*
98–9. S.D.] *F2 (after l. 97); not in F1.*
94. and] *F;* or *Hanmer, conj. Johnson.*

89. *affected*] inclined (from 'affect' meaning to 'like' or 'respond to').

94. *a fool, and a physician*] 'A fool or a physician' was a common phrase (Tilley M125); in adapting it, Quickly, as usual, is wiser than she knows, in that the phrase both describes Caius and states the choice between Slender and Caius.

96. *once*] (Probably) some time; cf. *1H4*, v. ii. 73, and *Cæs.*, iv. iii. 191—although occasionally the word is used merely as an intensive with an imperative.

105. *speciously*] Quickly's error, repeated at iv. v. 106, for 'specially'.

106–8. *I must . . . slack it*] No allowance whatever for theatrical illusion is made by those who complain either that Quickly has had no time to be given this errand (which, after all, Mistress Page and Mistress Ford planned in iii. iii. 176–84) or that she does in fact 'slack it' since she apparently leaves it until nearly eight o'clock 'the following morning'. 'Double time' is frequent in *Wiv.*

SCENE V

Enter FALSTAFF.

Fal. Bardolph, I say!

[*Enter* BARDOLPH.]

Bard. Here, sir.

Fal. Go fetch me a quart of sack; put a toast in 't. [*Exit Bard.*] Have I lived to be carried in a basket, like a barrow of butcher's offal, and to be thrown in the Thames? Well, if I be served such another trick, I'll have my brains ta'en out and buttered, and give them to a dog for a New Year's gift. The rogues slighted me into the river with as little remorse as they would have drowned a blind bitch's puppies, fifteen i' th' litter; and you may know by my size that I have a kind of alacrity in sinking: if the bottom

Scene v

SCENE v] *F; Scene* XV. *The Garter-Inn. Pope.* S.D.] *Q; Enter Falstaffe, Bardolfe, Quickly, Ford. F; Enter* Falstaff *and* Bardolph. *Rowe.* 1. S.D.] *As New Camb.; not in F.* 3–4. S.D.] *Theobald; not in F.* 4–6. Have . . . Thames?] *F;* Haue I liued to be carried in a basket and throwne into the Thames like a barow of Butchers offoll. *Q.* 9. slighted] *F;* slided *Q;* sleighted *conj. New Camb.* 10. blind bitch's] *As F;* bitch's blind *Theobald.*

3. *toast*] Toast was commonly put in both beer (to put a 'head' on it) and wine.

5. *barrow*] barrowful. Wheatley follows Daniel in preferring the Q reading, not seeing that 'barrow' could mean the contents of a barrow rather than the barrow itself.

7. *buttered*] Hart quotes lines from *The Pilgrim* (1621)—'The thing is mad, / Abominably mad, her brains are buttered'—that suggest that 'buttered brains was a synonym for foolishness'.

8. *New Year's gift*] Gifts were customarily given on 1 January (which was New Year's Day even when it was the practice not to change the year number, in reckoning dates, until Lady Day, 25 March).

9. *slighted*] Elsewhere in Shakespeare (e.g. *2H4*, v. ii. 94) 'slight' means 'treat with contempt' or 'treat as insignificant' and perhaps that is what it means here, though in a different construction. Q has 'the rogues slided me in' which—if it is not a mishearing or a misunderstanding—may indicate that F 'slighted' is an error, or that Shakespeare did intend a kind of pun.

11–12. *you may know . . . sinking*] The literal-minded duly point out that, according to the laws of physics, size and speed in sinking are not necessarily related. Dorset was later to make a delightful use of Shakespeare's phrase in his satire 'To Mr Edward Howard' —'So in this way of writing, without thinking, / Thou hast a strange alacrity in sinking'.

were as deep as hell, I should down. I had been drowned but that the shore was shelvy and shallow—a death that I abhor: for the water swells a man; and what a thing should I have been when I had been swelled! I should have been a mountain of mummy.

[*Enter* BARDOLPH *with sack.*]

Bard. Here's Mistress Quickly, sir, to speak with you.

Fal. Come, let me pour in some sack to the Thames water: for my belly's as cold as if I had swallowed snowballs for pills to cool the reins. Call her in.

Bard. Come in, woman!

Enter MISTRESS QUICKLY.

Quick. By your leave; I cry you mercy. Give your worship good morrow.

Fal. Take away these chalices. Go brew me a pottle of sack finely.

Bard. With eggs, sir?

Fal. Simple of itself; I'll no pullet-sperm in my brewage. [*Exit Bardolph.*] How now?

Quick. Marry, sir, I come to your worship from Mistress Ford.

Fal. Mistress Ford! I have had ford enough; I was thrown into the ford; I have my belly full of ford.

17. S.D.] *As Capell; not in F; Enter* Bardolph. *Theobald.* 22. S.D.] *Q; not in F.* 28. pullet-sperm] *F* (Pullet-Spersme). 29. S.D.] *Capell; not in F.*

14. *shelvy*] 'Shelves' in *3H6*, v. iv. 23, *Lucr.*, 335, and at least twice in Marlowe's (and Nashe's) *Dido* means sandbanks (once it is perhaps used of reefs or rocks): *O.E.D.* 'shelf' *sb.*[2] Falstaff may thus mean that the bed of the river had sandbanks so that the water was not deep; alternatively he could mean that the bank 'shelved' or sloped gradually (*O.E.D.* 'shelve' *v.*[3] 1).

17. *mummy*] Perhaps just 'dead flesh', as *O.E.D.* takes it (obviously Falstaff is not thinking of a desiccated body) but the word was also applied to 'a pulpy substance or mass' (*O.E.D.* *sb.*[1] 1. c).

21. *reins*] kidneys.

24. *morrow*] morning—and as the subsequent exchange with Ford shows, it *is* morning, about 8 a.m. See III. iv. 106–8 and note.

25. *chalices*] drinking cups or goblets (as in *Ham.*, IV. vii. 161)—but Falstaff, complaining that from such goblets he cannot get more than a sip, may also be thinking of the sacramental vessels.

pottle] half a gallon, or a vessel of that size (as in II. i. 203).

28. *Simple*] pure, 'straight'.

Quick. Alas the day, good heart, that was not her fault! She does so take on with her men; they mistook their erection.

Fal. So did I mine, to build upon a foolish woman's promise.

Quick. Well, she laments, sir, for it, that it would yearn your heart to see it. Her husband goes this morning a-birding; she desires you once more to come to her, between eight and nine. I must carry her word quickly; she'll make you amends, I warrant you.

Fal. Well, I will visit her; tell her so. And bid her think what a man is; let her consider his frailty, and then judge of my merit.

Quick. I will tell her.

Fal. Do so. Between nine and ten, sayst thou?

Quick. Eight and nine, sir.

Fal. Well, be gone; I will not miss her.

Quick. Peace be with you, sir. *Exit.*

Fal. I marvel I hear not of Master Brook; he sent me word to stay within. I like his money well.—O, here he comes.

Enter FORD *as* BROOK.

Ford. Bless you, sir!

Fal. Now, Master Brook, you come to know what hath passed between me and Ford's wife?

Ford. That, indeed, Sir John, is my business.

Fal. Master Brook, I will not lie to you: I was at her house the hour she appointed me.

Ford. And sped you, sir?

51. S.D.] *Q; not in F.* 54. S.D.] *As Q; not in F.*

35. *does so take on with*] The phrase is used again in IV. ii. 18: shows how angry she is with.

36. *erection*] Quickly's version of direction (instruction).

39. *yearn*] move to compassion (*O.E.D.* v.[1] 7). Hilda Hulme (p. 125) suspects a further indecency, on the meaning 'to become erect'.

45. *consider his frailty*] Falstaff, like the devil, can quote—or adapt—Scripture: 'the flesh is frail', then as now, was a popular variation on the Biblical 'the flesh is weak' (Tilley F363).

50. *miss*] fail.

61. *sped you*] did you succeed (past tense of the verb 'to speed')—no doubt with special emphasis on sexual success.

Fal. Very ill-favouredly, Master Brook.

Ford. How so, sir? Did she change her determination?

Fal. No, Master Brook, but the peaking cornuto her husband, Master Brook, dwelling in a continual larum of jealousy, comes me in the instant of our encounter, after we had embraced, kissed, protested, and, as it were, spoke the prologue of our comedy; and at his heels a rabble of his companions, thither provoked and instigated by his distemper, and, forsooth, to search his house for his wife's love.

Ford. What, while you were there?

Fal. While I was there.

Ford. And did he search for you, and could not find you?

Fal. You shall hear. As good luck would have it, comes in one Mistress Page; gives intelligence of Ford's approach; and, in her invention and Ford's wife's distraction, they conveyed me into a buck-basket—

Ford. A buck-basket?

Fal. Yes, a buck-basket!—rammed me in with foul shirts and smocks, socks, foul stockings, greasy napkins, that, Master Brook, there was the rankest compound of villainous smell that ever offended nostril.

77. in] *F;* by *Q.* 78. distraction] *F;* direction *Hanmer, conj. Warburton.* 80 Yes] *F1;* By the Lord *Q;* Yea *F2.* 81. greasy] *F;* and greasie *Rowe.*

62. *ill-favouredly*] i.e. unpleasantly or disagreeably (the corresponding adjective, used before in I. i. 275, usually means 'ugly').

64. *peaking*] sneaking, skulking, or mean-spirited (*O.E.D.* 1). The quibble seen by some editors on the 'peak' of the (cuckold's) horn may be imaginary.

cornuto] horned beast, cuckold. ('Cornute', an anglicized form of the Italian word, is also found.)

66. *larum*] A common aphetic form of 'alarum': alarm.

me] Another instance of the 'ethic dative' in Falstaff's speech. Cf. I. iii. 52 and note.

67. *encounter*] Often, but by no means always, in Shakespeare means 'amatory meeting'. The tone of the word is best suggested in *Troil.*, IV. v. 58–9, by the derivative 'encounterer': 'these encounterers, so glib of tongue, / That give accosting welcome ere it comes'—part of Ulysses' scornful description of Cressida.

protested] made protestations (of affection).

70. *distemper*] lack of 'temper' (in the sense of balance).

78. *distraction*] Q confirms the F reading and so rules out the emendation 'direction'.

80. *rammed*] There is probably a quibble on 'ram' and 'buck', each meaning the male of certain horned species.

82. *that*] with the result that.

Ford. And how long lay you there?

Fal. Nay, you shall hear, Master Brook, what I have suffered to bring this woman to evil, for your good. Being thus crammed in the basket, a couple of Ford's knaves, his hinds, were called forth by their mistress to carry me in the name of foul clothes to Datchet Lane; they took me on their shoulders; met the jealous knave their master in the door, who asked them once or twice what they had in their basket. I quaked for fear lest the lunatic knave would have searched it; but fate, ordaining he should be a cuckold, held his hand. Well, on went he for a search, and away went I for foul clothes. But mark the sequel, Master Brook: I suffered the pangs of three several deaths. First, an intolerable fright, to be detected with a jealous rotten bell-wether; next, to be compassed like a good bilbo in the circumference of a peck, hilt to point, heel to head; and then to be stopped in like a strong distillation with stinking clothes that fretted in their own grease—think of that—a man

100. with] *F;* by *Rowe*[3].

89. *knaves, his hinds*] Originally 'hind', like 'knave', meant only 'servant', particularly a farm-servant, but it was commonly used in a derisory way to mean 'boor'.

93–4. *who . . . basket*] See III. iii. 166–7 and note.

95–6. *fate . . . cuckold*] Falstaff is alluding to the maxim that 'cuckolds come by destiny' (Tilley C889).

100. *with*] by.

101. *rotten*] rotting (with disease).

bell-wether] the castrated male sheep that wore a bell round its neck and was used to lead the flock: hence, often, leader of the 'mob'—and Falstaff sees Ford as that too (cf. l. 69).

compassed] Not 'encompassed' but 'curved' (*O.E.D.* 'compass' *v.*[1] v.14)—'head to foot', as Falstaff goes on to explain, since he had to curl up to fit into the basket.

102. *good bilbo*] Part of the test of quality in the bilbo or 'Bilboa' sword (cf. I. i. 146 and note) would be to bend it 'hilt to point' to make sure that it would not snap.

peck] a vessel that would hold a 'peck', a quarter of a bushel, of dry goods.

103. *stopped*] stuffed (*O.E.D.* 'stop' *v.* 1).

104. *distillation*] Here, that which has been, or is being, distilled—i.e. condensed after being converted into vapour by heat.

105. *fretted*] fermented (*O.E.D.* 'fret' *v.*[1] 7, 10)—and did so in their own 'grease', not needing the addition of Falstaff's. Cf. the image in II. i. 65–6, which Falstaff unwittingly is repeating.

of my kidney—think of that—that am as subject to heat as butter; a man of continual dissolution and thaw: it was a miracle to 'scape suffocation. And in the height of this bath, when I was more than half stewed in grease, like a Dutch dish, to be thrown into the Thames and cooled, glowing hot, in that surge, like a horse-shoe—think of that—hissing hot—think of that, Master Brook!

Ford. In good sadness, sir, I am sorry that for my sake you have suffered all this. My suit, then, is desperate: you'll undertake her no more?

Fal. Master Brook, I will be thrown into Etna, as I have been into Thames, ere I will leave her thus. Her husband is this morning gone a-birding; I have received from her another embassy of meeting. 'Twixt eight and nine is the hour, Master Brook.

Ford. 'Tis past eight already, sir.

Fal. Is it? I will then address me to my appointment. Come to me at your convenient leisure and you shall know how I speed; and the conclusion shall be crowned with your enjoying her. Adieu. You shall have her, Master Brook; Master Brook, you shall cuckold Ford. *Exit.*

Ford. Hum! Ha! Is this a vision? Is this a dream? Do I sleep? Master Ford, awake; awake, Master Ford:

112. surge] *F* (serge); forge *conj. Capell* (*1783*). 128. *Exit*] *Q; not in F.*

106. *of my kidney*] The phrase survives in colloquial use to mean 'make-up' or, sometimes, 'type', but in Falstaff's use it is, of course, particularly vivid as carrying on the physical images of fat, blubber, and grease.

107. *dissolution*] dissolving, turning into liquid.

110. *Dutch dish*] Presumably the cooking of the Low Countries was proverbially oily or 'greasy'.

112. *surge*] The word had once meant simply 'stream' (*O.E.D. sb.* 1. a) but had come to have its modern meaning of violently moving water and so adds to the comic exaggeration when applied to the Thames, so placid until Falstaff is tipped in.

114. *sadness*] seriousness (the normal Elizabethan meaning).

117–18. *Etna . . . Thames*] A brilliant adaptation of 'go through fire and water'.

120. *embassy*] ambassador, or party of ambassadors; and even though used elsewhere by Shakespeare of messages of love, has a deliberately comic effect of incongruity here since it refers to Mistress Quickly.

127–8. *Brook . . . Ford*] Again a neat verbal jest is ruined if 'Broome' replaces 'Brook'.

there's a hole made in your best coat, Master Ford. This 'tis to be married; this 'tis to have linen and buck-baskets! Well, I will proclaim myself what I am. I will now take the lecher; he is at my house; he cannot 'scape me; 'tis impossible he should; he cannot creep into a halfpenny purse, nor into a pepper-box; but, lest the devil that guides him should aid him, I will search impossible places. Though what I am I cannot avoid, yet to be what I would not shall not make me tame: if I have horns to make one mad, let the proverb go with me—I'll be horn-mad. *Exit.*

141. one] *F;* me *Halliwell, conj. Dyce* (*Remarks*).

131. *a hole made . . . coat*] 'To pick a hole in a man's coat' was a proverbial phrase (Tilley H522) meaning to find a fault in somebody who was thought of, or who thought of himself, as impeccable. Cf. *H5,* III. vi. 88–9.

136. *halfpenny purse*] A small purse for carrying halfpennies and other such coins. Cf. *LLL.*, v. i. 77, 'thou halfpenny purse of wit'.

142. *horn-mad*] See note on I. iv. 45.

ACT IV

SCENE I

Enter MISTRESS PAGE, [MISTRESS] QUICKLY, *and* WILLIAM.

Mrs. Page. Is he at Master Ford's already, think'st thou?

Quick. Sure he is by this, or will be presently; but truly he is very courageous mad about his throwing into the water. Mistress Ford desires you to come suddenly.

Mrs. Page. I'll be with her by and by: I'll but bring my young man here to school. Look, where his master comes; 'tis a playing-day, I see.

[*Enter* EVANS.]

How now, Sir Hugh, no school to-day?

Evans. No; Master Slender is let the boys leave to play.

Quick. Blessing of his heart!

Mrs. Page. Sir Hugh, my husband says my son profits nothing in the world at his book. I pray you, ask him some questions in his accidence.

ACT IV

Scene I

ACT IV SCENE I] *F;* Act IV. Scene I. Page'*s house. Pope; Act IV. Scene I. A Street. Capell.* S.D.] *Rowe; Enter Mistris Page, Quickly, William, Euans. F.* 7. S.D.] *Rowe* (*after l. 8*)*; not in F.* 9. let] *F;* get *Collier*[2].

iv. i] For comment on this scene, as probably intended for an educated audience, see Introduction, p. xxix. It avoids two successive Falstaff scenes. Q, which has nothing corresponding to iv. i, gets over the difficulty by transposing iii. iv and iii. v, and (necessarily) by omitting the mention in the original iii. iv of Quickly's errand to Falstaff.

2. *presently*] immediately (as in iii. iii. 81). 'By and by' (l. 5) has weakened in meaning in exactly the same way.

3. *courageous*] Perhaps Quickly intended another word (but it is hardly likely to have been 'outrageous' as Hart and others say). As usual, her malapropism is, ironically, appropriate.

9.] Apparently, distinguished visitors to schools had the same privilege as they have today, of 'asking' for a holiday for the pupils.

13. *accidence*] the part of grammar that deals with the inflexions of

Evans. Come hither, William. Hold up your head; come.

Mrs. Page. Come on, sirrah, hold up your head. Answer your master, be not afraid.

Evans. William, how many numbers is in nouns?

Will. Two.

Quick. Truly I thought there had been one number more, because they say 'Od's nouns'.

Evans. Peace your tattlings! What is 'fair', William?

Will. *Pulcher.*

Quick. Polecats? There are fairer things than polecats, sure.

Evans. You are a very simplicity 'oman: I pray you, peace.—What is *lapis*, William?

Will. A stone.

Evans. And what is 'a stone', William?

Will. A pebble.

Evans. No, it is *lapis*: I pray you remember in your prain.

Will. *Lapis.*

Evans. That is a good William. What is he, William, that does lend articles?

words. Here, of course, in the practice of Elizabethan schools, the language in question is Latin; and William is almost certainly being tested on the opening pages of the text-book that Edward VI commanded to be used in all schools, *A Shorte Introduction of Grammar* ('for the bryngynge vp of all those that entende to atteyne the knowlege of the Latine tongue'), by William Lilly and John Colet, first published in 1549 and often reprinted. Such 'rehersing of the wordes' is recommended to the schoolmaster, in the preface.

15. *sirrah*] Cf. I. iii. 75 and III. ii. 18 and notes.

18. *Two*] William is correct: as Lilly told him, 'In Nounes be two Numbers, the Singular and the Plurall'.

20. *Od's nouns*] Quickly has misunderstood the common expletive, which is a corruption of '(By) God's (i.e. Christ's) wounds' ('nouns' being pronounced with the vowel [u:]).

22. pulcher] One of Lilly's examples of an adjective or 'Noune Adiective'.

23. *Polecats*] Quickly's confusion is more easily understood if, as is probable, the Elizabethan pronunciation of the first syllable rhymed with 'pull', but again she is giving herself away: polecats were notorious for their odour—and the word was slang for 'prostitutes'.

26. lapis] This is the noun that Lilly uses to exemplify a singular form and also the third declension; and the schoolmaster is advised in the preface to have the pupil both turn the Latin into English and turn the English back into Latin.

29. *pebble*] The F spelling 'peeble' probably indicates William's pronunciation (a common one), and makes clearer the joke ('stone', of course, also meant 'testicle').

Will. Articles are borrowed of the pronoun, and be thus declined: *Singulariter nominativo hic, hæc, hoc.*

Evans. *Nominativo hig, hag, hog.* Pray you mark: *genitivo huius.* Well, what is your accusative case?

Will. *Accusativo hinc.*

Evans. I pray you have your remembrance, child: *accusativo hing, hang, hog.*

Quick. 'Hang-hog' is Latin for bacon, I warrant you.

Evans. Leave your prabbles, 'oman.—What is the focative case, William?

Will. O—*vocativo*, O.

Evans. Remember, William: focative is *caret.*

Quick. And that's a good root.

38. *hinc*] *F;* hunc *Halliwell.* 40. *hing*] *F;* hung *Pope.* 41. Latin] *F3* (Latine); latten *F1.*

34–5.] More text-book material—and William has learnt it off, word for word from his edition of Lilly (probably 1577), without understanding any of it. Evans continues the quotation from Lilly with his '*genitivo huius*' in ll. 36–7.

35. nominativo] This, the form used in Lilly's text-book, is the ablative case of the Latin word for 'nominative' and means '*in* the nominative' (case), as *genitivo* and *accusativo* in ll. 36 and 38–9 mean 'in the genitive' and 'in the accusative'.

40. hing, hang, hog] i.e. *hinc, hanc, hoc.* William has given only the masculine accusative, and has given it incorrectly (it should be *hunc*). Evans adds the feminine and neuter forms but repeats William's error (unless Pope's emendation is to be accepted—and it surely spoils the joke).

41. *Hang-hog*] Quickly's miraculous inference is not necessarily more amusing if, with Zachary Grey (I. 110–11) and Halliwell, one sees a reference to Sir Nicholas Bacon's rejoinder to one Hog, a prisoner who claimed kinship and asked that the sentence of death passed on him should therefore be commuted: 'you and I cannot be of kindred unless you be hang'd; for Hog is not Bacon, till it be well hang'd'.

42. *prabbles*] Elsewhere (see I. i. 51–2 and note) Evans speaks of 'pribbles and prabbles' and means 'quarrels'. Here 'silly objections', even 'prattling'.

43. *focative*] Evans's mispronunciation of 'vocative'—which, unfortunately, in conjunction with William's reply, suggests a 'four-letter word'.

44.] F prints all three words in italic, its way of drawing attention to William's learnt-off replies; but it also has l. 50 in italic, and l. 44 is funnier if William's 'O' is intended to show his distress at not being able to give an answer, and thereby giving an intelligible one, that the vocative is the form used in address—'O woman' (or whatever the noun may be). Alternatively, Baldwin (I. 561–5) thinks that William's mind goes back to Lilly's section on the vocative of nouns, where the example cited is 'O magister, *O mayster*'.

45. caret] Latin for 'is missing' (regularly used by Lilly in such contexts—e.g. 'vocatiuo caret') and, perhaps, 'is *caret*' shows how little Latin even Evans has learnt. Quickly thinks he has said 'carrot'—but that was also a slang term for the penis (Partridge, p. 84).

Evans. 'Oman, forbear.

Mrs. Page. Peace.

Evans. What is your genitive case plural, William?

Will. Genitive case?

Evans. Ay.

Will. Genitive *horum, harum, horum*.

Quick. Vengeance of Ginny's case; fie on her! Never name her, child, if she be a whore.

Evans. For shame, 'oman.

Quick. You do ill to teach the child such words.—He teaches him to hick and to hack, which they'll do fast enough of themselves, and to call 'horum'—fie upon you!

Evans. 'Oman, art thou lunatics? Hast thou no understandings for thy cases, and the numbers of the genders? Thou art as foolish Christian creatures as I would desires.

Mrs. Page. [*To Quickly*] Prithee hold thy peace.

Evans. Show me now, William, some declensions of your pronouns.

Will. Forsooth, I have forgot.

Evans. It is *qui*, *quæ*, *quod*: if you forget your *quies*, your *quæs*, and your *quods*, you must be preeches. Go your ways, and play; go.

Mrs. Page. He is a better scholar than I thought he was.

Evans. He is a good sprag memory. Farewell, Mistress Page.

52. Genitive] *F;* Genitivo *Singer*. 53. Ginny's] *This ed.;* Ginyes *F; Giney's Theobald;* Jenny's *Capell;* Jinny's *Ridley*. 60. lunatics] *Capell;* Lunaties *F;* Lunacies *Rowe*. 61. of] *F;* and *Collier*[2]. the] *F;* thy *conj. Grant White*. 64. *To Quickly*] *Munro; not in F*. 68. *quæ*] *Pope; que F*. 69. *quæs*] *Pope; Ques F*. preeches] *F;* preeched *conj. Grant White*.

53. *Vengeance of*] A mild asseveration: 'a plague on'.

case] Another slang term—this time, for the female pudend.

57. *to hick and to hack*] (Apparently) to hiccup from excessive drinking and to take sexual pleasure where it can be found: cf. II. i. 50 and note.

67. *I have forgot*] Or, possibly, William has not reached pp. 16 and 17 of his Lilly.

68–9. quies . . . quæs . . . quods] If pronounced by Evans as 'keys . . . case . . . cods', the words would suggest to an Elizabethan audience still further indecencies: 'case' as in l. 53, 'cods' for 'testicles', and 'keys' for the part that 'unlocks' the 'case'.

69. *preeches*] breeches—i.e. breeched, meaning whipped.

72. *sprag*] Perhaps Evans's pronunciation of 'sprack', but Wright records

Mrs. Page. Adieu, good Sir Hugh. [*Exit Evans.*] Get you home, boy. Come, we stay too long. *Exeunt.*

SCENE II

Enter FALSTAFF *and* MISTRESS FORD.

Fal. Mistress Ford, your sorrow hath eaten up my sufferance. I see you are obsequious in your love, and I profess requital to a hair's breadth, not only, Mistress Ford, in the simple office of love, but in all the accoutrement, complement, and ceremony of it. But are you sure of your husband now?

Mrs. Ford. He's a-birding, sweet Sir John.

Mrs. Page. [*Within*] What ho, gossip Ford! What ho!

Mrs. Ford. Step into th' chamber, Sir John. [*Exit Falstaff.*]

[*Enter* MISTRESS PAGE.]

74. S.D.] *Steevens*[3]*; not in F.*

Scene II

SCENE II] *F;* Scene II. Ford'*s House. Pope;* [4.2] *The hall in Master Ford's house; the buck-basket in a corner New Camb.* S.D.] *Rowe; Enter Falstoffe, Mist. Ford, Mist. Page, Seruants, Ford, Page, Caius, Euans, Shallow. F.* 5. accoutrement] *Capell;* accustrement *F1;* accoustrement *F2.* 8. *Within*] *Rowe; not in F.* 9. *Exit Falstaff*] *Rowe; not in F.* *Enter . . . Page*] *As F2; not in F1.*

later uses of 'sprag' in the same sense of 'lively' or 'smart'.

Scene II

1–2. *your sorrow . . . sufferance*] i.e. my suffering is completely insignificant in comparison with your sorrow, and I have forgotten it.

2. *obsequious*] compliant, anxious to please (*O.E.D.* 1).

3. *to a hair's breadth*] Already a stock phrase (Tilley H29).

4. *office*] function or (perhaps) deed, act.

5. *accoutrement*] There would be a strong case for preserving F's 'accustrement' as an older form of the word rather than an old spelling. It normally means 'apparel' (or 'equipment'), as in *AYL.*, III. ii. 402, and is rather odd here—but of course Falstaff is using his precious, wooing, manner as in III. iii.

complement] This also is hard to paraphrase, for the word did mean consummation (*O.E.D. sb.* 3) as well as accompaniment; and in view of 'ceremony' in the same word-group, it may be meant in the wider sense of elaborate forms of polite address ('complement' and 'compliment' were not always distinguished).

8. *gossip*] A term of affectionate greeting used by one woman to another (*O.E.D. sb.* 2). From the OE *godsibb*, the word once also meant a godfather or godmother.

Mrs. Page. How now, sweetheart, who's at home besides yourself?

Mrs. Ford. Why, none but mine own people.

Mrs. Page. Indeed?

Mrs. Ford. No, certainly.—[*Aside to her*] Speak louder.

Mrs. Page. Truly, I am so glad you have nobody here.

Mrs. Ford. Why?

Mrs. Page. Why, woman, your husband is in his old lines again: he so takes on yonder with my husband; so rails against all married mankind; so curses all Eve's daughters, of what complexion soever; and so buffets himself on the forehead, crying, 'Peer out, peer out!', that any madness I ever yet beheld seemed but tameness, civility, and patience to this his distemper he is in now. I am glad the fat knight is not here.

Mrs. Ford. Why, does he talk of him?

Mrs. Page. Of none but him, and swears he was carried out, the last time he searched for him, in a basket; protests to my husband he is now here, and hath drawn him and the rest of their company from their sport, to make another experiment of his suspicion. But I am glad the knight is not here; now he shall see his own foolery.

Mrs. Ford. How near is he, Mistress Page?

Mrs. Page. Hard by, at street end; he will be here anon.

Mrs. Ford. I am undone: the knight is here.

Mrs. Page. Why, then, you are utterly shamed, and he's but a dead man. What a woman are you? Away

14. S.D.] *As Theobald; not in F.* 17. lines] *F;* vaine *Q;* lunes *Theobald.*

17. *lines*] The Q reading 'in his old vaine againe' confirms F 'lines' and almost rules out the emendation 'lunes' (fits of lunacy).

18. *takes on*] is angry. Cf. III. v. 35.

21. *crying, 'Peer out . . . '*] i.e. calling on the horns of the cuckold to appear (perhaps quoting an old children's rhyme, in which the words are addressed to the snail).

23. *to*] compared to.

35. *street end*] This is either an alternative form of the possessive or the construction (Abbott 430) where a kind of compound noun replaces the expected possessive. It is frequent with a proper noun, as in 'Carthage Queen' (*MND.*, I. i. 173) or 'These should be Carthage walls' (Marlowe and Nashe's *Dido*, II. i. 1).

anon] at once. Like 'presently' and 'by and by', the word has lost force (and is consequently often misunderstood: cf. *1H4*, II. iv. 31–112).

with him, away with him; better shame than murder.

Mrs. Ford. Which way should he go? How should I bestow him? Shall I put him into the basket again?

[*Enter* FALSTAFF.]

Fal. No, I'll come no more i' th' basket. May I not go out ere he come?

Mrs. Page. Alas, three of Master Ford's brothers watch the door with pistols, that none shall issue out; otherwise you might slip away ere he came. But what make you here?

Fal. What shall I do? I'll creep up into the chimney.

Mrs. Ford. There they always use to discharge their birding-pieces. Creep into the kill-hole.

Fal. Where is it?

Mrs. Ford. He will seek there, on my word. Neither press, coffer, chest, trunk, well, vault, but he hath an abstract for the remembrance of such places and goes to them by his note. There is no hiding you in the house.

Fal. I'll go out, then.

42. S.D.] *As F2; not in F1.* 51.] *F;* birding-pieces. / *Mrs. Page.* Creep into the kiln-hole. *Dyce, conj. Malone.* kill-hole] *F;* kiln-hole *Capell.*

42. *the basket*] *New Camb.* is undoubtedly right in having the buck-basket on the stage from the beginning of the scene (unless it is 'discovered', by the drawing of a curtain, at this point). Ll. 103–4 prove that the servants do not carry it on at l. 98. The Quarto version, which begins the scene with lines corresponding to 99–101, probably implies a recollection that the basket had to be brought on the stage before Falstaff enters.

48. *what make you*] what are you doing.

50–1. *discharge their birding-pieces*] Because it was a safe way to discharge the fire-arms or to dislodge the soot (or both). For the method of hunting birds, cf. note on III. iii. 214. The frequent references to 'birding pieces' confirm that a recognizable type of gun was used specifically for this 'sport'.

51. *Creep into the kill-hole*] Malone conjectured that these words should be given to Mistress Page. He referred to Mistress Ford's vetoing of the proposal, in l. 53; but saw also that Mistress Ford could be tantalizing Falstaff by pretending to change her mind. (Ralph Crane's speech prefixes, not always clearly distinguished and sometimes not in line with the relevant speech, may well have caused confusion. Cf. l. 59, note.) The 'kill-hole' is the door or opening of the kiln or oven.

53. *press*] cupboard, as in III. iii. 195.

55. *abstract*] list or catalogue.

Mrs. Page. If you go out in your own semblance, you die, Sir John—unless you go out disguised.

Mrs. Ford. How might we disguise him?

Mrs. Page. Alas the day, I know not: there is no woman's gown big enough for him; otherwise he might put on a hat, a muffler, and a kerchief, and so escape.

Fal. Good hearts, devise something: any extremity rather than a mischief.

Mrs. Ford. My maid's aunt, the fat woman of Brainford, has a gown above.

Mrs. Page. On my word, it will serve him. She's as big as he is; and there's her thrummed hat, and her muffler too. Run up, Sir John.

Mrs. Ford. Go, go, sweet Sir John; Mistress Page and I will look some linen for your head.

Mrs. Page. Quick, quick! We'll come dress you straight; put on the gown the while. [*Exit Falstaff.*]

Mrs. Ford. I would my husband would meet him in this shape. He cannot abide the old woman of Brainford; he swears she's a witch, forbade her my house, and hath threatened to beat her.

59–60. *Mrs. Page.* If . . . disguised.] *Malone; Mist. Ford.* If . . . disguis'd. *F; Mistress Ford.* If . . . Sir John. / *Mistress Page.* Unless you go disguised. *conj. Greg.* 61. *Mrs. Ford.* How . . . him?] *F1;* How . . . him? *F2.* 67. Brainford] *F;* Brentford *Capell.* 75. S.D.] *As F2; not in F1.*

59. Mrs. Page] Redistribution of some words from F is necessary, since F gives Mistress Ford two successive speeches. Sir Walter Greg, in a private letter recorded in the 1954 *New Cambridge*, p. 134, suggested that only 'unless you go out disguised' should be given to Mistress Page; and Wilson accepted this.

64. *muffler*] a scarf 'to cover part of the face and the neck' (*O.E.D.* 1. a).

kerchief] a form of cover for the head (*O.E.D.* 1) rather than neckerchief (*O.E.D.* 2), for Falstaff is dressed in a muffler *and* 'some linen for your head' (l. 73) which is, presumably, the kerchief.

65. *Good hearts*] A term of affection, probably more commonly used by women to other women.

67. *fat woman of Brainford*] For possible reference to a recorded resident of Brainford, see Introduction, p. lxii. Brainford is Brentford, then a village (on the Thames, about half-way between Windsor and London), now a suburb of London.

70. *thrummed hat*] 'Thrums' are 'the ends of the warp-threads left unwoven and remaining attached to the loom when the web is cut off' or waste yarn (*O.E.D.* 'thrum' *sb.*[2] 1, 2)—but the verb was used not only of the adapting of such material but also of fringing generally (*v.*[2] b). A fringed hat would be more appropriate here as offering more cover for the face.

Mrs. Page. Heaven guide him to thy husband's cudgel; and the devil guide his cudgel afterwards!

Mrs. Ford. But is my husband coming?

Mrs. Page. Ay, in good sadness, is he, and talks of the basket too, howsoever he hath had intelligence.

Mrs. Ford. We'll try that: for I'll appoint my men to carry the basket again, to meet him at the door with it, as they did last time.

Mrs. Page. Nay, but he'll be here presently; let's go dress him like the witch of Brainford.

Mrs. Ford. I'll first direct my men what they shall do with the basket. Go up; I'll bring linen for him straight.

Mrs. Page. Hang him, dishonest varlet, we cannot misuse him enough.

We'll leave a proof, by that which we will do,
Wives may be merry and yet honest too.
We do not act that often jest and laugh;
'Tis old, but true: 'Still swine eats all the draff'.

[*Exit.*]

[*Enter* JOHN *and* ROBERT.]

Mrs. Ford. Go, sirs, take the basket again on your shoulders. Your master is hard at door; if he bid you set it down, obey him. Quickly, dispatch. [*Exit.*]

John. Come, come, take it up.

92.] *Capell adds* 'Exit'. 93–4.] *Prose as Pope;* Hang . . . Varlet, / We . . . misuse enough: *F.* 94. him] *F2; not in F1.* 98. draff] *F* (draugh). *Exit*] *Capell; not in F.* *Enter John and Robert.*] *This ed.; not in F1; Enter M. Ford, Page, Priest, Shallow, the two men carries the basket, and Ford meets it. Q; Enter Ser. F2 (after l. 101); Enter Servants with the Basket. Rowe (after l. 101); Re-enter Mistress* Ford *with her two Men. Capell.* 101. *Exit*] *Capell; not in F; Exeunt* Mrs. *Page* and Mrs. *Ford. Theobald.* 102, 104. *John*] *This ed.; 1 Ser. F.*

83. *in good sadness*] in all seriousness.

84. *intelligence*] information—as in l. 136.

85. *try*] test.

93. *dishonest*] Probably in a stronger sense, the opposite of 'honest' (l. 96) meaning 'chaste'.

97.] i.e. women who jest and laugh are not the immoral ones; and our mirth is not assumed for ulterior purposes.

98. *Still swine . . . draff*] A proverb (Tilley S681). 'Still' means 'quiet', and 'draff' 'dregs' or 'hog's-wash'. The saying is used in a comparable way by Heywood in *If You Know Not Me You Know Nobody*, Part 2: 'The still sowe eats all the draffe; and no question the most smoother toungued fellow, the more arrant knave'.

100. *hard at door*] right at the door, close to it. (*O.E.D.* 'hard' *adv.* 6). Cf. 'hard by', in l. 35 above.

Robert. Pray heaven it be not full of knight again.

John. I hope not; I had as lief bear so much lead.

[*Enter* FORD, PAGE, SHALLOW, CAIUS, *and* EVANS.]

Ford. Ay, but if it prove true, Master Page, have you any way then to unfool me again?—Set down the basket, villain! Somebody call my wife. Youth in a basket! O you pandarly rascals, there's a knot, a ging, a pack, a conspiracy against me. Now shall the devil be shamed.—What, wife, I say! Come, come forth: behold what honest clothes you send forth to bleaching!

Page. Why, this passes, Master Ford; you are not to go loose any longer, you must be pinioned.

Evans. Why, this is lunatics; this is mad as a mad dog.

Shal. Indeed, Master Ford, this is not well, indeed.

Ford. So say I too, sir.

[*Enter* MISTRESS FORD.]

Come hither, Mistress Ford—Mistress Ford, the honest woman, the modest wife, the virtuous creature, that hath the jealous fool to her husband! I suspect without cause, mistress, do I?

Mrs. Ford. Heaven be my witness you do, if you suspect me in any dishonesty.

103. *Robert*] *This ed.; 2 Ser. F.* 104. as lief] *F2;* liefe as *F1.* S.D.] *Rowe; not in F.* 107. villain] *F;* villains *Collier*[2]. 109. ging] *F2;* gin *F1;* gang *Rowe.* 117. S.D.] *Hanmer; not in F; after l. 115 Theobald.*

104. S.D. Caius] Actually the main 'justification' for bringing Caius on here is that he appears in the corresponding III. iii; he does not speak. Q does not mention him in its version of the scene; but cf. III. iii. 219 and IV. ii. 29–31.

105ff.] Ford is obviously replying to a query by Page whether he is not making a fool of himself: the stress is on the 'un' of 'unfool' (which is apparently of Shakespeare's coining).

107–8. *Youth in a basket*] Proverbial (Tilley Y51) for a triumphant lover—but Tilley is able to cite only the two examples given by Hart.

108. *knot*] gang. Cf. III. ii. 46 and note.

109. *ging*] gang or pack. This F2 reading makes good sense—but F1's 'gin' is not completely impossible, meaning snare or trap.

109–10. *Now . . . shamed*] i.e. the truth will be known—an allusion to the proverb (Tilley T566) 'Speak the truth and shame the devil'.

113. *passes*] surpasses, is beyond belief. ('Passing' was used in the same way for 'surpassingly', as in 'passing strange'.) The phrase is repeated in l. 126.

Ford. Well said, brazen-face, hold it out.—Come forth, sirrah! [*Pulling clothes out of the basket.*]

Page. This passes!

Mrs. Ford. Are you not ashamed? Let the clothes alone.

Ford. I shall find you anon.

Evans. 'Tis unreasonable; will you take up your wife's clothes? Come, away.

Ford. Empty the basket, I say!

Mrs. Ford. Why, man, why?

Ford. Master Page, as I am a man, there was one conveyed out of my house yesterday in this basket: why may not he be there again? In my house I am sure he is; my intelligence is true, my jealousy is reasonable. Pluck me out all the linen.

Mrs. Ford. If you find a man there, he shall die a flea's death.

Page. Here's no man.

Shal. By my fidelity, this is not well, Master Ford; this wrongs you.

Evans. Master Ford, you must pray, and not follow the imaginations of your own heart: this is jealousies.

Ford. Well, he's not here I seek for.

Page. No, nor nowhere else but in your brain.

Ford. Help to search my house this one time. If I find not what I seek, show no colour for my extremity; let

125. S.D.] *As Rowe; not in F.* 130. Come, away] *F;* Come away *Rowe.* 132. *Mrs. Ford*] *F; Page conj. Lambrechts.*

124. *hold it out*] Cf. *LLL.*, v. ii. 395, Can any face of brass hold longer out?', i.e. remain unchanged for a longer time. The different but corresponding modern idiom is 'keep it up'.

136. *intelligence*] information (a surviving meaning).

137. *me*] The ethic dative again.

141. *By my fidelity*] upon my word, by my faith. (Even the oaths uttered by Shallow can sound precious.)

142. *wrongs you*] i.e. is unworthy of you. Cf. III. iii. 192.

143. *you must pray*] Because Evans thinks that Ford is possessed by the devil. Page had made the same assumption in III. iii. 199 (and it is noteworthy that many of the phrases in IV. ii echo, probably deliberately, those of Ford's earlier search).

143–4. *the imaginations of your own heart*] Evans is alluding to Jeremiah 13:10.

148. *show no colour*] May mean either 'offer no excuse or explanation' (*O.E.D.* 'colour' *sb.* III) or 'do not defend, take the part of' (comparing 'show the colours'). Cf. *Cæs.*, II. i. 28–30.

extremity] going to extremes or, perhaps, extravagance (*O.E.D.* 5).

me for ever be your table-sport; let them say of me, 'As jealous as Ford, that searched a hollow walnut for his wife's leman'. Satisfy me once more; once more search with me.

[*Exeunt John and Robert with the basket.*]

Mrs. Ford. What, ho, Mistress Page, come you and the old woman down; my husband will come into the chamber.

Ford. Old woman? What old woman's that?

Mrs. Ford. Why, it is my maid's aunt of Brainford.

Ford. A witch, a quean, an old cozening quean! Have I not forbid her my house? She comes of errands, does she? We are simple men; we do not know what's brought to pass under the profession of fortune-telling. She works by charms, by spells, by th' figure, and such daubery as this is, beyond our element; we know nothing. Come down, you witch, you hag, you; come down, I say!

152. S.D.] *This ed.; not in F, Q.* 157.] *F;* Why my maidens Ant, *Gilliā* of *Brainford. Q.* 163. daubery] *F* (dawbry). is,] *F;* is *Wheatley.*

149. *table-sport*] the subject of your dinner-table jokes.

150. *a hollow walnut*] the proverbial unlikely small hiding-place.

151. *leman*] lover (often, unlawful lover). Shakespeare may be using the word here—and in *Tw.N.*, II. iii. 26, and *2H4*, v. iii. 49—as a conscious archaism (Byron, of course, revived it in *Childe Harold*).

157.] By naming the old woman 'Gillian', Q makes more probable some reference to a real (or proverbial) person. See Introduction, p. lxii, and cf. l. 168 and note.

158. *cozening*] cheating—both because of her fortune-telling and because he suspects her 'errands' of being immoral.

quean] disreputable female (of any kind, though often used of harlots).

162–3. *by th' figure*] by drawing the appropriate diagrams—no doubt including the 'lines, circles, letters, and characters' that Marlowe's Faustus names as the 'heavenly' 'metaphysics of magicians / And necromantic books' (Scene I, 48–50). In astrology, 'figure' was also used for diagrams of the 'aspects' of the planets, or a horoscope. These interpretations seem more probable than an allusion to the witch's frequent use of a wax figure of her victim on which to cast spells etc. But see next note.

163. *daubery*] Although 'daub' could mean to cover with clay (and perhaps therefore to model in clay) and also to paint inartistically (as the model would no doubt have been painted), 'daubery' here probably derives rather from 'daub' as meaning 'put on a false show' (*O.E.D. v.* 7. b) and so means 'trickery' generally.

163–4. *beyond our element*] *Either* 'beyond our legitimate sphere of activity or knowledge' *or*, spoken ironically, 'beyond our feeble understanding' (cf. 'out of one's element').

Mrs. Ford. Nay, good, sweet husband!—Good gentlemen, let him not strike the old woman.

Enter FALSTAFF *in woman's clothes, and* MISTRESS PAGE.

Mrs. Page. Come, Mother Prat, come, give me your hand.

Ford. I'll prat her. [*Beating him*] Out of my door, you witch, you rag, you baggage, you polecat, you runnion, out, out! I'll conjure you, I'll fortune-tell you. [*Exit Falstaff.*]

Mrs. Page. Are you not ashamed? I think you have killed the poor woman.

Mrs. Ford. Nay, he will do it. 'Tis a goodly credit for you!

Ford. Hang her, witch!

Evans. By yea and no, I think the 'oman is a witch indeed. I like not when a 'oman has a great peard; I spy a great peard under his muffler.

Ford. Will you follow, gentlemen? I beseech you, follow; see but the issue of my jealousy; if I cry out

167. not] *Q3; not in F.* S.D.] Q (*Enter Falstaffe disguised like an old woman, and misteris Page with him, Ford beates him, and hee runnes away.*)*; not in F1; Enter Fal. F2.* 170. S.D.] *As Rowe* (*after* '*witch*')*; not in F.* 171. rag] *F1* (Ragge)*;* Hagge *Q3;* Rag *F2;* Hag *F3.* 172. runnion] *F;* ronyon *Capell.* 173. S.D.] *F2; not in F1.* 181. his] *F;* her *Q.*

168. *Mother Prat*] The name is not found in Q or in any other recorded allusion to Gillian of Brainford.

170. *prat*] Hart thought that this was an instance of the more or less meaningless repetition, in a threat, of a word previously used (like 'fortune-tell' in l. 172); *New Cambridge* compares 'prat(s)' defined by *O.E.D.* (*sb.*²) as 'buttocks'. But cf. *O.E.D.* 'prat' *v.* meaning 'to practise tricks'—which would be exactly parallel to 'I'll conjure you' in l. 172.

171. *rag*] Emendation is unnecessary: 'rag' is similarly applied in *Tim.*, IV. iii. 271, to somebody worthless.

polecat] See note on IV. i. 23.

172. *runnion*] The word—also used contemptuously of a woman, by the First Witch, in *Mac.*, I. iii. 6, in the form 'ronyon'—is probably from MF *rongne,* F *rogne,* the mange or scurf, whence *rongneux,* scurvy (cf. 'the roynish clown' in *AYL.*, II. ii. 8), although *O.E.D.* is uncertain and is content to say 'an abusive term applied to a woman'.

181. *his*] Emendation of F is again superfluous: Evans in his excitement gets his pronouns mixed—and so is wiser than he knows. Certainly Evans does not suspect the truth: as Hart shows, citing e.g. *Mac.*, I. iii. 46, beards were thought to be common among witches.

thus upon no trail, never trust me when I open again.

Page. Let's obey his humour a little further: come gentlemen. *Exeunt Ford, Page, Shallow, Caius, and Evans.*

Mrs. Page. Trust me, he beat him most pitifully.

Mrs. Ford. Nay, by th' mass, that he did not: he beat him most unpitifully, methought.

Mrs. Page. I'll have the cudgel hallowed and hung o'er the altar; it hath done meritorious service.

Mrs. Ford. What think you: may we, with the warrant of womanhood and the witness of a good conscience, pursue him with any further revenge?

Mrs Page. The spirit of wantonness is sure scared out of him; if the devil have him not in fee-simple, with fine and recovery, he will never, I think, in the way of waste attempt us again.

Mrs. Ford. Shall we tell our husbands how we have served him?

Mrs. Page. Yes, by all means—if it be but to scrape the figures out of your husband's brains. If they can find in their hearts the poor unvirtuous fat knight shall be any further afflicted, we two will still be the ministers.

187. S.D.] Q (*Exit omnes*)*; not in F1; Exeunt F2.*

184. *upon no trail*] when there is not in fact a scent for the hounds to follow (and 'cry out' is the technical hunting term for the barking of the dogs).

open] give tongue when following a scent (*O.E.D. v.* II. 21)—a regular hunting term, thus carrying on the image of 'upon no trail'.

186. *obey his humour*] accede to his 'distempered', unbalanced requests.

196. *wantonness*] lust (i.e. a stronger sense than the current one).

197. *in fee-simple*] The legal term for absolute possession, for ever, with no flaw in the title and no 'limitation'.

197–8. *with fine and recovery*] Both 'fine' and 'recovery' have more than one meaning in law, but almost certainly the reference here is to the processes, based on legal fiction, by which an entailed estate is transferred. Mistress Page would thus mean, in short, that unless the devil's title to Falstaff is now final, beyond any possibility of change, Falstaff will not err in this way again. (Elizabethans were particularly interested in legal procedure, and Shakespeare's knowledge of law is not exceptional.)

199. *waste*] Yet another legal term: roughly, any unauthorized act of damage or destruction by a tenant, one who does not have full legal ownership—and so correctly applied to Falstaff's relations with the merry wives.

203. *figures*] imaginings (distinct from the use of 'figure' in l. 163).

206. *ministers*] Perhaps again in a

Mrs. Ford. I'll warrant they'll have him publicly shamed; and methinks there would be no period to the jest should he not be publicly shamed.

Mrs. Page. Come, to the forge with it, then; shape it: I would not have things cool. *Exeunt.*

SCENE III

Enter HOST *and* BARDOLPH.

Bard. Sir, the German desires to have three of your horses: the Duke himself will be to-morrow at court, and they are going to meet him.

Host. What duke should that be comes so secretly? I hear not of him in the court. Let me speak with the gentlemen. They speak English?

210. it, then; shape] *as Hudson;* it, then shape *F;* it then, shape *Hanmer.*

Scene III

SCENE III] *F;* Scene VI. *Changes to the* Garter-Inn. *Pope.* 1. German desires] *F; Germans* desire *Capell.*

legal sense: the officers whose duty it is to ad*minister* the law.

208. *period*] full-stop, end.

Scene III

IV. iii] For the problems of interpreting this scene, see Introduction, pp. xlvi ff. Briefly, one must deduce that Caius and Evans, carrying out their threat to take vengeance on the Host, have hired somebody (some commentators would say Pistol, Nym, and John Rugby) to impersonate the retainers of a German duke and hire the Host's horses—perhaps without paying the hire and certainly proposing not to return them. The German duke may be Count Mömpelgard. It is even more debatable whether the holding of Falstaff's horses as security (v. v. 115–16) is linked with this; indeed it is not clear whether Ford–Brook (v. v. 238–40) does finally release Falstaff from the obligation to pay the money for which the horses have been held.

1. *German desires*] Most editors accept the emendation 'Germans desire' but where all is so cryptic, alteration is most unwise. Obviously there is more than one retainer (Q says 'heere be three Gentlemen come from the Duke the Stanger sir, would haue your horse') but perhaps there is one spokesman.

4. *What duke . . . secretly?*] The line has more meaning if Hotson's theory is accepted—that the play was written for a ceremony to which Count Mömpelgard, Duke of Würtemberg, was carefully not invited: he 'comes so secretly' that he does not come at all. See Introduction, p. xlvii. *Pace New Cambridge*, there is no contradiction with ll. 9–10: the Host has reservations for the retainers, not for the Duke who would no doubt have more aristocratic lodgings.

Bard. Ay, sir; I'll call him to you.
Host. They shall have my horses, but I'll make them pay; I'll sauce them. They have had my house a week at command; I have turned away my other guests. They must come off; I'll sauce them. Come. *Exeunt.*

SCENE IV

Enter PAGE, FORD, MISTRESS PAGE, MISTRESS FORD, *and* EVANS.

Evans. 'Tis one of the best discretions of a 'oman as ever I did look upon.
Page. And did he send you both these letters at an instant?
Mrs. Page. Within a quarter of an hour.
Ford. Pardon me, wife. Henceforth do what thou wilt:
I rather will suspect the sun with cold

7. him] *F;* them *Q.* 9. house] *Q;* houses *F.* 11. come off] *F;* compt off *Theobald, conj. Warburton;* count off *Hanmer, conj. Warburton;* not come off *Capell.*

Scene IV

SCENE IV] *F;* Scene VII. *Changes to* Ford'*s house. Pope.* S.D.] *F; Enter Ford, Page, their wiues, Shallow, and Slender. Syr Hu. Q.* 7. cold] *Rowe;* gold *F.*

7. *him*] The F pronoun is retained, consistently with 'German' in l. 1. Q, equally consistently, has Bardolph say 'Ile call them to you sir'.

9. *sauce*] The metaphor is more probably from seasoning food (cf. *AYL.*, III. v. 69, 'I'll sauce her with bitter words') than, as Hilda Hulme suggests, pp. 45–6, from paying more for the sauce than for the food. *New Cambridge* is surely right in preserving the image by paraphrasing 'make it hot for them'. *O.E.D.* cites only this passage for the meaning 'charge extortionate prices', comparing the much later phrase 'to pay sauce'.

9–10. *at command*] Generally explained as 'reserved for their use upon arrival' but Schmidt's paraphrase 'at pleasure' is supported by many parallels from other plays, and makes sense in that the Host would be less likely to 'turn away' his other guests before the 'Germans' arrived. Perhaps, however, he would have known more about them if they had already been in residence.

11. *come off*] 'pay up' (*O.E.D.*).

Scene IV

6–16. The verse form here, and in most of the scene, may be intended to elevate the tone. Some, however, see signs of revision or of the 'source' play.

7. *suspect . . . with*] suspect . . . of. (Hart glosses 'suspect' as 'accuse', comparing *Oth.*, IV. ii. 145–7—where also the word may surely *mean* 'suspect'. *O.E.D.* gives him no support.)

cold] *New Cambridge* suggests that F's

Than thee with wantonness; now doth thy honour
 stand,
In him that was of late an heretic,
As firm as faith.

Page. 'Tis well, 'tis well; no more.
Be not as extreme in submission
As in offence.
But let our plot go forward: let our wives
Yet once again, to make us public sport,
Appoint a meeting with this old fat fellow,
Where we may take him, and disgrace him for it.

Ford. There is no better way than that they spoke of.

Page. How? To send him word they'll meet him in the Park at midnight? Fie, fie, he'll never come.

Evans. You say he has been thrown in the rivers, and has been grievously peaten, as an old 'oman: methinks there should be terrors in him that he should not come; methinks his flesh is punished, he shall have no desires.

Page. So think I too.

Mrs. Ford. Devise but how you'll use him when he comes,
And let us two devise to bring him thither.

Mrs. Page. There is an old tale goes that Herne the hunter,
Sometime a keeper here in Windsor Forest,

11–12.] *As Capell; one line F.* 28–9.] *As Q3;* There . . . the / Hunter (sometime . . . Forrest) / *F.*

'gold' must be 'an error of dictation'—but compositors' minds do sometimes wander and there is always the possibility of 'foul case'.

9. *heretic*] unbeliever, or one who held false beliefs.

28–45.] Two problems present themselves here: that Q calls the hunter 'Horne' and that it specifies that Falstaff is to be disguised like him, whereas Page in F refers to 'this shape' (l. 44), leaving the audience to infer what the 'shape' is, at least until Mistress Page in l. 63 speaks of dishorning the 'spirit'. (v. i. 5–6 later mentions horns and chain.) As the collation on l. 42 shows, Theobald incorporated two lines from Q in his text, and most editors import at least the second. See Introduction, p. xxxvi. The relevant lines in Q (which gives no other account of 'Horne') are: 'Oft haue you heard since *Horne* the hunter dyed, / That women to affright their litle children, / Ses that he walkes in shape of a great stagge. / Now for that *Falstaffe* hath bene so deceiued, / As that he dares not venture to the house, / Weele send him word to meet vs in the field, / Disguised like *Horne*, with huge horns on his head, / The houre shalbe iust betweene twelue and one, / And at that time we will meet him both'.

29. *Sometime*] once, formerly.

Doth all the winter-time, at still midnight,
Walk round about an oak, with great ragg'd horns,
And there he blasts the tree, and takes the cattle,
And makes milch-kine yield blood, and shakes a chain
In a most hideous and dreadful manner.
You have heard of such a spirit, and well you know
The superstitious idle-headed eld
Receiv'd, and did deliver to our age,
This tale of Herne the hunter for a truth.

Page. Why, yet there want not many that do fear
In deep of night to walk by this Herne's oak.
But what of this?

Mrs. Ford. Marry, this is our device,
That Falstaff at that oak shall meet with us.

Page. Well, let it not be doubted but he'll come;
And in this shape when you have brought him thither,
What shall be done with him? What is your plot?

Mrs. Page. That likewise have we thought upon, and thus:
Nan Page (my daughter) and my little son
And three or four more of their growth we'll dress
Like urchins, ouphs, and fairies, green and white,

31. ragg'd] *F1* (rag'd-), *F2;* ragged *Rowe;* jag'd *Capell.* 32. tree] *F;* trees *Hanmer.* 33. makes] *F2;* make *F1.* 42. us.] *F;* us. / We'll send him word to meet us in the Field, / Disguis'd like *Herne*, with huge Horns on his Head. *Theobald (from Q, which has 'Horne', not 'Herne');* us, / Disguis'd like *Herne*, with huge horns on his head. *Capell.* 43. come;] *As F* (come,); come, *Capell.* 44. shape when] *F2;* shape, when *F1;* shape; when *Capell.*

31. *ragg'd*] shaggy, rough or jagged (*O.E.D. a.*[1] I. 1, 2)—used by Shakespeare several times of rocks.

32. *blasts*] Either 'blights' (*O.E.D. v.* 5) or 'kills as if with lightning'. The word was especially associated with evil supernatural influence; cf. *Ham.*, I. iv. 41, 'airs from heaven or blasts from hell'.

takes] 'possesses', bewitches ('taking' is similarly used of a malign influence, as in *Lr.*, III. iv. 61).

33. *shakes a chain*] Then, as now, a presumed habit of ghosts. Cf. v. i. 5.

36. *eld*] ancients (in the sense of people of earlier ages, as suggested by *O.E.D. sb.*[2] 5. b).

39. *want not*] fail not, are.

43. *let it not be doubted*] Some commentators have felt that Page is too easily persuaded and that the text must have been cut. Dramatic illusion, however, allows for a playwright to omit part of a sequence of evidence, and especially in the comedies Shakespeare relies on this.

48. *growth*] size, age.

49. *urchins*] goblins or elves (*O.E.D.* I. c).

ouphs] The same word as oaph, auph,

With rounds of waxen tapers on their heads,
And rattles in their hands; upon a sudden,
As Falstaff, she, and I are newly met,
Let them from forth a sawpit rush at once
With some diffused song; upon their sight,
We two in great amazedness will fly;
Then let them all encircle him about,
And fairy-like to pinch the unclean knight,
And ask him why, that hour of fairy revel,
In their so sacred paths he dares to tread
In shape profane.

Mrs. Ford. And till he tell the truth,
Let the supposed fairies pinch him sound,
And burn him with their tapers.

Mrs. Page. The truth being known,
We'll all present ourselves, dis-horn the spirit,
And mock him home to Windsor.

Ford. The children must
Be practis'd well to this, or they'll ne'er do 't.

Evans. I will teach the children their behaviours; and I will be like a jack-an-apes also, to burn the knight with my taber.

57. to pinch] *F; too, pinch Warburton;* to—pinch *Steevens*[2], *conj. Tyrwhitt.*
60. *Mrs. Ford*] *Rowe; Ford F.*

or auf: children of elves (magical dwarfs) and particularly changelings, substituted by fairies for human children.

54. *diffused*] divided among them, as a kind of part-song. *New Cambridge* compares the S.D. 'Burthen (dispersedly)' in *Tp.*, I. ii. 382. (The other 'explanation' is 'wild' or 'irregular'.)

57. *to pinch*] 'To' may seem unusual after 'let', but the construction is not unlike others described in Abbott 349. Cf. also 'thou . . . / didst let . . . / thy rude hand to act / The deed', *John*, IV. ii. 237–41. Cf. also 'to marry' in l. 84 and 'to pinch' in IV. vi. 43. For 'pinch', cf. V. v. 46 and 103 S.D., and notes.

61. *sound*] soundly.

63. *dis-horn*] Greg, in the letter to Wilson quoted in *New Cambridge* p. 134 (see note on IV. ii. 59), argued that 'There would be little point in saying "take off his horns"—it must mean "strip him of his Horne disguise"' (and so maintained that the name must be 'Horne'). To take off the dressed-up Falstaff's horns, however, is symbolic enough of exposing him in his true character.

67. *jack-an-apes*] monkey (see I. iv. 102 and note). Q has it that in the last scene Evans is dressed 'like a Satyre' and some editors insert a S.D. accordingly—and *New Cambridge* actually says that 'a satyr . . . was a kind of "ape"'. Falstaff's 'Heavens defend me from that Welsh *fairy*' (V. v. 82) hardly suggests that the satyr-disguise was intended in the F version, even if it

Ford. That will be excellent. I'll go buy them vizards.
Mrs. Page. My Nan shall be the queen of all the fairies,
Finely attired in a robe of white.
Page. That silk will I go buy.—[*Aside*] And in that time
Shall Master Slender steal my Nan away,
And marry her at Eton.—Go, send to Falstaff
straight.
Ford. Nay, I'll to him again in name of Brook;
He'll tell me all his purpose. Sure, he'll come.
Mrs. Page. Fear not you that. Go get us properties
And tricking for our fairies.
Evans. Let us about it: it is admirable pleasures and fery
honest knaveries. [*Exeunt Page, Ford, and Evans.*]
Mrs. Page. Go, Mistress Ford,
Send quickly to Sir John to know his mind.
[*Exit Mistress Ford.*]
I'll to the Doctor, he hath my good will,
And none but he to marry with Nan Page.
That Slender, though well landed, is an idiot;
And he my husband best of all affects.
The Doctor is well money'd, and his friends
Potent at court: he, none but he, shall have her,
Though twenty thousand worthier come to crave
her. [*Exit.*]

69.] *As one line, Pope;* That . . . excellent, / Ile . . . vizards. *F.* 70–1.] *As Rowe*[3]*; as prose F.* 72. *Aside*] *Pope* (*after l. 73*)*; not in F.* time] *F;* tire *Theobald.* 79–80.] *Prose as Pope;* Let . . . it, / It . . . knaueries. *F.* 80. S.D.] *Rowe; not in F.* 82. quickly] *F; Quickly Theobald.* S.D.] *Rowe; not in F.* 84. he to] *F;* he, to *Pope.* 89. S.D.] *F2; not in F1.*

does not rule out the possibility. ('Welsh goat' in v. v. 138 probably has no reference to costume at all.) Hart may be right in deducing, with the support of a passage in Nashe, that 'jack-an-apes' also meant an evil spirit (or evil fairy).

69. *vizards*] visors or masks (cf. IV. vi. 39).

74. *Eton*] Eton is within sight of Windsor, across the river.

77. *properties*] In the sense in which it is still used in the theatre, of any portable article necessary in the production.

78. *tricking*] adornments (the verb 'trick' commonly means 'dress up').

85. *well landed*] possessed of much land (as compared with the 'well moneyed' Caius, who has no landed inheritance).

86. *affects*] likes, approves.

SCENE V

Enter HOST *and* SIMPLE.

Host. What wouldst thou have, boor? What, thick-skin? Speak, breathe, discuss; brief, short, quick, snap.

Sim. Marry, sir, I come to speak with Sir John Falstaff from Master Slender.

Host. There's his chamber, his house, his castle, his standing-bed, and truckle-bed; 'tis painted about with the story of the Prodigal, fresh and new. Go, knock and call; he'll speak like an Anthropophaginian unto thee; knock, I say.

Sim. There's an old woman, a fat woman, gone up into his chamber. I'll be so bold as stay, sir, till she come down; I come to speak with her, indeed.

Host. Ha? A fat woman? The knight may be robbed; I'll call.—Bully knight, bully Sir John! Speak from thy lungs military. Art thou there? It is thine host, thine Ephesian, calls.

Scene V

SCENE V] *F;* Scene VIII. *The* Garter-Inn. *Pope.* S.D.] *Q; Enter Host, Simple, Falstaffe, Bardolfe, Euans, Caius, Quickly. F.*

1. *thick-skin*] blockhead or bumpkin. Cf. *MND.*, III. ii. 13.

2. *discuss*] disclose, speak up. Cf. I. iii. 89 and note.

snap] Apparently an adjective or adverb, connected with the verb 'snip' or 'snap', and meaning 'sudden(ly)' or 'rapid(ly)'. The closest parallel is *LLL.*, V. i. 62–3, 'a quick venue of wit! snip, snap, quick and home!'

5. *castle*] There is no need to suspect an allusion to Falstaff's original name, Oldcastle, in *1H4*. A man's home is still his castle.

6. *truckle-bed*] a small low bed on 'truckles', i.e. castors, that could be run under a normal bed when not in use.

'tis painted . . .] It is not quite clear whether the Host is referring to the painted hangings round the bed or round the room; both were known. In wealthier homes, woven tapestry was used.

7. *the Prodigal*] the Prodigal Son of Christ's parable, as told in Luke 15.

8–9. *Anthropophaginian*] Strictly, a cannibal, an eater of human flesh. The noun is familiar from Othello's traveller's tales to Desdemona of 'the Cannibals that each other eat, / The Anthropophagi and men whose heads / Do grow beneath their shoulders' (I. iii. 143–5). Nashe (in *Christ's Tears*) and Dekker (in *The Wonderful Year*) also use forms of the word, the latter contributing the added information that the 'Anthropophagi are Scithians'. *If* the Host knows what the word means, he must be ironically cheering Simple up with the expectation that Falstaff will really 'bite his head off'.

16. *Ephesian*] The word is generally explained as 'boon companion', on a

Fal. [*Above*] How now, mine host?

Host. Here's a Bohemian-Tartar tarries the coming down of thy fat woman. Let her descend, bully, let her descend; my chambers are honourable. Fie! Privacy? Fie!

Enter FALSTAFF.

Fal. There was, mine host, an old fat woman even now with me, but she's gone.

Sim. Pray you, sir, was 't not the wise woman of Brainford?

Fal. Ay, marry, was it, mussel-shell: what would you with her?

Sim. My master, sir, my master Slender, sent to her, seeing her go thorough the streets, to know, sir, whether one Nym, sir, that beguiled him of a chain, had the chain or no.

Fal. I spake with the old woman about it.

Sim. And what says she, I pray, sir?

17. *Above*] *As Theobald; not in F; Enter* Falstaff. *Rowe.* 21. S.D.] *Q* (*after l. 23*); *not in F.* 28. My . . . Slender] *F* (My Master (Sir) my master *Slender*,); My master, sir, master Slender *Steevens*[2].

supposed analogy with 'Corinthian' (Corinth being noted for loose living); and the same explanation is given of *2H4*, II. ii. 164, where Prince Hal asks the Page what company Falstaff is keeping and is told 'Ephesians, my lord, of the old church'. In *Sewanee Review*, LXVII, 1959, 204–19, however, J. A. Bryant has suggested that much more is involved in *H4*: Hal's famous self-commitment, in his early soliloquy, to 'redeeming time when men think least I will' is seen to be a quotation from Ephesians 5:16; the theme is identified with Paul's plea to the Ephesians 4:22, 'that ye put off concerning the former conversation the old man which is corrupt according to the deceitful lusts'. 'Ephesians' in *2H4* therefore presumably means, specifically, Ephesians in need of salvation. Whether any of this deeper meaning carries over, ironically, to the Host's description of himself (as such an unregenerate sinner) is an open question.

18. *Bohemian-Tartar*] The Tartars, proverbially savages, are not normally associated with Bohemia. The Host enjoys making up epithets, as perhaps does Pistol: 'Phrygian Turk' in I. iii. 84 is a close parallel.

tarries] awaits.

26. *mussel-shell*] Johnson explained, reasonably enough, that Simple is so christened because he is standing with his mouth open; Hart, objecting—in a rather literal way—that this image would apply only to the whole mussel, with *two* shells, preferred to think that the reference was to 'an empty worthless object'. *New Cambridge*'s suggestion of a further possible pun on 'muzzle' (it accepts the emendation 'tyke', i.e. mongrel, in l. 51) piles one hypothesis on another.

Fal. Marry, she says that the very same man that beguiled Master Slender of his chain cozened him of it.

Sim. I would I could have spoken with the woman herself; I had other things to have spoken with her too, from him.

Fal. What are they? Let us know.

Host. Ay, come; quick.

Sim. I may not conceal them, sir.

Host. Conceal them, or thou diest.

Sim. Why, sir, they were nothing but about Mistress Anne Page, to know if it were my master's fortune to have her or no.

Fal. 'Tis, 'tis his fortune.

Sim. What, sir?

Fal. To have her, or no. Go; say the woman told me so.

Sim. May I be bold to say so, sir?

Fal. Ay, sir; like who more bold.

Sim. I thank your worship; I shall make my master glad with these tidings. [*Exit.*]

Host. Thou art clerkly, thou art clerkly, Sir John. Was there a wise woman with thee?

Fal. Ay, that there was, mine host; one that hath taught me more wit than ever I learned before in my life; and I paid nothing for it neither, but was paid for my learning.

Enter BARDOLPH.

42. *Sim.*] *Rowe; Fal. F.* conceal] *F;* reveal *conj. Farmer.* 43. or] *F;* and *Hanmer.* 51. Ay, sir; like] *F* (I Sir: like) *; I* tike *Q;* Ay, sir Tike; like *Steevens*², *conj. Farmer;* Ay, sir Tike; *Reed.* 53. *Exit*] *Rowe; not in F.* 59. S.D.] *Q; not in F.*

42.] Rowe's emendation, giving the line to Simple, not Falstaff, seems inescapable, but there is no need to emend 'conceal' to 'reveal', which Simple undoubtedly means: one character after another in this comedy falls into malapropism. The Host echoes Simple's word ironically in the next line.

51. *like who more bold*] Emendation is unnecessary (and Q's 'tike' is either, as Hart argued, a simple misprint, or a reporter's groping attempt to 'improve'). The F reading is ably defended by Sisson, *N.R.*, p. 72, as idiomatic and meaning 'as bold as the boldest'.

54. *clerkly*] learned like a clerk (scholar).

58. *was paid*] was rewarded, by being thrashed. Falstaff is ringing the changes on the popular maxim 'Bought wit is best' (Tilley W545).

Bard. Out, alas sir, cozenage, mere cozenage!

Host. Where be my horses? Speak well of them, varletto.

Bard. Run away with the cozeners: for so soon as I came beyond Eton, they threw me off, from behind one of them, in a slough of mire; and set spurs and away, like three German devils, three Doctor Faustuses.

Host. They are gone but to meet the Duke, villain; do not say they be fled. Germans are honest men.

Enter EVANS.

Evans. Where is mine host?

Host. What is the matter, sir?

Evans. Have a care of your entertainments: there is a friend of mine come to town tells me there is three cozen-Germans that has cozened all the hosts of

62. with] *F;* with by *Collier*[2]. 67. S.D.] *Q (after ll. 78–84); not in F.* 71–2. three cozen-Germans] *F* (three Cozen-Iermans)*;* three sorts of cosen garmombles *Q.*

60. *cozenage*] double-dealing.

mere] absolute—as in the often misunderstood line in the 'Seven ages of man' speech in *AYL.*, II. vii. 165, 'second childishness and mere oblivion'.

61. *varletto*] 'Varlet' is too simple for the Host.

62. *the cozeners*] There is no doubting the identification of these with the 'gentlemen' who hired the Host's horses in IV. iii. (q.v.).

64. *slough*] marsh or bog—and Wheatley's suggestion of a pun on Slough, then a mere village, near Windsor, is not unattractive.

65. *Doctor Faustuses*] Another reference to Marlowe's famous play (see note on I. i. 120)—this time to the titular hero, the German scholar who sold his soul to the devil in return for magical power. There may be particular reference to (a) the scenes (xiii and xiv, ed. J. D. Jump) in which Faustus's vengeance on three men who try to murder him involves having one (or perhaps all three) of them dragged through 'a lake of mud and dirt'; and (b) the scene (xv) in which he sells a horse to a 'horse-courser' and changes it into straw when the courser disobeys instructions by riding the horse into water.

67. *Germans . . . men*] The speech, not in Q, so far from 'softening down' the Mömpelgard allusion, as *New Cambridge* believes, would presumably have raised a laugh from a 'knowing' court audience.

68–84.] It seems clear that Evans and Caius, who warn the Host to avoid what has already happened, do so by malice aforethought, having arranged the loss themselves. Each, significantly, uses the hypocritical 'I tell you for good will'.

70. *entertainments*] Not, probably, supplies or equipment but, in Evans's version of English, those whom you 'entertain'—'guests' at the Inn.

72. *cozen-Germans*] A quibble on 'cousins-german(e)' or 'cousin-german(e)s' (full cousins) and on cozening-Germans, rogues pretending to be Germans, and even 'cousin-Germans', i.e. German 'relations'. (There

Readins, of Maidenhead, of Colebrook, of horses and money. I tell you for good will, look you; you are wise, and full of gibes and vlouting-stocks, and 'tis not convenient you should be cozened. Fare you well. *Exit.*

Enter CAIUS.

Caius. Vere is mine host de Jarteer?

Host. Here, Master Doctor, in perplexity and doubtful dilemma.

Caius. I cannot tell vat is dat; but it is tell-a me dat you make grand preparation for a Duke de Jamanie: by my trot, dere is no Duke that the court is know to come. I tell you for good will; adieu. *Exit.*

Host. Hue and cry, villain, go!—Assist me, knight, I am undone!—Fly, run, hue and cry, villain, I am undone! *Exeunt Host [and Bardolph].*

77. *Exit*] *Q; not in F.* *Enter Caius*] *Q (before ll. 68–77); not in F.* 84. *Exit*] *Q; not in F.* 85. Hue] *Rowe;* Huy *F.* 86. hue] *Rowe;* huy *F.* 87. S.D.] *Capell; not in F; Exit Q.*

was a proverb 'Call me cousin but cozen me not'—Tilley C739.) The notorious Q reading, 'three sorts of cosen garmombles', may retain a kind of bad pun on, or anagram of, Mömpelgard, perhaps a relic of an authentic text but more probably a substitution made by a reporter who remembered only that there had been a joke involving the Duke. The word 'garmombles', or something like it, did exist; Nashe uses the similar 'geremumble' at least twice, as a term of abuse: in *Strange News* he calls Gabriel Harvey 'the foresaid fanaticall *Phobetor, geremumble, tirleriwhisco,* or what you will', and in *Nashe's Lenten Stuff* he employs 'geremumble' as a verb, meaning apparently to garbage (gut) fish (I. 321 and III. 207).

73. *Readins*] Reading, a village not far from Windsor (Maidenhead and Colebrook or Colnbrook were others); now of course a large town.

75. *gibes*] Evans may or may not mean this. If he does mean it, he is referring sarcastically to the Host's gibes at him in III. i. Certainly 'vlouting-stocks' recalls his words to Caius on that occasion, 'Pray you let us not be laughing-stocks to other men's humours' (ll. 78–9) and 'he has made us his vlouting-stog' (l. 108).

79. *doubtful*] Either 'doubting' (*O.E.D.* 2) or 'apprehensive' (*O.E.D.* 5).

82. *Jamanie*] i.e. Germany. Shakespeare may be indicating the pronunciation but there is reason for thinking that 'Iarman' may have been his own normal spelling of the word. Compare F's 'Iermans' in l. 72. The point was made by R. C. Bald (*Shakespeare Survey* II. 58).

83–4. *no Duke . . . come*] See IV. iii. 4 and note.

85. *villain . . . knight*] 'Villain' is addressed to Bardolph, as before (l. 66); 'knight' to Falstaff—who, as he proceeds to say, is too sorry for himself to worry about other people's troubles.

Fal. I would all the world might be cozened, for I have been cozened and beaten too. If it should come to the ear of the court how I have been transformed, and how my transformation hath been washed and cudgelled, they would melt me out of my fat drop by drop, and liquor fishermen's boots with me; I warrant they would whip me with their fine wits till I were as crest-fallen as a dried pear. I never prospered since I forswore myself at primero. Well, if my wind were but long enough, I would repent.

Enter MISTRESS QUICKLY.

Now, whence come you?

Quick. From the two parties, forsooth.

Fal. The devil take one party, and his dam the other, and so they shall be both bestowed. I have suffered more for their sakes—more than the villainous inconstancy of man's disposition is able to bear.

Quick. And have not they suffered? Yes, I warrant, speciously one of them: Mistress Ford, good heart, is beaten black and blue, that you cannot see a white spot about her.

Fal. What tell'st thou me of black and blue? I was beaten myself into all the colours of the rainbow; and I was like to be apprehended for the witch of Brainford. But that my admirable dexterity of wit,

97. long enough] *F;* long inough to say my prayers *Q.* 98. S.D.] *Q (after l. 99); not in F.*

93. *liquor*] oil or grease (as boots are sometimes oiled today to make them resistant to water).

95. *as crest-fallen . . . pear*] A daringly mixed metaphor, of course: 'crest-fallen' describes the defeated cock, and 'fallen' provides the link to the image of the pear that has fallen to the ground and shrivelled up.

96. *forswore myself*] (Presumably) cheated, by lying about the cards I held.

primero] a popular game of cards.

97. *long enough*] The additional words imported by many editors from Q no doubt make the joke obvious—and for that reason are unlikely to have been written by Shakespeare for Falstaff.

101.] Cf. I. i. 135 and note.

102. *bestowed*] placed, and looked after.

106. *speciously*] specially (as before, in III. iv. 105).

my counterfeiting the action of an old woman, delivered me, the knave constable had set me i' th' stocks, i' th' common stocks, for a witch.

Quick. Sir, let me speak with you in your chamber: you shall hear how things go and, I warrant, to your content. Here is a letter will say somewhat. Good hearts, what ado here is to bring you together! Sure, one of you does not serve heaven well, that you are so crossed.

Fal. Come up into my chamber. *Exeunt.*

SCENE VI

Enter FENTON *and* HOST.

Host. Master Fenton, talk not to me, my mind is heavy. I will give over all.

Fent. Yet hear me speak. Assist me in my purpose
And, as I am a gentleman, I'll give thee
A hundred pound in gold more than your loss.

Host. I will hear you, Master Fenton; and I will, at the least, keep your counsel.

Fent. From time to time I have acquainted you
With the dear love I bear to fair Anne Page,
Who mutually hath answer'd my affection,
So far forth as herself might be her chooser,
Even to my wish. I have a letter from her
Of such contents as you will wonder at,
The mirth whereof so larded with my matter

113. an old] *F; a wood Theobald;* a wode *Hanmer.*

Scene VI

SCENE VI] *F; Scene VI. Another Room. Capell.*

113. *an old woman*] i.e. an ordinary old lady, as distinct from 'a witch'.

121. *crossed*] thwarted (*O.E.D.* 'cross' *v.* 12, 14).

122.] It will be seen that Shakespeare does not attempt the particularly difficult task of showing how Falstaff could have been persuaded to risk a third meeting with Mistress Ford; he is content to indicate the direction that Quickly's lies might have taken.

Scene VI

2. *give over*] give up.

14. *larded with my matter*] mixed or

That neither singly can be manifested
Without the show of both. Fat Falstaff
Hath a great scene; the image of the jest
I'll show you here at large. Hark, good mine host.
To-night at Herne's oak, just 'twixt twelve and one,
Must my sweet Nan present the Fairy Queen—
The purpose why, is here—in which disguise,
While other jests are something rank on foot,
Her father hath commanded her to slip
Away with Slender, and with him at Eton
Immediately to marry; she hath consented.
Now, sir, her mother, even strong against that match,
And firm for Doctor Caius, hath appointed
That he shall likewise shuffle her away,
While other sports are tasking of their minds,

16. Fat] *F1;* fat Sir *Iohn F2;* wherein fat *Malone* (*as Q*). 17. great scene] *F;* mightie scare *Q;* great scene in it *Capell;* great share *Dyce*²*;* great scare *Craig.* 25–6.] *This ed.;* Immediately . . . Now Sir, / Her . . . match *F;* Immediately . . . consented: / Now, Sir, / Her . . . match, *Malone.* 26. even strong] *F;* ever strong *Pope;* still *Q.* 27. Caius] *F; Cayus,* in a robe of red *Q.*

interpenetrated with the problem I am discussing with you. Fenton's language hereabouts is extremely formal—even stilted.

16–17. *Fat Falstaff . . . scene*] *New Cambridge,* which argues that throughout the play there are signs that Falstaff replaced a character in the 'source play' who must have been a different kind of wooer, maintains that 'verse and sense are improved' if the passage is read without these words—and that the same is true of the corresponding Q line 'Wherein fat *Falstaffe* had [sic] a mightie scare'. What the Q line does prove is that the reporter was trying to recall a text like F.

17–18. *the image . . . at large*] i.e. I'll describe to you in detail the form the jest will take.

20. *present*] act the part of.

21. *here*] Perhaps Fenton points to the letter from Anne.

22. *something rank*] somewhat overabundantly. 'Rank' is used as an adverb, as in *Troil.,* I. iii. 196.

26.] The rearrangement of the F lines adopted here involves no problems, of 'patchwork' or otherwise; many a line in Elizabethan drama has twelve syllables of which the term of address (such as 'My lord') forms the first two.

even] Pope's emendation 'ever' may well be correct but is not essential; and Q's 'still against that match' could be an attempted recalling of either. Wheatley maintained that 'even' means 'equally'.

27.] Q's mention of a *red* dress here gives the best reason for thinking that red was the third colour involved in the multiple intrigue of Act v, but neither F nor Q is consistent in its account of what actually happens. See Introduction, pp. xxx-xxxii.

28. *shuffle*] smuggle or steal, 'remove . . . in a hurried, secret, or underhand manner' (*O.E.D. v.* 5. b).

29. *tasking of*] employing (the modern idiom is 'taxing').

And at the dean'ry, where a priest attends,
Straight marry her; to this her mother's plot
She seemingly obedient likewise hath
Made promise to the Doctor. Now, thus it rests:
Her father means she shall be all in white;
And in that habit, when Slender sees his time
To take her by the hand and bid her go,
She shall go with him: her mother hath intended,
The better to denote her to the Doctor—
For they must all be mask'd and vizarded—
That quaint in green she shall be loose enrob'd,
With ribands pendant flaring 'bout her head;
And when the Doctor spies his vantage ripe,
To pinch her by the hand, and, on that token,
The maid hath given consent to go with him.

Host. Which means she to deceive, father or mother?

Fent. Both, my good host, to go along with me:
And here it rests—that you'll procure the vicar
To stay for me at church, 'twixt twelve and one,
And, in the lawful name of marrying,
To give our hearts united ceremony.

Host. Well, husband your device; I'll to the vicar.
Bring you the maid, you shall not lack a priest.

Fent. So shall I evermore be bound to thee;
Besides, I'll make a present recompense. *Exeunt.*

38. denote] *Capell, conj. Steevens;* deuote *F1* (*probably a turned* '*n*'); devote *F2*.
49. in] *F* (*corrected*); id (*uncorrected*).

30. *dean'ry*] Hart takes this to mean the deanery attached to St George's Chapel (in the grounds of Windsor Castle). The alternative is to believe that the word is used very loosely of a parsonage.

40. *quaint*] neat(ly) or pleasant(ly). The word had no pejorative implication at all in Elizabethan usage, as is perhaps adequately shown by *Ado*, III. iv. 22–3, 'for a fine, quaint, graceful, and excellent fashion, yours is worth ten on 't'.

41. *pendant*] hanging down (from her hair or head-dress).

flaring] waving all round.

43. *To pinch*] For the use of the full infinitive, cf. IV. iv. 57 and note.

token] agreed signal.

50. *give . . . ceremony*] Again Fenton's language is so formal as to seem stilted or precious; he can only mean 'unite us with the full sanction of religious rites'.

51. *husband your device*] look after your (own part of the) plan. For 'husband' used in a similar context to mean 'manage' a plan involving trickery, cf. *Shr.*, *Ind.* I. 68. Conceivably the Host also intends a pun—but the Host in this scene is a strangely chastened version of the earlier character.

54. *present*] immediate.

ACT V

SCENE I

Enter FALSTAFF *and* [MISTRESS] QUICKLY.

Fal. Prithee no more prattling; go. I'll hold. This is the third time; I hope good luck lies in odd numbers. Away, go! They say there is divinity in odd numbers, either in nativity, chance, or death. Away!

Quick. I'll provide you a chain, and I'll do what I can to get you a pair of horns.

Fal. Away, I say, time wears; hold up your head, and mince. [*Exit Mistress Quickly.*]

[*Enter* FORD *as* BROOK]

How now, Master Brook? Master Brook, the matter will be known to-night, or never. Be you in the Park about midnight, at Herne's oak, and you shall see wonders.

ACT V

Scene I

ACT V SCENE I] *F; Act V Scene I. A Room in the garter Inn. Capell.* S.D.] *Rowe; Enter Falstoffe, Quickly, and Ford. F.* 2–4. I hope . . . death] *As F;* They say there is good luck in old numbers *Q.* 8. *Exit Mistress Quickly*] *Rowe* (*after l. 6*)*; not in F.* *Enter Ford as Brook*] *As Rowe; not in F.*

1. *hold*] meet the commitment, keep the appointment (cf. *O.E.D.* 'hold' *v.* I. 9).

1–4. *This is the third time . . . death*] Falstaff is alluding to the group of proverbs best known from 'third time lucky'. Tilley cites 'There is luck in odd numbers' (L582); 'all things thrive at thrice' (T175); and 'the third time pays for all' (T319—quoted in *Tw.N.*, v. i. 40).

3. *divinity*] Perhaps 'divination' (*O.E.D.* 5); more probably, 'divine power' (*O.E.D.* 3), as in *Ham.*, v. ii. 10.

7. *wears*] is running out (*O.E.D.* *v.*[1] IV. 19).

8. *mince*] When used of speech or walking, the verb normally has a pejorative sense in Shakespeare, implying affectation; cf. also Portia's smiling boast that when she and Nerissa are disguised as males, 'I'll prove the prettier fellow of the two, / . . . and turn two mincing steps / Into a manly stride' (*Mer.V.*, III. iv. 64–8).

Ford. Went you not to her yesterday, sir, as you told me you had appointed?

Fal. I went to her, Master Brook, as you see, like a poor old man, but I came from her, Master Brook, like a poor old woman. That same knave Ford, her husband, hath the finest mad devil of jealousy in him, Master Brook, that ever governed frenzy. I will tell you he beat me grievously, in the shape of a woman; for in the shape of man, Master Brook, I fear not Goliath with a weaver's beam, because I know also life is a shuttle. I am in haste; go along with me: I'll tell you all, Master Brook. Since I plucked geese, played truant, and whipped top, I knew not what 'twas to be beaten, till lately. Follow me; I'll tell you strange things of this knave Ford, on whom to-night I will be revenged, and I will deliver his wife into your hand. Follow. Strange things in hand, Master Brook! Follow. *Exeunt.*

SCENE II

Enter PAGE, SHALLOW, *and* SLENDER.

Page. Come, come, we'll couch i' th' castle-ditch till we

22. Goliath] *Steevens*[3]*;* Goliah *Ff.*

Scene II

SCENE II] *F;* Act V. Scene I. Windsor-Park. *Pope; Scene II. A Street. Capell.*

22. *Goliath . . . beam*] The comparison of Goliath's spear to a weaver's beam is made in I Samuel 17 : 7, and at least twice thereafter in the Old Testament; cf. also I Chronicles 11 : 23.

22–3. *also life is a shuttle*] As 'also' indicates, Falstaff is adding another half-quotation from the Bible about a weaver, this time from Job 7 : 6: 'My days are swifter than a weaver's shuttle, and are spent without hope'.

24. *plucked geese*] Apparently plucking feathers from a living goose, to use the feathers for some game, was a schoolboy prank.

25. *whipped top*] made my top spin and continue spinning by lashing it with a whip.

Scene II

1. *couch*] lie hidden.

castle-ditch] Some editors identify this as the Castle-ditch, on one side of Windsor Castle.

see the light of our fairies. Remember, son Slender, my daughter.

Slen. Ay, forsooth; I have spoke with her, and we have a nay-word how to know one another: I come to her in white, and cry 'mum'; she cries 'budget'; and by that we know one another.

Shal. That's good too; but what needs either your 'mum' or her 'budget'? The white will decipher her well enough. It hath struck ten o'clock.

Page. The night is dark; light and spirits will become it well. Heaven prosper our sport! No man means evil but the devil, and we shall know him by his horns. Let's away; follow me. *Exeunt.*

SCENE III

Enter MISTRESS PAGE, MISTRESS FORD, *and* DOCTOR CAIUS.

Mrs. Page. Master Doctor, my daughter is in green: when you see your time, take her by the hand, away with her to the deanery, and dispatch it quickly. Go before into the Park; we two must go together.

3. my daughter] *F2;* my *F1.*

Scene III

SCENE III] *F; Scene III. Another Street, leading to the Park. Capell;* Scene III. *The Street in Windsor. Malone.*

3. *daughter*] F1 has a blank space where this, or some similar word, should be. Apparently the compositor's attention was distracted, or type was dropped. There is no corresponding scene in Q, but F2's addition is acceptable.

5. *nay-word*] pass-word (as in II. ii. 121).

6. *mum . . . budget*] Slender (or Anne, in irony) has chosen an appropriately childish greeting. 'Mumbudget' (related to the surviving 'mum's the word'—Tilley M1310) was used of an inability or a refusal to speak (Tilley M1311); *O.E.D.* conjectures, with convincing citations, that it was 'the name of some children's game in which silence was required'. Thomas Hardy later uses 'to come mum-budgeting' in the sense of 'to come secretly'.

8. *what needs*] what is the need for; cf. Apemantus' indignant 'What needs these feasts, pomps and vain-glories?' (*Tim.*, I. ii. 248–9).

11. *become*] suit.

13. *devil . . . horns*] A neat adaptation of 'the devil is known by his horns' (Tilley D252).

Caius. I know vat I have to do. Adieu. [*Exit.*]

Mrs. Page. Fare you well, sir.—My husband will not rejoice so much at the abuse of Falstaff as he will chafe at the Doctor's marrying my daughter; but 'tis no matter: better a little chiding than a great deal of heartbreak.

Mrs. Ford. Where is Nan now? And her troop of fairies? And the Welsh devil Hugh?

Mrs. Page. They are all couched in a pit hard by Herne's oak, with obscured lights, which, at the very instant of Falstaff's and our meeting, they will at once display to the night.

Mrs. Ford. That cannot choose but amaze him.

Mrs. Page. If he be not amazed, he will be mocked; if he be amazed, he will every way be mocked.

Mrs. Ford. We'll betray him finely.

Mrs. Page. Against such lewdsters and their lechery

5. *Exit*] *F2; not in F1.* 12. Welsh devil Hugh] *As Capell;* Welch-deuill Herne *F; Welch*-deuill *Herne Q3; Welch* devil *Evans Theobald;* Welsh devil *Hart.*

9–10. *better . . . heartbreak*] This may be a proverb, or Mistress Page's variation on one. There are several that could be relevant, including 'Better once a mischief than always an inconvenience' (Tilley M995) and 'Better a snotty child than his nose wiped off' (C296).

12. *Welsh devil Hugh*] The F reading 'Welch-deuill Herne' is retained by *New Cambridge*, as 'Welsh devil-hern', and defended on the argument that Evans was dressed as a satyr [which is far from certain], that 'a satyr was a kind of devil, for the Elizabethans' [which is debatable], and that 'thus he was a "devil-hern" in two senses: (i) "hern" or "harn"=brain; here used of the head, v. N.E.D. "harn", (ii) his function was to "devil" Herne–Falstaff'. This is not easily acceptable. Nor, *pace* Hart, is there particular significance in the fact that 'Herne', unlike most proper names, is not in italics in F; on the same page, [E5v], 'Ioue' and 'Iupiter' are in roman, not italic. Capell's emendation 'Hugh' may be accepted on the assumption either that the compositor had read ahead and had in his mind 'Herne's' from l. 13, or that the later line had caught his eye. Some support is lent to the emendation by Ford's 'Well said, fairy Hugh' in v. v. 132 and Falstaff's 'Heavens defend me from that Welsh fairy' in v. v. 82.

17. *amaze*] Probably 'terrify' or 'frighten', but the other frequent meaning in Elizabethan English is 'bewilder', which can hardly be ruled out here.

18. *mocked*] *New Cambridge* sees a quibble here and in l. 19, on the two senses of 'deceived' and 'ridiculed'.

21. *lewdsters*] The meaning is obvious but no earlier use of the word has been recorded.

21–2.] No doubt the couplet is to give the effect of epigram, and to sound authoritative.

Those that betray them do no treachery.

Mrs. Ford. The hour draws on. To the oak, to the oak!

Exeunt.

SCENE IV

Enter EVANS [*disguised*] *and* [WILLIAM *and other children as*] *Fairies.*

Evans. Trib, trib, fairies; come; and remember your parts. Be pold, I pray you; follow me into the pit; and when I give the watch-'ords, do as I pid you. Come, come; trib, trib. *Exeunt.*

SCENE V

Enter FALSTAFF [*disguised as Herne*] *wearing a buck's head.*

Fal. The Windsor bell hath struck twelve; the minute draws on. Now, the hot-blooded gods assist me! Remember, Jove, thou wast a bull for thy Europa;

Scene IV

SCENE IV] *F; Scene IV. The Park. Capell.* S.D.] *As Camb.; Enter Euans and Fairies. F; Enter Sir* Hugh, Pistol, Quickly, Anne Page, *and Others, vizarded, and disguis'd for Fairies. Capell; The Fairies approach, dancing . . . : Sir Hugh Evans . . .; Pistol . . .; Quickly . . .; Anne Page with William, and many other boys . . . New Camb.*

Scene V

SCENE V] *F; Scene V. Another Part of the Park. Capell.* S.D.] *As Q (Enter sir Iohn with a Bucks head vpon him); Enter Falstaffe, Mistris Page, Mistris Ford, Euans, Anne Page, Fairies, Page, Ford, Quickly, Slender, Fenton, Caius, Pistoll. F.* 1. struck] *F* (stroke). 2. hot-blooded gods] *Rowe*[3]; hot-bloodied-Gods *F1*; hot-bloodied-god *F4*; hot-blooded God *Rowe*[1-2].

Scene IV

S.D.] Some editors bring on Pistol, Anne, and Quickly, but the S.D. in F does not name them. For Evans's disguise, see IV. iv. 67 and note.

1. *Trib*] i.e. trip, or as Falstaff might have said, 'mince'.

Scene V

3. *Jove . . . Europa*] Jove–Jupiter–Zeus fell in love with Europa, daughter of the King of Tyre, changed himself into a bull, and when she climbed upon his back, swam across the sea with her to Crete.

love set on thy horns. O powerful love, that in some respects makes a beast a man; in some other, a man a beast. You were also, Jupiter, a swan for the love of Leda. O omnipotent love, how near the god drew to the complexion of a goose! A fault done first in the form of a beast: O Jove, a beastly fault! And then another fault in the semblance of a fowl: think on 't, Jove, a foul fault! When gods have hot backs, what shall poor men do? For me, I am here a Windsor stag, and the fattest, I think, i' th' forest. Send me a cool rut-time, Jove, or who can blame me to piss my tallow?—Who comes here? My doe?

Enter MISTRESS FORD *and* MISTRESS PAGE.

Mrs. Ford. Sir John! Art thou there, my deer, my male deer?

Fal. My doe with the black scut? Let the sky rain potatoes; let it thunder to the tune of 'Greensleeves', hail kissing-comfits, and snow eringoes; let there

15. S.D.] *Q; not in F.*

6–7. *Jupiter . . . Leda*] To rape Leda, Jupiter disguised himself as a swan.

8. *complexion*] Probably a quibble on the two senses, appearance and disposition or nature.

8, 9, 10, 11. *fault*] Hilda Hulme, p. 112, shows that 'fault' often had the stronger meaning of 'sin' (particularly sexual sin).

11. *hot*] lustful.

14–15. *cool . . . tallow*] Falstaff wants cool weather because lust—carrying on the thought of l. 11—is hot and likely to cause his 'tallow' or fat to melt. Ray, citing as proverbial 'He has piss'd his tallow', comments that 'this is spoken of bucks who grow lean after rutting time, and may be applied to men'. If there is a specific reference to the belief that the male deer at rutting time ate red mushrooms or toadstools to cause it to urinate freely, to relieve the 'heat' (in both senses), Shakespeare's authority may well have been Turberville, ch. 17, first cited by Farmer.

16, 17. *deer*] There is, of course, a quibble on 'dear' (frequent in Shakespeare: cf. e.g. *1H4*, v. iv. 107–8); and cf. l. 23 and note.

18. *scut*] The normal meaning is the short tail of the rabbit or deer—itself no elegant phrase to apply to Mistress Ford—but it seems also to have come to mean the pudend.

19. *potatoes*] For another reference to the common belief in the aphrodisiac power of potatoes—odd as that seems today—cf. *Troil.*, v. ii. 56.

Greensleeves] Named because it is a love song; cf. II. i. 61 and note.

20. *kissing-comfits*] perfumed 'comfits' (sweetmeats of preserved fruit, sugar-plums) to sweeten the breath.

eringoes] candied roots of the seaholly, *Eryngium maritinum*, also considered to be aphrodisiac.

come a tempest of provocation, I will shelter me here.

Mrs. Ford. Mistress Page is come with me, sweetheart.

Fal. Divide me like a bribed buck, each a haunch; I will keep my sides to myself, my shoulders for the fellow of this walk—and my horns I bequeath your husbands. Am I a woodman, ha? Speak I like Herne the hunter? Why, now is Cupid a child of conscience: he makes restitution. As I am a true spirit, welcome! *Noise of horns within.*

Mrs. Page. Alas, what noise?

Mrs. Ford. Heaven forgive our sins!

Fal. What should this be?

Mrs. Ford.
Mrs. Page. } Away, away! *They run off.*

Fal. I think the devil will not have me damned, lest the

22.] *Capell adds 'embracing her'.* 24. bribed] *F* (brib'd-); bribe- *Theobald.* 30. S.D.] *As Q* (*There is a noise of hornes, the two women run away.*); *not in F.* 34. S.D.] *As Rowe; not in F.* 35–7.] *Prose as Pope;* I . . . damn'd, / Least . . . fire; / He . . . thus. *F.*

21. *provocation*] i.e. sexual temptation or excitation. The inferiority of Q in this scene cannot be better shown than by quoting the lines 'Welcome Ladies' and 'This makes amends for all' that virtually replace, from ll. 18–22, 'Let the sky . . . here'.

23. *sweetheart*] No doubt there is a quibble on 'hart', as on 'deer' in ll. 16 and 17. The F spelling 'sweet hart' may be intended to indicate this.

24. *bribed buck*] Following up *O.E.D.*'s demonstration that 'bribed' could mean 'stolen' (*ppl. a.* and 'bribe' *v.* 1), *New Cambridge* interprets the F phrase to mean a stolen buck which had to be cut up quickly and divided among the poachers if the theft was not to be discovered by the keeper; but ll. 24–6 perhaps imply that it is the keeper who has been bribed to allow the deer to be taken. The breaking-up of the deer was a regular part of the hunting ritual.

25–6. *fellow of this walk*] the keeper responsible for this particular 'walk' or part of Windsor Forest. (He was entitled to the right shoulder of a deer legitimately killed.) Hart sees a quibble on the sense of the male deer who uses this section of the forest as his domain; *New Cambridge* suggests one on the meaning that Falstaff 'will keep his shoulders to fight the keeper, should he appear'—but neither seems probable. As Falstaff goes on to say, he is trying to speak like Herne or any good hunter, in the jargon of the hunt. *The Book of Saint Albans*, cited by Kinnear, advises the beginner to learn the language if he wishes to be 'counted a perfect woodman'.

27. *woodman*] forester or hunter—but because of the quibble on the object of the 'hunt' (the 'deer' or 'dear'), it came to mean also one who pursued women: cf. *Meas.*, IV. iii. 170.

29. *makes restitution*] i.e. restores that of which I was previously wrongly deprived—yourself.

oil that's in me should set hell on fire; he would never else cross me thus.

Enter EVANS [*disguised as before;* PISTOL *as Hobgoblin*]; MISTRESS QUICKLY *as the Fairy Queen;* [ANNE PAGE *and*] *children as Fairies* [*with tapers*].

Quick. Fairies, black, gray, green, and white,
You moonshine revellers, and shades of night,
You orphan heirs of fixed destiny,
Attend your office and your quality.
Crier Hobgoblin, make the fairy oyes.
Pist. Elves, list your names; silence, you airy toys.

37. S.D.] *This ed.; Enter Fairies. F; Enter sir Hugh like a Satyre, and boyes drest like Fayries, mistresse Quickly, like the Queene of Fayries: they sing a song about him, and afterward speake. Q; Enter Sir* Hugh Evans, *like a satyr*; Mrs. Quickly, *and* Pistol; Anne Page, *as the Fairy Queen, attended by her brother and others, dressed like fairies, with waxen tapers on their heads. Malone.* 38, 91. *Quick.*] *As F* (*Qui.*)*; Queen / Collier, conj. Harness; Anne / Halliwell, conj. Harness.* 40. orphan heirs] *F;* Ouphen-heirs *Theobald, conj. Warburton;* ouphs, and heirs *Keightley.* 43. *Pist.*] *F; Eva. Theobald; Puck conj. Harness.*

37. S.D.] It is worthy of note that F's '*Enter Fairies*' is the only entry it gives *within* a scene during the whole play; the 'copy' may thus have been different here. F's speech prefixes ('*Qui.*' at ll. 38 and 91 and '*Qu.*' at 56 and 85), together with Q's S.D. and five speech prefixes '*Quic.*', are the authority for Quickly's playing the Fairy Queen. (The full Q S.D. seems to rule out the theory that the speech prefixes mean no more than that the one boy-actor played both parts.) She has replaced Anne, as part of the counter-scheming. The rhyming couplets are used to give the effect of incantation.

39. *shades*] spirits, spectres.

40.] The line has given rise to much comment, involving emendation and conjecture about wider meanings of 'orphan' as 'friendless'. Fairies, however, did not normally have parents, and were 'orphan' in that sense; and perhaps they were 'heirs of fixed destiny' in that different fairies had different fixed functions, times, and places (e.g. the fairies being addressed can come out only at night).

41. *Attend*] attend to, perform.

office] duty.

quality] profession or calling (*O.E.D.* 5)—as in *Gent.*, IV. i. 58.

42. *Crier . . . oyes*] 'Crier' as in 'town crier': one who 'cries' 'oyes' or 'oyez' ('hear ye'). The corresponding line in Q (which differs too much in this scene to be collated in the ordinary way) is 'Giue them their charge *Puck* ere they part away'. 'Hobgoblin' was an alternative name for Puck or Robin Goodfellow.

43. Pist.] Pistol does not appear at all in this scene in Q, and the corresponding lines, in two speeches, are given to Evans. Again it is possible, but unlikely, that the F speech prefix meant only that the actor who played Pistol played Hobgoblin here. The masque tradition of actors stepping out of their parts may explain how Pistol (and Quickly and Evans) now speak without their previous characteristic idiom.

airy toys] creatures as insubstantial

Cricket, to Windsor chimneys shalt thou leap;
Where fires thou find'st unrak'd and hearths unswept,
There pinch the maids as blue as bilberry:
Our radiant Queen hates sluts and sluttery.
Fal. They are fairies; he that speaks to them shall die.
I'll wink and couch: no man their works must eye.
[*Lies face downwards.*]
Evans. Where's Bead? Go you, and where you find a maid
That ere she sleep has thrice her prayers said
Raise up the organs of her fantasy,
Sleep she as sound as careless infancy;
But those as sleep and think not on their sins,

44. shalt thou leap] *F;* when thoust leapt *Collier*[2]. 49. S.D.] *This ed.; not in F; Lyes down upon his Face Rowe.* 50. Bead] *F* (*Bede*)*; Pead Q.* 52. Raise] *F;* Rein *Hanmer, conj. Warburton;* Rouse *Collier*[2]. fantasy,] *F;* fantasie; *Theobald.*

as the air. 'Toys' sometimes had the sense of 'objects lacking substance', sometimes that of 'idle fancies' (cf. I. iv. 40). Theseus' 'I never may believe / These antique fables nor these fairy toys' (*MND.*, v. i. 2–3) suggests that 'fairy' and 'toy' were associated in Shakespeare's mind.

44. *Cricket*] Apparently one of the traditional personal names for a fairy.

45. *unrak'd*] not properly 'raked' to keep smouldering over-night and be still alight in the morning.

46. *pinch the maids . . .*] A traditional occupation, or function, of fairies. (Caliban dreads the pinches of Prospero's spirits in *Temp.*; and Nashe in *The Terrors of the Night*, quoted by Hart, has 'The Robin-good-fellowes, elfes, Fairies, Hobgoblins of our latter age . . . pincht maids in their sleep that swept not their houses cleane . . .'. Cf. also *Err.*, II. ii. 191–4.)

bilberry] The bilberry (or 'whortleberry') is a particularly deep blue.

47. *Queen*] Probably the word refers both to the Fairy Queen and to the Queen in Windsor Castle—Elizabeth herself.

sluts] Used in the weaker sense, implying only untidiness or slovenliness (*O.E.D.* 1).

48–9.] If Falstaff, unexpectedly, also speaks in rhyme, that is probably not because Shakespeare forgot to adapt earlier material but because the play is intended to become less realistic as it takes on more of the character of a masque.

49. *wink and couch*] close my eyes and hide by lying down.

50. Evans] The speech of Evans, like that of Quickly and Pistol, loses its former character so far as the appearance of the words on the page is concerned—but the actor is apparently relied on to continue with the accent, for Falstaff (ll. 82–3) identifies Evans as a 'Welsh fairy'.

Bead] Q has Evans call one fairy 'Pead', another 'Peane', showing that the reporter understood the name that F spells 'Bede' to mean 'Bead'—which is, of course, appropriate for a small fairy.

52.] i.e. give her imagination free rein, let her have pleasing dreams—perhaps with a quibble.

53. *Sleep she*] though she is sleeping. The alternative is to replace F's comma after l. 52 by a semi-colon and interpret as 'may she sleep'.

careless] carefree.

54. *as*] who.

Pinch them, arms, legs, backs, shoulders, sides, and
shins.

Quick. About, about;
Search Windsor Castle, elves, within and out;
Strew good luck, ouphs, on every sacred room
That it may stand till the perpetual doom
In state as wholesome as in state 'tis fit,
Worthy the owner, and the owner it;
The several chairs of order look you scour
With juice of balm and every precious flower;
Each fair instalment, coat, and sev'ral crest,
With loyal blazon, evermore be blest;
And nightly, meadow-fairies, look you sing,
Like to the Garter's compass, in a ring:
Th' expressure that it bears, green let it be,

56, 85. *Quick.*] *As F (Qu.); Queen / Collier; Anne / Halliwell.* 60. state as] *F;* site as *Hanmer.* 62. several] *F* (seuerall). 63. balm . . . flower;] *As Rowe;* Balme; . . . flowre, *F.* 64. sev'ral] *F* (seu'rall). 66. nightly, meadow-fairies] *As Capell;* Nightly-meadow-Fairies *F.*

59. *the perpetual doom*] the final judgment; Day of Judgment. Hart suggested that in these lines there may be an allusion to Elizabeth's motto *semper eadem* ('always the same').

60.] i.e. as 'healthy' in state (condition) as it is fitting in state (dignity).

61. *and the owner it*] and the owner worthy of—indeed the only appropriate owner of—it.

62. *several chairs of order*] various stalls (in the choir of St George's Chapel, Windsor) assigned (one each) to the knights who are members of the Order of the Garter. Each knight's crest, helmet, and mantlings are above his stall; and his banner is on a stave projecting from the wall above these.

63. *balm*] Originally the aromatic gum of specific trees, 'balm' was used of aromatic herbs and indeed of practically any fragrant plant or oil. It was customary to perfume rooms for special occasions; and the allusion here is almost certainly to the coming ceremony of installing the new Knights of the Garter. See Introduction, pp. xliv ff.

64. *instalment*] place where one is installed; here the individual stall of the particular knight.

coat] coat of arms, referring either to that on the banner or to the stall-plate nailed to the back of the stall.

crest] 'A figure or device (originally borne by a knight on his helmet) placed on a wreath, coronet, or chapeau, and borne above the shield and helmet in a coat of arms' (*O.E.D. sb.* 3); also used of the helmet itself. The crests of the Garter Knights are set on the helmets.

65. *blazon*] Used both of the heraldic shield and of the banner bearing the coat of arms. The verbal construction in ll. 64–5 is not 'be blest with' but 'be blest, as well as the loyal blazon'.

67. *compass*] circle, circumference (*O.E.D. sb.* IV).

in a ring] An easy order for the fairies, who normally danced in a 'fairy ring'.

68. *expressure*] expression (cf. *Troil.*, III. iii. 203–4, 'an operation more divine / Than breath or pen can give expressure to') and so, conceivably,

More fertile-fresh than all the field to see;
And *Honi soit qui mal y pense* write
In em'rald tufts, flowers purple, blue, and white,
Like sapphire, pearl, and rich embroidery
Buckled below fair knighthood's bending knee:
Fairies use flowers for their charactery.
Away, disperse; but till 'tis one o'clock,
Our dance of custom round about the oak
Of Herne the hunter, let us not forget.

Evans. Pray you, lock hand in hand; yourselves in order set;
And twenty glow-worms shall our lanterns be
To guide our measure round about the tree.
But, stay, I smell a man of middle earth!

Fal. Heavens defend me from that Welsh fairy, lest he transform me to a piece of cheese!

Pist. Vile worm, thou wast o'erlook'd even in thy birth.

Quick. With trial-fire touch me his finger-end:
If he be chaste, the flame will back descend,
And turn him to no pain; but if he start,
It is the flesh of a corrupted heart.

69. More] *F2;* Mote *F1.* 71. em'rald tufts] *F* (Emrold-tuffes). 82–3.] *Prose as Pope;* Heauens . . . Fairy, / Least . . . Cheese. *F.*

impression or imprint. The fairy ring manifests itself in grass greener and fresher looking than is the other grass. The Garter ribbon itself is blue, as Shakespeare possibly recognizes in ll. 71–3, and the motto is normally, but not invariably, in gold lettering.

70. Honi soit . . . pense] Evil be to him who evil thinks—the motto of the Order of the Garter, woven into the garter itself.

74. *charactery*] script. It is not clear whether in this line 'flowers' is to be pronounced as a monosyllable (F does spell 'Flowres' both here and in l. 71) and 'charactery' as four syllables, with the main stress on the second, or whether 'flowers' has two syllables and 'charactery' three, with the main stress on the first.

76. *dance of custom*] customary dance.

81. *middle earth*] Described by *O.E.D.* as 'an etymologizing perversion' of ME *middelerd*, the term was originally used because the earth was theoretically midway between heaven and hell; it came to be applied to the 'real' or human world as distinct e.g. from the world of fairy.

82–3.] See notes on I. ii. 12 and V. v. 50; and cf. ll. 138–40.

84. *o'erlook'd*] looked at by one with the evil eye, and so bewitched, destined for evil (*O.E.D.* 'overlook' *v.* 7—discussed also by Hilda Hulme, pp. 19–20).

85. *trial-fire*] Hart quotes from Fletcher's *Faithful Shepherdess* a parallel passage (a flame 'which will burn him if he lust'). Fletcher may only have been imitating Shakespeare, but there may well have been such a popular superstition, ingeniously adapted for the purpose of Falstaff's 'trial'.

me] Another example of the ethic dative.

Pist. A trial, come.
Evans. Come, will this wood take fire?
[*They burn him with their tapers.*]
Fal. Oh, oh, oh!
Quick. Corrupt, corrupt, and tainted in desire!
About him, fairies, sing a scornful rhyme;
And, as you trip, still pinch him to your time.

Song.

Fie on sinful fantasy,
Fie on lust and luxury!
Lust is but a bloody fire,
Kindled with unchaste desire,
Fed in heart, whose flames aspire,
As thoughts do blow them, higher and higher.
Pinch him, fairies, mutually;
Pinch him for his villainy;
Pinch him, and burn him, and turn him about,
Till candles and starlight and moonshine be out.

During this song they pinch Falstaff. Doctor Caius comes one way, and steals away a fairy in green; Slender another way, and takes off a fairy in white; and Fenton comes, and steals away Anne Page. A noise of hunting is heard within. The Fairies run away. Falstaff pulls off his buck's head, and rises.

89. S.D.] *As Q; not in F; They burn him with their Tapers, and pinch him.* Rowe (*before* 'Come'). 103. *During . . . rises.*] *As Steevens, after Theobald; not in F; Here they pinch him, and sing about him, & the Doctor comes one way & steales away a boy in red. And Slender another way he takes a boy in greene: And Fenton steales misteris Anne, being in white. And a noyse of hunting is made within: and all the Fairies runne away. Falstaffe pulles of his bucks head, and rises vp.* Q; *He offers to run out.* Rowe.

89. *wood*] The reference can hardly be, as some editors suggest, to Falstaff's horns, made of oak (if they were); the word must be used ironically, of his finger.

94. *fantasy*] imaginings, and so aspiration.

95. *luxury*] All but synonymous with 'lust'; lechery.

96. *bloody fire*] fire in the blood.

98. *aspire*] rise up, like smoke (*O.E.D.* III. 5).

100. *mutually*] together, in unison (*O.E.D.* 2).

103. S.D. During . . . rises] This is based on Q but differs from it, largely because Q again gets the colours mixed. Earlier editors point out that the scene may have been influenced by IV. iii of Lyly's *Endimion* in which, while dancing and singing such words as 'pinch him, pinch him, black and blue', the fairies pinch Corsites. (Although *Endimion* was published in

Enter PAGE, FORD, MISTRESS PAGE, *and* MISTRESS FORD.

Page. Nay, do not fly; I think we have watch'd you now.
Will none but Herne the hunter serve your turn?
Mrs. Page. I pray you, come, hold up the jest no higher.
Now, good Sir John, how like you Windsor wives?
[*Pointing to the horns*] See you these, husband? Do not these fair yokes
Become the forest better than the town?
Ford. Now, sir, who's a cuckold now? Master Brook, Falstaff's a knave, a cuckoldly knave; here are his horns, Master Brook; and, Master Brook, he hath enjoyed nothing of Ford's but his buck-basket, his cudgel, and twenty pounds of money, which must be paid to Master Brook; his horses are arrested for it, Master Brook.

103. *Enter Page . . . Mistress Ford.*] *As Capell; not in F; And enters* M. *Page,* M. *Ford, and their wiues,* M. *Shallow, Sir Hugh. Q; Enter* Page, Ford, *&c. They lay hold on him. Rowe; Enter Page, Ford, Mistress Page, Mistress Ford, and Sir Hugh Evans. Alexander.* 104–5.] *Verse as Rowe; prose F.* 108. S.D.] *Hanmer; not in F.* yokes] *F1* (yoakes)*;* Okes *F2.* 110–12.] *Prose as Pope;* Now . . . now? / Mr *Broome* . . . Cuckoldly knaue, / Heere . . . hornes Master *Broome:* / And . . . *F.*

1591, the words of the song first appear in the play in Blount's edition of 1632, and their authorship and date are open to question.)

S.D. Enter . . . Ford] Q also brings on Shallow and Evans (who has not left the stage, unless he ran away with the 'fairies', as Pistol and Mistress Quickly presumably did), and gives Shallow the words 'God saue you sir *Iohn Falstaffe*' in reply to Falstaff's first speech. F has neither entrance nor dialogue for Shallow, but his presence would be natural enough in the finale. Perhaps also the Q S.D. implies that Evans left the stage to drop his disguise; it may conceivably be relevant, as Hart suggested, that he resumes his Welsh accent hereafter (but see note on l. 43). Neither Pistol nor Quickly speaks again in Q or F, and they could hardly be included in Mistress Page's final invitation (ll. 238–40). In Q the dialogue begins after the S.D. with a speech by Falstaff that includes another attempt to link the action with the *H4* plays: 'What hunting at this time of night? / Ile lay my life the mad Prince of *Wales* / Is stealing his fathers Deare'.

104. *watch'd*] caught by spying upon or lying in wait for; cf. *2H6*, I. iv. 45 and 58.

106. *hold up*] keep up, maintain.

108. *yokes*] Falstaff's horns, so called apparently because they resemble the oxen's yoke in shape. See l. 121 and note. Hart's suggestions that the 'horns' were made of 'oak' and that there is a pun on 'oak' are unconvincing. (It would presumably be easier for Quickly—see v. i—to obtain for him the mounted head of a buck or the horns from one.)

109. *Become*] suit.

110–16.] Ford's mockery of Falstaff includes a parody of his style, with, particularly, the over-frequent use of 'Master Brook'.

115. *arrested*] seized by law, to be

Mrs. Ford. Sir John, we have had ill luck: we could never meet. I will never take you for my love again, but I will always count you my deer.

Fal. I do begin to perceive that I am made an ass.

Ford. Ay, and an ox too: both the proofs are extant.

Fal. And these are not fairies? I was three or four times in the thought they were not fairies; and yet the guiltiness of my mind, the sudden surprise of my powers, drove the grossness of the foppery into a received belief, in despite of the teeth of all rhyme and reason, that they were fairies. See now how wit may be made a Jack-a-Lent, when 'tis upon ill employment!

118. meet] *F;* mate *New Camb.* 122. And . . . fairies? I] *Prose as Pope;* And . . . Fairies: / I . . . *F.*

held until the debt is paid. This is what Mistress Ford said would be Falstaff's punishment, at II. i. 93–4. There is no direct connection between this part of the plot and the stealing of the Host's horses; and indeed the plan that some editors see—to replace the Host's own horses by letting him have Falstaff's—would contradict, not enhance, the plans for vengeance on the Host made by Evans and Caius. At most, Falstaff's loss of his horses is an ironic parallel to the Host's. In Q Mistress Ford does later ask her husband to let Falstaff off his debt; F leaves the question open.

118. *meet*] *New Cambridge*'s emendation 'mate' is defended by the argument that 'they had "met" three times, but never "mated"'. 'But', as C. J. Sisson says, *N.R.*, p. 73, 'surely there are meetings and meetings'. The two words may have been closer in pronunciation than they are today and conceivably a quibble is involved.

121. *an ox too*] *New Cambridge* says that 'to make an ox of one' means 'to make one a fool' and compares *Troil.*, v. i. 66, which does not necessarily support this. May the reference not be to a proverb that Tilley does list, O107: 'an ox is taken by the horns and a man by the tongue'? Certainly 'both the proofs' in the second half of the line refers to the horns; and the 'ox' image refers back to 'yokes' in l. 108.

extant] Another quibble, on the surviving meaning 'still in existence' and the literal meaning 'standing up', 'protuberant' (*O.E.D. adj.* 1).

124. *guiltiness . . .*] Hart complains that 'this is most un-Falstaffian language' and *New Cambridge* adds that 'the passage must be a relic of the old play'. Alternatively one may see Shakespeare skilfully modulating into the key of the final passages—perhaps at the cost of consistency in characterization but not necessarily so: this is not the first time in the Falstaff plays that Falstaff has admitted to being the dupe ('Ah, no more of that, Hal, an thou lovest me!') and the balancing of the phrases sounds 'authentic'.

125. *powers*] mind and senses.

foppery] cheating (cf. *O.E.D.* 'fop' *v.* 2—the same as 'fob' in 'fob off').

126–7. *in despite . . . reason*] 'In spite of the teeth' (originally, perhaps, the teeth of an animal) was a proverbial phrase (Tilley S764), as, of course, was 'neither rhyme nor reason'.

128. *Jack-a-Lent*] See note on III. iii. 23.

Evans. Sir John Falstaff, serve Got, and leave your desires, and fairies will not pinse you.

Ford. Well said, fairy Hugh.

Evans. And leave you your jealousies too, I pray you.

Ford. I will never mistrust my wife again, till thou art able to woo her in good English.

Fal. Have I laid my brain in the sun and dried it, that it wants matter to prevent so gross o'er-reaching as this? Am I ridden with a Welsh goat too? Shall I have a cockscomb of frieze? 'Tis time I were choked with a piece of toasted cheese.

Evans. Seese is not good to give putter; your belly is all putter.

Fal. 'Seese' and 'putter'? Have I lived to stand at the taunt of one that makes fritters of English? This is enough to be the decay of lust and late-walking through the realm.

Mrs. Page. Why, Sir John, do you think, though we would have thrust virtue out of our hearts by the head and shoulders, and have given ourselves without scruple to hell, that ever the devil could have made you our delight?

Ford. What, a hodge-pudding? A bag of flax?

Mrs. Page. A puffed man?

Page. Old, cold, withered, and of intolerable entrails?

152. hodge-pudding] *F;* hog's pudding *Pope;* hog-pudding *Collier.* flax] *F;* flux *conj. New Camb.*

137. *wants*] lacks.

138. *ridden with a Welsh goat*] There were said to be many goats in Wales, and the devil was said to transform himself often into a goat. There need be no direct allusion to Evans's costume.

139. *cockscomb of frieze*] a jester's cap, made of frieze, a coarse woollen cloth variously thought to be typical of Wales and of Ireland (both being considered poverty-stricken). Cf. *The Two Noble Kinsmen*, III. v. 8, 'You most coarse frieze capacities'.

140. *cheese*] See note on I. ii. 12 (the Welsh fondness for cheese).

144. *fritters*] Literally, pieces of fried batter. (The other meaning, 'shreds' or 'fragments', would seem to have been later.)

148–9. *thrust . . . shoulders*] 'To thrust out (or in) by the head and shoulders' was a stock phrase (Tilley H274).

152. *hodge-pudding*] a pudding or sausage made of 'hodge' or pig's entrails (cf. II. i. 31, and l. 154 below).

bag of flax] sack full of flax, or flax-pods (from which linseed is extracted). Emendation is unnecessary: Hal calls Falstaff 'wool-sack' in *1H4*, II. iv. 148.

154. *intolerable*] No doubt again with a quibble: excessive (*O.E.D.* 1.c) and

Ford. And one that is as slanderous as Satan?

Page. And as poor as Job?

Ford. And as wicked as his wife?

Evans. And given to fornications, and to taverns, and sack, and wine, and metheglins, and to drinkings, and swearings, and starings, pribbles and prabbles?

Fal. Well, I am your theme: you have the start of me. I am dejected; I am not able to answer the Welsh flannel; ignorance itself is a plummet o'er me; use me as you will.

Ford. Marry, sir, we'll bring you to Windsor to one Master Brook that you have cozened of money, to whom you should have been a pandar. Over and above that you have suffered, I think to repay that money will be a biting affliction.

164. is a plummet o'er me] *F;* has a plume o' me *conj. Johnson;* is a planet o'er me *conj. Farmer.* 170.] *Theobald inserts, from Q,* 'Mrs *Ford.* Nay, husband, let That go to make amends: / Forgive that Summ, and so we'll all be Friends.'

impossible to bear or carry (literally).

155–7.] The allusions are to Satan as the slanderer of Job (Job, 1:9–11 and 2:4–5) and probably, as Noble points out (p. 272), to a marginal gloss on 2:9 in the Bishop's Bible (1568 and 1572): 'A cruel temptation of an euyl and vngodly wife'.

159. *metheglins*] The plural is perhaps Evans's own (unless it is the variant 'metheglings') but 'metheglin' is the well-known name of a potent spiced mead, first concocted in Wales. Cf. Wasp's insults in Jonson's *Bartholomew Fair*, IV. vi. 47–51, 'You are a welsh Cuckold . . . You stinke of leeks, *Metheglyn*, and cheese'.

160. *swearings, and starings*] Hart shows, by relevant quotations from Nashe, that 'swearing and staring' was 'evidently an established phrase': 'staring' meant 'glaring' or 'raving' as if mad (*O.E.D.* 'stare' *v.* 3.a).

160–1. *pribbles and prabbles*] Evans falls back on another ready-made phrase: cf. I. i. 51–2 and note.

162. *your theme*] the subject of your jests.

you have the start of me] A standard phrase (Tilley S828); the modern idiom might be 'have the advantage over me' or 'have the whip hand'.

163. *dejected*] Probably yet another quibble on secondary and primary meanings: downcast and cast down (in status if not physically).

163–4. *Welsh flannel*] Cf. l. 139 and note. (A conjecture that the English word 'flannel' is a corruption of Welsh *gwlanen* is called 'plausible' by *O.E.D.*, which sees some difficulties in the theory.)

164. *plummet*] *New Cambridge* saw another quibble, 'plummet' being (1) the nautical apparatus for testing depth (and apparently Falstaff means that he has now sunk even deeper than the plummet: ignorant people—like Evans—can find him out to be more ignorant) and (2) plumbet, defined by *O.E.D.* as 'a woollen fabric' (and thus a 'flannel').

Page. Yet be cheerful, knight: thou shalt eat a posset to-night at my house, where I will desire thee to laugh at my wife that now laughs at thee. Tell her Master Slender hath married her daughter.

Mrs. Page. [*Aside*] Doctors doubt that; if Anne Page be my daughter, she is, by this, Doctor Caius' wife.

Enter SLENDER.

Slen. Whoa, ho, ho, father Page!

Page. Son, how now? How now, son? Have you dispatched?

Slen. Dispatched? I'll make the best in Gloucestershire know on 't; would I were hanged, la, else!

Page. Of what, son?

Slen. I came yonder at Eton to marry Mistress Anne Page, and she's a great lubberly boy. If it had not been i' th' church, I would have swinged him, or he should have swinged me. If I did not think it had been Anne Page, would I might never stir—and 'tis a postmaster's boy!

Page. Upon my life, then, you took the wrong.

Slen. What need you tell me that? I think so, when I took a boy for a girl. If I had been married to him, for all he was in woman's apparel, I would not have had him.

Page. Why, this is your own folly. Did not I tell you how you should know my daughter by her garments?

175. *Aside*] *Theobald; not in F.* 176. S.D.] *Q; not in F.*

171. *eat a posset*] See note on I. iv. 7. 'Eat' is used in a general sense: the modern idiom would be 'take'.

175. *Doctors doubt that*] Apparently proverbial; cf. 'You need not doubt, you are no doctor'. Tilley D425, and 'That is but one doctor's opinion', D426. The pun on 'daughter' and 'doctor' suspected by Hart may not be there.

176. Enter Slender] Q reverses the order of the entries of Slender and Caius.

179. *dispatched*] settled the business (*O.E.D.* 'dispatch' *v.* II. 10).

185. *swinged*] thrashed. *New Cambridge* sees a (somewhat improbable) quibble on the sense 'have sexual intercourse', citing *O.E.D.* 'swinge' *v.*[1] I. e.

187. *would . . . stir*] Not Slender's invention but a stock phrase ('I would I might never stir else', Tilley S861).

188. *postmaster's*] The postmaster was the official in charge of the post-messengers or post-horses.

Slen. I went to her in white, and cried 'mum', and she cried 'budget', as Anne and I had appointed; and yet it was not Anne, but a postmaster's boy.

Mrs. Page. Good George, be not angry: I knew of your purpose, turned my daughter into green, and indeed she is now with the Doctor at the deanery, and there married.

Enter CAIUS.

Caius. Vere is Mistress Page? By gar, I am cozened: I ha' married *un garçon*, a boy; *un paysan*, by gar; a boy; it is not Anne Page; by gar, I am cozened.

Mrs. Page. Why, did you take her in green?

Caius. Ay, by gar, and 'tis a boy; by gar, I'll raise all Windsor. [*Exit.*]

Ford. This is strange. Who hath got the right Anne?

Page. My heart misgives me: here comes Master Fenton.

Enter FENTON *and* ANNE PAGE.

How now, Master Fenton?

Anne. Pardon, good father; good my mother, pardon.

Page. Now, mistress, how chance you went not with Master Slender?

Mrs. Page. Why went you not with Master Doctor, maid?

Fent. You do amaze her. Hear the truth of it.
You would have married her most shamefully,
Where there was no proportion held in love.

196. white] *Rowe*[3]*;* greene *F;* red *Q.* 200. green] *Rowe*[3]*;* white *F.* 202. *Enter Caius*] *Q; not in F.* 204. *un garçon*] *Capell;* oon Garsoon *F1;* one Garsoon *F2.* *un paysan*] *As Capell;* oon pesant *F.* 206. take] *F;* not take *Pope.* green] *Pope;* white *F.* 207. by gar, and] *Hanmer;* bee gar, and *F.* by gar, I'll] *Hanmer;* be gar, Ile *F.* 208. *Exit*] *Capell; not in F.* 211. S.D.] *Q; not in F.*

196. *white*] Why F should have mixed up the colours here and in l. 200 is not clear. A desperate hypothesis would be that the scribe, thinking that Slender was bound to get his instructions wrong, made the alteration in l. 196 and then changed 200 to be consistent (but of course Mistress Page could not rely on Slender's being wrong). Q adds to the confusion by saying 'red' (it has no line corresponding to 200).

204. paysan] peasant or rustic.

217. *amaze*] bewilder (here by asking two questions simultaneously). Cf. l. 228.

The truth is, she and I, long since contracted,
Are now so sure that nothing can dissolve us.
Th' offence is holy that she hath committed,
And this deceit loses the name of craft,
Of disobedience, or unduteous title,
Since therein she doth evitate and shun
A thousand irreligious cursed hours
Which forced marriage would have brought upon her.

Ford. Stand not amaz'd; here is no remedy.
In love the heavens themselves do guide the state;
Money buys lands, and wives are sold by fate.

Fal. I am glad, though you have ta'en a special stand to
strike at me, that your arrow hath glanced.

Page. Well, what remedy? Fenton, heaven give thee joy!
What cannot be eschew'd must be embrac'd.

Fal. When night-dogs run, all sorts of deer are chas'd.

Mrs. Page. Well, I will muse no further. Master Fenton,
Heaven give you many, many merry days!
Good husband, let us every one go home,
And laugh this sport o'er by a country fire,
Sir John and all.

Ford. Let it be so.—Sir John,
To Master Brook you yet shall hold your word,
For he to-night shall lie with Mistress Ford. *Exeunt.*

224. title] *F;* guile *Collier*[2]. 233–4.] *Verse as Rowe*[3]*; prose F.* 240. so.—Sir John,] *As Theobald;* so (Sir *Iohn*:) *F;* so, Sir *John*: *Rowe.*

221. *sure*] firmly bound together.

225. *evitate*] avoid. Fenton, speaking in a high moral tone, is again using formal language.

229–30.] The rhyming couplet indicates the finality of the epigrammatic statement; the second line is a variant of the proverb 'Marriage and hanging go by destiny' (cf. Tilley M682).

231. *stand*] hunter's hiding place from which to shoot. Cf. e.g. *3H6*, III. i. 3.

234.] A variation on proverbs such as 'What cannot be cured must be endured' (Tilley C922): 'eschew'd' means 'avoided'; 'embrac'd', 'accepted'.

235.] This sounds like a proverb but Tilley does not list any closely parallel to it. The meaning and relevance at least are clear: when dogs run loose at night, out of control, the hunting will not be according to the rules; and so those who set out to deceive each other over Anne's marriage cannot complain that matters were taken out of their hands, that they wanted to hunt true 'deer' but acquired unexpected trophies.

236. *muse*] Either 'wonder' or 'complain' (*O.E.D. v.* 3, 6).